THE TELEVISION PLAYS
1965–1984

TOM STOPPARD

The Television Plays
1965–1984

faber and faber
LONDON · BOSTON

This collection first published in 1993 by
Faber and Faber Limited
3 Queen Square London WC1N 3AU

Photoset by Parker Typesetting Service, Leicester
Printed by Clays Ltd, St Ives plc

A CIP record for this book is available from the British Library
ISBN 0 571 16568 0 [cased]
0 571 16570 2 [paper]

2 4 6 8 10 9 7 5 3 1

CONTENTS

INTRODUCTION

These six plays for television span nearly twenty years, but not evenly. The first four were written close together (1965–7); *Professional Foul* followed after a ten-year gap, and *Squaring the Circle* seven years after that. My case history as a writer for television understates my interest in plays on screen but is fair comment otherwise. I wanted to be in the theatre. The first play I wrote, in 1960, was meant for the stage, and the next plays, for radio and TV, were – I hoped – stepping stones towards getting a play on the boards. 1967, the beginning of the ten-year gap, was the year of my first professional stage production in England.

This is not a philosophical claim for the value of one medium over another. It is simply the way I felt, and there were many like me in those early Osborne, Wesker and Pinter years, when bliss was it to be performed but to be *staged* was very heaven.

A Separate Peace was one half of an hour-long programme consisting of a documentary and a play which were supposed to illuminate each other. The documentary (which I made with Christopher Martin) was about chess. I now doubt that chess and the desire to escape from the world are good metaphors for each other.

Teeth, a Roald Dahl-type story (as I hoped), I take this opportunity to dedicate to my much more recent and much nicer dentist. *Another Moon Called Earth* contributed a good deal to *Jumpers*: a woman who won't get out of bed, a husband working in the next room, a death, a visiting detective. Penelope in this play pushes someone out of the window and I began *Jumpers* thinking that Dottie was going to be the murderer of McFee.

Neutral Ground is based on *Philoctetes* by Sophocles. It was written for a proposed Granda TV series based on myths and legends. The series never happened but three years later the play was taken off the shelf and transmitted on its own, the only vestige of its original inspiration being the hero's egregious name of Philo.

Leaving aside weightier matters, *Professional Foul* serves as a good example of the concealed difficulty in the most-asked question: 'How long does it take to write?' When does one start counting? I had promised to deliver a play by the last day of 1976 to mark Amnesty International's Prisoner of Conscience Year (1977). On that day, after months of trying, I had nothing to show, nothing begun and nothing in mind. A visit to the USSR (not Czechoslovakia) finally produced a ghost of a plot, and after that the play was written in two or three weeks, including turning a ballroom dancing team into the England Football squad.

By comparison, the writing, rewriting, production and post-production troubles of *Squaring the Circle* were an endless saga (described in the Introduction to the play's first publication). Whether it is a play at all, rather than a drama-documentary, is a question, through perhaps not a vital one.

T.S. 1993

A SEPARATE PEACE

CHARACTERS

JOHN BROWN
NURSE
DOCTOR
NURSE MAGGIE COATES
MATRON
NURSE JONES

A Separate Peace was first transmitted in August 1966 by the
BBC. The cast included:

JOHN BROWN	Peter Jeffrey
NURSE MAGGIE COATES	Hannah Gordon
DOCTOR	Ronald Hines
PRODUCER	Ronald Mason
DIRECTOR	Alan Gibson

*The office of the Beechwood Nursing Home. Behind the reception
counter sits a uniformed nurse. It is 2.30 a.m. A car pulls up outside.*
JOHN BROWN *enters. He is a biggish man, with a well-lined face:
calm, pleasant. He is wearing a nondescript suit and overcoat, and
carrying two zipped travelling bags. Looking around, he notes the
neatness, the quiet, the flowers, the nice nurse, and is quietly pleased.*

BROWN: Very nice.

NURSE: Good evening . . .

BROWN: 'Evening. A lovely night. Morning.

NURSE: Yes . . . Mr . . .?

BROWN: I'm sorry to be so late.

NURSE: (*Shuffling papers*) Were you expected earlier?

BROWN: No. I telephoned.

NURSE: Yes?

BROWN: Yes. You have a room for Mr Brown.

NURSE: Oh! – Have you brought him?

BROWN: I brought myself. Got a taxi by the station. I
      telephoned from there.

NURSE: You said it was an emergency.

BROWN: That's right. Do you know what time it is?

NURSE: It's half-past two.

BROWN: That's right. An emergency.

NURSE: (*Aggrieved*) I woke the house doctor.

BROWN: A kind thought. But it's all right. Do you want me to
      sign in?

NURSE: What is the nature of your emergency, Mr Brown?

BROWN: I need a place to stay.

NURSE: Are you ill?

BROWN: No.

NURSE: But this is a private hospital . . .
      (BROWN *smiles for the first time.*)

BROWN: The best kind. What is a hospital without privacy? It's
      the privacy I'm after – that and the clean linen . . . (*A*

5

thought strikes him.) I've got money.

NURSE: . . . the Beechwood Nursing Home.

BROWN: I require nursing. I need to be nursed for a bit. Yes. Where do I sign?

NURSE: I'm sorry, but admissions have to be arranged in advance except in the case of a genuine emergency – I have no authority –

BROWN: What do you want with authority? A nice person like you.
(*Moves.*) Where have you put me?

NURSE: (*Moves with him*) And *you* have no authority –

BROWN: (*Halts*) That's true. That's one thing I've never had.
(*He looks at her flatly.*) I've come a long way.

NURSE: (*Wary*) Would you wait for just one moment?

BROWN: (*Relaxes*) Certainly. Have you got a sign-in book? Must abide by the regulations. Should I pay in advance?

NURSE: No, that's quite all right.

BROWN: I've got it – I've got it all in here –
(*He starts trying to open one of the zipped cases, it jams and he hurts his finger. He recoils sharply and puts his finger in his mouth. The* DOCTOR *arrives, dishevelled from being roused.*)

NURSE: Doctor – this is Mr Brown.

DOCTOR: Good evening. What seems to be the trouble?

BROWN: Caught my finger.

DOCTOR: May I see?
(BROWN *holds out his finger. The* DOCTOR *studies it, looks up.*)
(*Guardedly.*) Have you come far?

BROWN: Yes. I've been travelling all day.
(*The* DOCTOR *glances at the* NURSE.)
Not with my finger. I did that just now. Zip stuck.

DOCTOR: Oh. And what – er –

NURSE: Mr Brown says there's nothing wrong with him.

BROWN: That's right – I –

NURSE: He just wants a bed.

BROWN: A room.

DOCTOR: But this isn't a hotel.

BROWN: Exactly.

DOCTOR: Exactly what?

BROWN: I don't follow you.

DOCTOR: Perhaps I'm confused. You see, I was asleep.

BROWN: It's all right. I understand. Well, if someone would show me to my room, I shan't disturb you any further.

DOCTOR: (*With a glance at the* NURSE) I don't believe we have any rooms free at the moment.

BROWN: Oh yes, this young lady arranged it.

NURSE: He telephoned from the station. He said it was an emergency.

DOCTOR: But you've come to the wrong place.

NURSE: No, this is the place all right. What's the matter?

DOCTOR: (*Pause*) Nothing – nothing's the matter. (*He nods at the* NURSE.) All right.

NURSE: Yes, doctor. (*Murmurs worriedly.*) I'll have to make an entry.

DOCTOR: Observation.

BROWN: (*Cheerfully*) I'm not much to look at.

NURSE: Let me take those for you, Mr Brown [*the cases*].

BROWN: No, no, don't you. (*Picks up cases.*) There's nothing the matter with me . . .

(BROWN *follows the* NURSE *inside. The* DOCTOR *watches them go, picks up Brown's form and reads it. Then he picks up the phone and starts to dial.*)

SCENE 2

Brown's private ward. A pleasant ward with a hospital bed and the usual furniture. One wall is almost all window and is curtained.

BROWN *and* NURSE *enter.* BROWN *puts his cases on the bed. He likes the room.*

BROWN: That's nice. I'll like it here. (*Peering through curtains*) What's the view?

NURSE: Well, it's the drive and the gardens.

BROWN: Gardens. A front room. What could be nicer?

(NURSE *starts to open case.*)

NURSE: Are your night things in here?

BROWN: Yes, I'll be very happy here.

(NURSE *opens the case, which is full of money – banknotes.*)

7

NURSE: Oh – I'm sorry –
    (BROWN *is not put out at all.*)
BROWN: What time is breakfast?
NURSE: Eight o'clock.
BROWN: Lunch?
NURSE: Twelve o'clock.
BROWN: Tea?
NURSE: Three o'clock.
BROWN: Supper?
NURSE: Half-past six.
BROWN: Cocoa?
NURSE: Nine.
BROWN: Like clockwork. Lovely.
    (*The* DOCTOR *enters with Brown's form and an adhesive*
    bandage.)
DOCTOR: Excuse me.
BROWN: I was just saying – everything's A1.
DOCTOR: I remembered your finger.
BROWN: I'd forgotten myself. It's nothing.
DOCTOR: Well, we'll just put this on overnight.
    (*He puts on the adhesive strip.*)
    I expect Matron will be along to discuss your case with you
    tomorrow.
BROWN: My finger?
DOCTOR: . . . Well, I expect she'd like to meet you.
BROWN: Be pleased to meet her.

SCENE 3

The hospital office. It is morning and the DOCTOR *is at the desk,*
telephoning.
DOCTOR: . . . I have absolutely no idea . . . The nurse said it
    looked like rather a lot . . . His savings, yes. No, I don't
    really want the police turning up at the bedside of any patient
    who doesn't arrive with a life history . . . I think we'd get
    more out of him than you would, given a little time . . . No,
    he's not being difficult at all . . . You don't need to worry
    about that – he seems quite happy . . .

Brown's private ward. BROWN *is in striped pyjamas, eating off a tray. A second nurse –* NURSE COATES (MAGGIE) *– is waiting for him to finish so that she can take his tray away.* MAGGIE *is pretty and warm.*

BROWN: The point is not breakfast in bed, but breakfast in bed without guilt – if you're not ill. Lunch in bed is more difficult, even for the rich. It's not any more expensive, but the disapproval is harder to ignore. To stay in bed for tea is almost impossible in decent society, and not to get up at all would probably bring in the authorities. But in a hospital it's not only understood – it's expected. That's the beauty of it. I'm not saying it's a great discovery – it's obvious really – but I'd say I'd got something.

MAGGIE: If you'd got something, there wouldn't be all this fuss.

BROWN: Is there a fuss?

(MAGGIE *doesn't answer.*)

I'm paying my way . . . Are you pretty full all the time?

MAGGIE: Not at the moment, not very.

BROWN: You'd think a place as nice as this would be very popular.

MAGGIE: Popular?

BROWN: I thought I might have to wait for a place, you know.

MAGGIE: Where do you live?

BROWN: I've never lived. Only stayed.

MAGGIE: You should settle down somewhere.

BROWN: Yes, I've been promising myself this.

MAGGIE: Have you got a family?

BROWN: I expect so.

MAGGIE: Where are they?

BROWN: I lost touch.

MAGGIE: You should find them.

BROWN: (*Smiles*) Their name's Brown.

(*The* MATRON *enters: she is not too old and quite pleasant.*)

MATRON: Good morning.

BROWN: Good morning to you. You must be Matron.

MATRON: That's right.

BROWN: I must congratulate you on your hospital, it's a lovely place you run here. Everyone is so nice.

MATRON: Well, thank you, Mr Brown. I'm glad you feel at home. (MAGGIE *takes Brown's tray*.)

BROWN: I never felt it there. Very good breakfast. Just what the doctor ordered. I hope he got a bit of a lie-in. (MAGGIE *exits with the tray, closing the door*.)

MATRON: Now, what's your problem, Mr Brown?

BROWN: I have no problems.

MATRON: Your complaint.

BROWN: I have no complaints either. Full marks.

MATRON: Most people who come here have something the *matter* with them.

BROWN: That must give you a lot of extra work.

MATRON: But it's what we're here for. You see, you can't really stay unless there's something wrong with you.

BROWN: I can pay.

MATRON: That's not the point.

BROWN: What is the point?

MATRON: This is a hospital. What are you after?

BROWN: (*Sadly*) My approach is too straightforward. An ordinary malingerer or a genuine hypochondriac wouldn't have all this trouble. They'd be accepted on their own terms. All I get is a lot of personal questions. (*Hopefully*.) Maybe I could *catch* something . . . But what difference would it make to you?

MATRON: We have to keep the beds free for people who need them.

BROWN: I need this room.

MATRON: I believe you, Mr Brown – but wouldn't another room like this one do? Somewhere else? You see, we deal with physical matters – of the body –

BROWN: There's nothing wrong with my *mind*. You won't find my name on any list.

MATRON: I know.

BROWN: (*Teasing*) How do you know? (*She doesn't answer*.) Go for the obvious, it's worth considering. I know what I like: a nice atmosphere – good food – clean rooms – no demands – cheerful staff – Well, it's *worth* the price. I won't be any trouble.

MATRON: Have you thought of going to a nice country hotel?

BROWN: Different kettle of fish altogether. I want to do nothing, and have nothing expected of me. That isn't possible out there. It worries them. They want to know what you're at – staying in your room all the time – they want to know what you're *doing*. But in a hospital it is understood that you're not doing anything, because everybody's in the same boat – it's the normal thing.

MATRON: But there's nothing wrong with you!

BROWN: That's why I'm *here*. If there was something wrong with me I could get into any old hospital – free. As it is, I'm quite happy to pay for *not* having anything wrong with me.

MATRON: But what do you want to do here?

BROWN: Nothing.

MATRON: You'll find that very boring.

BROWN: One must expect to be bored, in a hospital.

MATRON: Have you been in a hospital quite a lot?

BROWN: No. I've been saving up for it . . . (*He smiles.*)

SCENE 5

The hospital office. The DOCTOR *is phoning at a desk.*

DOCTOR: No luck? . . . Oh. Well, I don't know. The only plan we've got is to bore him out of here, but he's disturbingly self-sufficient . . . Mmmm, we've had a psychiatrist over . . . Well, he seemed amused . . . Both of them, actually; they were both amused . . . No, I shouldn't do that, he won't tell you anything. And there's one of our nurses – she's getting on very well with him . . . something's bound to come out soon . . .

SCENE 6

Brown's ward. BROWN *is in bed with a thermometer in his mouth.* MAGGIE *is taking his pulse. She removes the thermometer, scans it and shakes it.*

MAGGIE: I'm wasting my time here, you know.

BROWN: (*Disappointed*) Normal?

MAGGIE: You'll have to do better than that if you're going to stay.

BROWN: You're breaking my heart, Maggie.

MAGGIE: (*Almost lovingly*) Brownie, what are you doing to do with yourself?

BROWN: Maggie, Maggie . . . Why do you want me to do something?

MAGGIE: They've all got theories about you, you know.

BROWN: Theories?

MAGGIE: Train robber.

BROWN: That's a good one.

MAGGIE: Embezzler.

BROWN: Naturally.

MAGGIE: Eccentric millionaire.

BROWN: Wish I was. I'd have my own hospital, just for myself – with nurses, doctors, rubber floors, flowers, stretchers parked by the elevators, clean towels and fire regulations . . .

MAGGIE: It's generally agreed you're on the run.

BROWN: No, I've stopped.

MAGGIE: I think you're just lazy.

BROWN: I knew you were the clever one.

MAGGIE: (*Troubled, soft*) Tell me what's the matter, Brownie?

BROWN: I would if there was.

MAGGIE: What do you want to stay here for, then?

BROWN: I like you.

MAGGIE: You didn't know I was here.

BROWN: That's true. I came for the quiet and the routine. I came for the white calm, meals on trays and quiet efficiency, time passing and bringing nothing. That seemed enough. I never got it down to a person. But I like you – I like you very much.

MAGGIE: Well, I like you too, Brownie. But there's more in life than that.

(MATRON *enters*.)

MATRON: Good morning.

BROWN: Good morning, Matron.

MATRON: And how are we this morning?

BROWN: We're very well. How are you?

MATRON: (*Slightly taken aback*) *I'm* all right, thank you. Well, are you enjoying life?

BROWN: Yes, thank you, Matron.

MATRON: What have you been doing?

BROWN: Nothing.

MATRON: Now really, Mr Brown, this won't do, you know. Wouldn't you like to get up for a while? Have a walk in the garden? There's no reason why you shouldn't.

BROWN: No, I suppose not. But I didn't come here for that. I must have walked thousands of miles, in my time.

MATRON: It's not healthy to stay in bed all day.

BROWN: What do the other patients do?

MATRON: The other patients are here because they are not well.

BROWN: I thought patients did things . . . (*Vaguely*) made things.

MATRON: I suppose you wouldn't like to make paper flowers?

BROWN: What on earth for? You've got lots of real ones.

MATRON: *You* haven't got any.

BROWN: Well, no one knows I'm here.

MATRON: Then you must tell somebody.

BROWN: I don't want them to know.

MATRON: Who?

BROWN: Everybody.

MATRON: You'll soon get tired of sitting in bed.

BROWN: Then I'll sit by the window. I'm easily pleased.

MATRON: I can't let you languish away in here. You must do *something*.

BROWN: (*Sighs*) All right. What?

MATRON: We've got basket-weaving . . .?

BROWN: Then I'll be left alone, will I?

SCENE 7

The hospital office. The DOCTOR *is on the phone.*

DOCTOR: Well, *I* don't know – how many John Browns *are* there in Somerset House? . . . Good grief! . . . Of course, if it's any consolation it may not be his real name . . . I know it doesn't help . . . That's an idea, yes . . . His fingerprints . . . No, no,

I'll get them on a glass or something – Well, he might have been in trouble some time . . .

Brown's ward. BROWN *is working on a shapeless piece of basketry.*
MATRON *enters.*
MATRON: What is it?
BROWN: Basketwork.
MATRON: But what is it for?
BROWN: Therapy.
MATRON: You're making fun of me.
BROWN: It is functional on one level only. If that. *You'd* like me
    to make a sort of laundry basket and lower myself in it out of
    the window. That would be functional on *two* levels. At
    least.
    (*Regards the mess sadly.*) And I'm not even blind.
    (MATRON *silently dispossesses* BROWN *of his basketry.*)
MATRON: What about *painting*, Mr Brown?
    (*That strikes a chord.*)
BROWN: Painting . . . I used to do a bit of painting.
MATRON: Splendid. Would you do some for me?
BROWN: Paint in here?
MATRON: Nurse Coates will bring you materials.
BROWN: What colours do you like?
MATRON: I like all colours. Just paint what you fancy. Paint
    scenes from your own life.
BROWN: Clever! Should I paint my last place of employment?
MATRON: I'm trying to help you.
BROWN: I'm sorry. I know you are. But I don't need help.
    Everything's fine for me. (*Pause.*) Would you like me to
    paint the countryside?
MATRON: Yes, that would be nice.

The hospital office. The DOCTOR *is on the phone.*
DOCTOR: No . . . well, we haven't got anything against him really.

He's not doing any *harm*. No, he pays regularly. We can't really refuse . . . He's got lots left . . .

Brown's ward. BROWN *is painting a landscape all over one wall. He hasn't got very far, but one sees the beginnings of a simple pastoral scene, competent but amateurish.* MAGGIE *enters, carrying cut flowers in a vase.*

MAGGIE: Hello – (*She notices.*)

BROWN: I'll need some more paint.

MAGGIE: (*Horrified*) Brownie! I gave you drawing paper!

BROWN: I like space. I like the big sweep – the contours of hills all flowing.

MAGGIE: Matron will have a fit.

BROWN: What are the flowers?

MAGGIE: You don't deserve them.

BROWN: Who are they from?

MAGGIE: Me.

BROWN: Maggie!

MAGGIE: I didn't buy them.

BROWN: Pinched them?

MAGGIE: Picked them.

BROWN: A lovely thought. Put them over there. I should bring *you* flowers.

MAGGIE: I'm not ill.

BROWN: Nor am I. Do you like it?

MAGGIE: Very pretty.

BROWN: I'm only doing it to please Matron really. I could do with a bigger brush. There's more paint, is there? I'll need a lot of blue. It's going to be summer in here.

MAGGIE: It's summer outside. Isn't that good enough for you? (BROWN *stares out of the window: gardens, flowers, trees, hills.*)

BROWN: I couldn't stay out there. You don't get the benefits.

MAGGIE: (*Leaving*) I'll have to tell Matron, you know.

BROWN: You don't get the looking after. And the privacy. (*He considers.*) I'll have to take the curtains down.

The hospital office.

MATRON: What did the psychiatrist think?

DOCTOR: He likes him.

MATRON: (*Sour*) He's likeable.

DOCTOR: (*Thoughtfully*) I just thought I'd let him stay the night. I wanted to go back to bed and it seemed the easiest thing to do. I thought that in the morning . . . Well, I'm not sure what I thought would happen in the morning.

MATRON: He's not simple – he's giving nothing away. Not even to Nurse Coates.

DOCTOR: Well, keep her at it.

MATRON: She doesn't need much keeping.

SCENE 12

Brown's ward. BROWN *has painted a whole wall and is working on a second one.* MAGGIE *sits on the bed.*

MAGGIE: That was when I started nursing, after that.

BROWN: Funny. I would have thought your childhood was all to do with ponies and big stone-floored kitchens . . .

MAGGIE: Goes to show. What was your childhood like?

BROWN: Young . . . I wish I had more money.

MAGGIE: You've got a lot. You must have had a good job . . .?

BROWN: Centre forward for Arsenal.

MAGGIE: You're not fair! You don't give me anything in return.

BROWN: This painting's for you, Maggie . . . If I'd got four times as much money, I'd take four rooms and paint one for each season. But I've only got money for the summer.

MAGGIE: What will you do when it's gone?

BROWN: (*Seriously*) I don't know. Perhaps I'll get ill and have to go to a hospital. But I'll miss you, Maggie.

MAGGIE: If you had someone to look after you you wouldn't have this trouble.

BROWN: What trouble?

MAGGIE: If you had someone to cook your meals and do your laundry you'd be all right, wouldn't you?

BROWN: It's the things that go with it.

MAGGIE: You should have got married. I bet you had chances.

BROWN: Perhaps.

MAGGIE: It's not too late.

BROWN: You don't think so?

MAGGIE: You're attractive.

BROWN: What are you like when you're not in uniform? I can't think of you not being a nurse. It belongs to another world I'm not part of any more.

MAGGIE: What have you got about hospitals?

BROWN: A hospital is a very dependable place. Anything could be going on outside. Since I've been in here – there could be a war on, and for once it's got nothing to do with me. I don't even know about it. Fire, flood and misery of all kinds, across the world or over the hill, it can go on, but this is a private ward; I'm paying for it. (*Pause.*) The meals come in on trays, on the dot – the dust never settles before it's wiped – clean laundry at the appointed time – the matron does her round, not affected by anything outside. You need never know anything, it doesn't touch you.

MAGGIE: That's not true, Brownie.

BROWN: I know it's not.

MAGGIE: Then you shouldn't try and make it true.

BROWN: I know I shouldn't.
    (*Pause.*)

MAGGIE: Is that all there is to it, then?

BROWN: You've still got theories?

MAGGIE: There's a new one. You're a retired forger.

BROWN: Ha! The money's real enough.

MAGGIE: I know.

BROWN: How do you know?

MAGGIE: (*Shamefaced*) They had it checked.
    (BROWN *laughs*.)

BROWN: They've got to make it difficult. I've got to be a crook or a lunatic.

MAGGIE: Then why don't you tell them where you came from?

BROWN: They want to pass me on. But they don't know who to, or where. I'm happy here.

17

MAGGIE: Haven't you been happy anywhere else?

BROWN: Yes. I had a good four years of it once.

MAGGIE: In hospital?

BROWN: No, that was abroad.

MAGGIE: Where have you been?

BROWN: All over. I've been among French, Germans, Greeks, Turks, Arabs . . .

MAGGIE: What were you doing?

BROWN: Different things in different places. (*Smiles.*) I was painting in France.

MAGGIE: An artist?

BROWN: Oh very. Green and brown. I could turn a row of tanks into a leafy hedgerow. Not literally. Worse luck.

SCENE 13

The hospital office. The DOCTOR *is on the phone.*

DOCTOR: . . . He meant camouflage . . . Well, I realize that, but there are a number of points to narrow the field . . . Must be records of some kind . . . Service in France and Germany, probably Middle East . . .

SCENE 14

Brown's ward. BROWN *has painted two walls and is working on a third.*

MAGGIE: It's very nice, Brownie. Perhaps you'll be famous and people will come here to see your mural.

BROWN: I wouldn't let them in.

MAGGIE: After you're dead. In a hundred years.

BROWN: Yes, they could come in then.

MAGGIE: What will you do when you've finished the room?

BROWN: Go back to bed. It'll be nice in here. Hospital routine in a pastoral setting. That's kind of perfection, really.

MAGGIE: You could have put your bed in the garden.

BROWN: What's the date?

MAGGIE: The twenty-seventh.

BROWN: I've lasted well, haven't I?

18

MAGGIE: How old are you?

BROWN: Twice your age.

MAGGIE: Forty-four?

BROWN: And more. (*Looking close*.) What are you thinking?

MAGGIE: Before I was born, you were in the war.

BROWN: (*Moves*) Yes. Private Brown.

MAGGIE: Was it awful being in the war?

BROWN: I didn't like the first bit. But in the end it was very nice.

MAGGIE: What happened to you?

BROWN: I got taken prisoner . . . Four years.

MAGGIE: Is that when you were happy?

BROWN: Yes . . . Funny thing, that camp. Up to then it was all
    terrible. Chaos – all the pins must have fallen off the map,
    dive bombers and bullets. Oh dear, yes. The camp was like
    breathing out for the first time in months. I couldn't believe
    it. It was like winning, being captured. The war was still
    going on but I wasn't going to it any more. They gave us
    food, life was regulated, in a box of earth and wire and sky.
    On my second day I knew what it reminded me of.

MAGGIE: What?

BROWN: Here. It reminded me of here.

SCENE 15

The hospital office. Present are the DOCTOR, MATRON *and* MAGGIE.
The DOCTOR *holding a big book – a record of admissions, his finger on
a line.*

DOCTOR: John Brown. And an address. (*To* MAGGIE.) Well done.

MAGGIE: (*Troubled*) But does it make any difference?

MATRON: What was he doing round here?

DOCTOR: Staying with relatives – or holiday, we can find out.

MATRON: So long ago?

DOCTOR: Compound fracture – car accident. The driver paid for
    him . . . Well, something to go on at last!

MAGGIE: He hasn't done anything wrong, has he?

Brown's ward. The painting nearly covers the walls. BROWN *is finishing it off in one corner.*

BROWN: I was a regular, you see, and peace didn't match up to the war I'd had. There was too much going on.

MAGGIE: So what did you do then?

BROWN: This and that. Didn't fancy a lot. (*He paints.*) Shouldn't you be working, or something?

MAGGIE: I'll go if you like.

BROWN: I like you being here. Just wondered.

MAGGIE: Wondered what?

BROWN: I'm telling you about myself, aren't I? I shouldn't put you in that position – if they find out they'll blame you for not passing it on.

MAGGIE: But you haven't done anything wrong, have you, Brownie?

BROWN: Is that what you're here for?

MAGGIE: No.

(BROWN *finishes off the painting and stands back.*)

BROWN: There.

MAGGIE: It's lovely.

BROWN: Yes. Quite good. It'll be nice, to sit here inside my painting. I'll enjoy that.

SCENE 17

The hospital office. The DOCTOR *is on the phone.*

DOCTOR: . . . Brown. John Brown – yes, he was here before, a long time ago – we've got him in the records – Mmm – and an address. We'll start checking . . . there must be *somebody* . . .

SCENE 18

Brown's ward. The walls are covered with paintings. BROWN *is sitting on the bed. The door opens and a strange nurse –* NURSE JONES *– enters with Brown's lunch on a tray.*

JONES: Are you ready for lunch –? (*Sees the painting.*) My, my,

aren't you clever – it's better than anyone would have
thought.

BROWN: Where's Maggie?

JONES: Nurse Coates? I don't know.

BROWN: But – she's my nurse.

JONES: Yours? Well, she's everybody's.

BROWN: (*Worried*) You don't understand – she's looking after *me*,
you see.

(*The* DOCTOR *enters;* NURSE JONES *leaves.*)

DOCTOR: (*Cheerful*) Well, Mr Brown, good news.

BROWN: (*Wary*) Yes?

DOCTOR: You're going to have visitors.

BROWN: Visitors?

DOCTOR: Your sister Mabel and her husband. They were amazed
to hear from you.

BROWN: They didn't hear from *me*.

DOCTOR: They're travelling up tomorrow. All your friends had
been wondering where you'd got to –

BROWN: Where's Nurse Coates gone?

DOCTOR: Nowhere. She's round about. I think she's on nights
downstairs this week. I understand that you were here once
before – as a child.

BROWN: Yes. (*Angrily*) You couldn't leave well alone, could you?

DOCTOR: (*Pause; not phoney any more*) It's not enough, Mr
Brown. You've got to . . . *connect* . . .

SCENE 19

The hospital office. BROWN *appears, dressed, carrying his bags, from
the direction of his room. He sees* MAGGIE *and stops. She sees him.*

MAGGIE: Brownie! Where are you going?

BROWN: Back.

MAGGIE: Back where?

(*He does not answer.*)

You blame me?

BROWN: No. No. I don't *really*. You had to tell them, didn't you?

MAGGIE: I'm sorry – I –

BROWN: You thought it was for the best.

MAGGIE: Yes, I did. I still do. It's not good for you, what you're doing.

BROWN: How do you know? – *you* mean it wouldn't be good for *you*. How do you know what's good for me?

MAGGIE: They're coming tomorrow. Family, friends; isn't that good?

BROWN: I could have found them, if I'd wanted. I didn't come here for that. (*Comes up to her.*) They won. (*Looks out through the front doors.*) I feel I should breathe in before going out there.

MAGGIE: I can't let you go, Brownie.

BROWN: (*Gently mocking*) Regulations?

MAGGIE: I can't.

BROWN: I'm free to come and go. I'm paying.

MAGGIE: I know – but it *is* a hospital.

BROWN: (*Smiles briefly*) I'm not ill. Don't wake the doctor, he doesn't like being woken. (*Moves.*) Don't be sorry – I had a good time here with you. Do you think they'll leave my painting?

MAGGIE: Brownie . . .

BROWN: Trouble is, I've always been so *well*. If I'd been *sick* I would have been all right.

(*He goes out into the night.*)

TEETH

CHARACTERS

GEORGE POLLOCK
early thirties, a saloon-bar Lothario, handsome, big white smile

HARRY DUNN
the dentist; smaller, middle thirties, very clean and pink, light-framed spectacles; tight, even white smile

THE WIFE
thirty, white housecoat (dental receptionist), neat, hair in bun, good teeth

AGNES
young spinster, on the shelf, sad

FLORA
a bit older, same boat

Teeth was first transmitted in February 1967 by the BBC. The cast included:

GEORGE POLLOCK	John Stride
HARRY DUNN	John Wood
THE WIFE	Andre Melly
PRODUCER	Graeme McDonald
DIRECTOR	Alan Gibson

The waiting room.
Tatty furniture, ancient magazines.
Three people.

AGNES *and* FLORA *sit together, conspiratorially, on a settee, speaking quietly, on the borderline of audibility as far as* GEORGE POLLOCK *is concerned. From behind his illustrated paper he eavesdrops, his eyes switching over the top of his paper. That is to say, we see the paper first (it is* Woman's Own*) and then* GEORGE *peeps from behind it. We note, now or later, that he has been studying a bra-and-panty ad. But* AGNES *is coming through now.*

AGNES: The first thing I thought was – I'll have to kill myself now.

FLORA: No!

AGNES: Oh yes. I knew it was the end. And it was the real thing for me.

FLORA: He wasn't worth it.

AGNES: (*Sighs*) I don't know. There never was another for me.

FLORA: Plenty of fish in the sea, I say.

AGNES: Different kettle altogether. Yes, I seriously considered it. That'll teach him, I thought.

FLORA: What'll?

AGNES: *Killing* myself.

FLORA: Ah. Serve him right.

AGNES: Yes, it would've. You'll be sorry, I thought, Jack Stevens – *then* you'll know. (*Sighs again.*) Yes, I came close; I wouldn't be here today if we hadn't been all-electric.

FLORA: (*Nods sympathetically*) He was luckier than he knew.

AGNES: He would've carried his burden of guilt to his grave . . . instead of which he's got a very nice trading station in the China Seas. (*A reprise*) . . . You'll be sorry, Jack Stevens – then you'll know what you've done.

FLORA: What brought it about, then?

AGNES: (*Leans closer with meaningful intent*) Walked into the bathroom without knocking.

FLORA: No!

27

AGNES: Without so much as a by your leave.

FLORA: Disgusting.

AGNES: Said he didn't know I was in there.

FLORA: Well, he would, wouldn't he?

AGNES: And he did.

FLORA: What did you do?

AGNES: Turned my back quick as a flash. But he'd seen.

FLORA: He knew what he was doing all right.

AGNES: '*Agnes*,' he said, 'what have you done to your *teeth*?!' (*Pause.*)

FLORA: Teeth?

AGNES: I was brushing my teeth after dinner. It's only the two middle ones that come out – the rest's my own, what there is, but of course it's the *gap*, isn't it?

FLORA: Oh yes. It's the gap that'd give you away.

AGNES: (*Recalling it with tragic clarity*) 'Agnes, . . . what have you done to your *teeth*?!' . . . It wasn't the same after that with Jack Stevens. A week later he'd got his third mate's papers and he was taken away, over the horizon, by a dirty black tramp – yeh, Irene Castle from Cardiff, I still look out for her.

FLORA: Got all her own teeth, has she?

AGNES: 'sa boat.

(POLLOCK – *hereafter* GEORGE – *has allowed his curiosity to leave him exposed, ear cocked, eavesdropping. The two women catch him at it. He gives them a great white smile.*
The door into the reception room opens. The receptionist (the WIFE) *does not notice* GEORGE *at first and seems about to summon one of the two women. But* GEORGE *has stood up. The* WIFE *is somewhat taken aback but recovers. She changes the summons.*)

WIFE: Er . . . Mr Pollock . . .

(*The women stare at the queue-jumper* GEORGE *as he follows the* WIFE, *smiling.*)
(*To the women*) Mr Dunn won't keep you a moment . . .
(GEORGE *and the* WIFE *go into the reception room. As soon as the door is closed behind them, the* WIFE *turns to him in urgent enquiry, keeping her voice down.*)
What's the matter?

28

GEORGE: Nothing – I mean –

WIFE: You shouldn't come here –

> (*She glances at the second closed door, which leads into the surgery.*)

GEORGE: Why not?

WIFE: I'm not impressed – just because you've got a guilty conscience –

GEORGE: No . . .

WIFE: Well, you should have –

GEORGE: I'm sorry, lover – I was terribly disappointed myself – really disappointed.

WIFE: And don't call me lover –

GEORGE: I'm sorry – (*Tries to touch*) Who gave you those earrings –?

WIFE: (*Moves away*) You let me down –

GEORGE: I had to demonstrate a new line – there was big money involved – They [*earrings*] aren't real pearl, are they? Can't be –

WIFE: You've got another on the side – How many sides have you got?

GEORGE: Oh now, that's cynical, that is –

WIFE: Yesterday of all days –

GEORGE: Listen, you mustn't be so possessive – who gave you those earrings?

WIFE: A very good friend.

GEORGE: Don't give me that – you're a respectable married woman. It was Harry, was it?

WIFE: It was my birthday –

GEORGE: I know it was your birthday – I told you I couldn't get away.

WIFE: You can get away when it suits you – You're going off me.

GEORGE: How could I? – Think of last Saturday after tea – it doesn't add up –

WIFE: Lust –

GEORGE: Oh, I'm hurt –

WIFE: I knew it was a mistake –

GEORGE: Don't let's have regrets –

WIFE: Don't make me laugh –

29

GEORGE: Don't cry –

WIFE: You make me sick. I don't care anyway – I've been looking about, too, you know –

GEORGE: No, I bet it was Harry – Very nice, too – cultured, of course [*the earrings*] –

WIFE: Think you can get away with anything – *will you please stop grinning!*

GEORGE: Smiling – I've got a nice smile – Come here, you misguided sexy insatiable receptionist you –
(*He reaches to touch her; she recoils. Eyes on surgery door.*)

WIFE: For goodness' sake!

GEORGE: He can't hear us.

WIFE: Anyway, I'm working –

GEORGE: Live dangerously – let yourself go –

WIFE: Oh, give over –

GEORGE: You like my smile really – it's one of the two things you like about me –

WIFE: You're only like this when you're trying to make up –

GEORGE: We're friends again, aren't we?

WIFE: Are we?

GEORGE: Kiss and make up –

WIFE: Listen, you can't carry on like that here –

GEORGE: Don't worry about him –

WIFE: You've got to go now – you shouldn't have come – there are patients waiting –

GEORGE: I'm a patient –

WIFE: Please, George – they've got appointments –

GEORGE: I've got an appointment –

WIFE: You haven't –

GEORGE: Yes I have –

WIFE: What for?

GEORGE: Teeth.

WIFE: You've got toothache?

GEORGE: No, it's my check-up. Six-monthly.

WIFE: It's not. (*Going to her desk diary.*)

GEORGE: Yes it is – would you care to examine me?

WIFE: Oh, stop it, will you? – (*Scanning the diary*) I can't find it –

GEORGE: There was a reminder at the office –

WIFE: What reminder?

GEORGE: My appointment. I can see the system's cracking up – you can't keep your mind on it, or off the other.

WIFE: I thought you came to see *me* – I thought you came to be nice –

GEORGE: I am being nice – I'm charming the pants off you – that's what brought us together.

(*He advances, she backs, glancing at the surgery door.*)

WIFE: You make me ashamed.

(*The surgery door opens; the* WIFE *jumps;* HARRY DUNN *smiles.*)
Look who's here, Harry.

HARRY: Hello, George. Nice to see you.

GEORGE: How are you, Harry?

HARRY: Ready and waiting.

WIFE: I'm sorry – we were –

GEORGE: Having a natter.

HARRY: Right you are. Well, come on in. (*To the* WIFE) Tell you what – as it's George, while I'm just giving him the once-over, could you carry on with the files. I'll give you a buzz if there's any concrete to be mixed.

GEORGE: You won't find much wrong with *my* choppers.

HARRY: (*To the* WIFE) In flashing form, is he?

GEORGE: Ooh, he's wicked, isn't he?

(*The* WIFE *smiles wanly. The two men go into the surgery,* HARRY *closing the door.* HARRY *has a full complement of dental apparatus. It is a good-sized surgery, and the chair and machine sit in a good space, silent, waiting, ready for* GEORGE. HARRY *and* GEORGE *look at it a moment, as though the apparatus were a third occupant.*) Well . . .

(*He goes to meet it. Sits in the chair. There is some little 'business' over the first few lines of dialogue: principally,* HARRY *is sorting and readying a few shiny metal implements, and he fixes the paper-towel bib round* GEORGE's *neck.*

The machine is a modern one. Its body holds two or three squirters, rather like the nozzle of a petrol pump, only the rubber tube attached disappears into the machine when the nozzle is not in use: plus a swivel table for the tools: and the big praying-mantis leg of the high-speed drill.

HARRY *should make use of all his tools and nozzles, squirting air and water, swivelling, drilling, etc. The point is that* HARRY *is playing with* GEORGE. *The dental procedure does not have to be authentic or accurate. The director and actors can assume that there is nothing much wrong with* GEORGE's *teeth, and that there is a logical rationalization for using the machine indiscriminately for effect.*)

HARRY: Haven't seen you for a while.

GEORGE: No – you know how it is. I've hardly had time to turn round.

HARRY: Hard at it, are you?

GEORGE: My life's not my own.

HARRY: Yes, I was only saying to Prudence – we haven't seen George for ages.

GEORGE: Yes, we'll have to get together.

HARRY: Of course, we lead a very quiet life compared to yours, I expect.

GEORGE: I'm never at home.

HARRY: Out and about, on the town – that's George all over – I told Prudence.

GEORGE: On the job.

HARRY: Lovely work if you can get it. Mind you, we haven't had a lot of chance anyway – with Prudence going to the evening classes.

GEORGE: Oh yes.

HARRY: Did you know about that?

GEORGE: Er . . . no.

HARRY: Shows how long it is since we had you round. Now, let's have a look at you.

(GEORGE *opens his mouth.* HARRY *peers and probes . . .*)

. . . Yes, there's her flower-arranging . . . dressmaking – I don't know, she shouldn't be bored – I mean, she's a career woman really – but she's got to fill up her life. And then there's her charity work . . . did you know about her charity work?

GEORGE: (*Signifies denial*) Ughnugh.

HARRY: Must have been soon after we last saw you that she took it up. Helps with old people, once or twice a week, takes

32

them about, cheers them up, poor things. She's more out
than in . . . Still, it's only a matter of time till *I'm* an old
person so I expect she'll have more time for me then . . .
(*Smiles; withdraws.*)
(GEORGE *closes his mouth. Reaches for the mouthwash.*)

GEORGE: Well, mud in your eye, Harry – I see it's your round.
(GEORGE *washes out his mouth and sits back.*)

HARRY: No wonder she's so tired.

GEORGE: What?

HARRY: Prudence. Yes, I was only saying to her – it's about time
we had George and Mary round for a game of cards. We used
to enjoy that. Lovely girl, Mary – one of the best. Just as well
she's a working wife, I suppose.

GEORGE: How do you mean?

HARRY: How's *your* social life?

GEORGE: Oh, very quiet.

HARRY: Quiet evenings at home.

GEORGE: That sort of thing. Only I'm never there. That's why
they're quiet.
(*He starts to laugh, but has to open his mouth for* HARRY.)

HARRY: Yes, just as well for Mary – she's not the sort to sit
around the house . . .
(*He probes.*)
You've been letting yourself go a bit, haven't you?
(GEORGE'*s worried eyes.*)
I'm glad you came in today – this is a serious warning,
George. You think what people can't see isn't happening –
but it all comes out in the end. Your sins always find you out.
(GEORGE'*s eyes;* HARRY *probes.*)
I can spot the signs you know, a mile off, so you better watch
it, hadn't you? I must say, I wouldn't have thought it of you.
(*He withdraws long enough for –*)

GEORGE: Now hold on, Harry –
(HARRY *flicks on the spotlight. The glare is in* GEORGE'*s eyes.*
GEORGE *grips the sides of the chair.*)

HARRY: I'm giving you fair warning – and Mary wouldn't thank
you for it if it came to the worst, would she?

GEORGE: Look here –

(HARRY *squirts*.)

HARRY: Gums – it's your gums you have to watch, they're the ones doing it. You haven't been taking my advice – I told you: daily massage and woodpoints in the crannies. If your gums go then the lot goes. (*He withdraws*.) A serious warning, George.

GEORGE: Oh – (*In relief he takes a swig of water*.)

HARRY: You're not supposed to *drink* it.

GEORGE: My teeth are fine, Harry – I mean I don't want to teach you your job but – (*He has to open his mouth to say 'but' and in goes the steel*.)

HARRY: No pain? – there?

(*Jab*. GEORGE *jumps*.)

Yes, I thought as much.

GEORGE: You caught my gum there, Harry –

(HARRY *sighs and turns away, fiddling with his tools*.)

HARRY: Ah well . . . Yes, I've given it a bit of thought and I'm going to have it out.

GEORGE: What?

HARRY: I mean – she gets home absolutely dead beat. She just wants to go to sleep.

GEORGE: Oh. Well, I suppose it takes it out of her.

HARRY: The flower-arranging?

GEORGE: Oh well, I suppose it requires a certain concentration.

HARRY: You may be right. *You*'ve got the best of it.

GEORGE: Me?

HARRY: Well, entertaining clients and that sort of thing – at least you can take Mary along.

GEORGE: Oh, it's not her kind of thing. Business, you know. It's just hard work.

HARRY: Same boat, then.

GEORGE: Yes.

HARRY: Of course, women notice these things.

GEORGE: What?

HARRY: When you get home dead beat. Just want to go straight to sleep.

GEORGE: Oh yes.

HARRY: Same thing with me and Prudence. Only the other way round, of course. Makes one very tense, you know – and in my

34

job you've got to have a very steady hand, got to be cool and calm – (*He turns round with a wicked tool.*)

GEORGE: Harry! – (*He brings his voice down.*) There's nothing wrong, is there, Harry?

HARRY: Well, I've seen better, George. I don't know if I can save that one.

GEORGE: Don't be daft.

HARRY: Pink toothbrush – admit it.

GEORGE: What?

HARRY: They've been bleeding, when you brush your teeth.

GEORGE: Well, a bit, perhaps. Now and again.

HARRY: Pyorrhoea.

GEORGE: What?

HARRY: Setting in. (*Shakes his head.*) I've told you before, George – you've only got one set of teeth. Let them go once and they've gone for good. Now look at my teeth – (*He shows them*) I wasn't born with better teeth than you, but I look after them. I massage the gums. Use woodpoints on them. I've got a row of good strong white shiny teeth for that. See? Teeth are very important on every level. I mean, apart from anything else, it was my teeth that first attracted Prudence to me – she told me that.

(GEORGE *starts to speak but* HARRY *is in there: jab.* GEORGE *winces.*)

There – see that? Blood.

(GEORGE *starts to protest, to move.*)

Hey – hold on, mouth open, head still – I don't want to slip with this little number.

(GEORGE *freezes in alarm.* HARRY *starts to whistle softly.*)

. . . Yes, Prudence is very particular about teeth. I'm sure Mary's the same. She's got a lovely smile herself . . . Of course, I'm not saying that teeth are a key to a man's *character*, but it's the smile women look for. (*He withdraws.*) I mean, that swine Collins had good teeth, I'll give him that, and he took Prudence in completely.

GEORGE: What?

HARRY: Oh – have I spoken out of turn? Well, it's all water under the bridge now.

GEORGE: What is?

HARRY: Collins – a trainee from the dental hospital. Nasty piece of work. Thought I was an idiot.

GEORGE: Oh?

HARRY: Well, you know what Prudence is – very impressionable, a bit young and dizzy, a sitting duck for a bastard like Collins – I wouldn't tell Mary about this, you know, women don't like each other to know when they've made a bit of a fool of themselves – but there was a little something between Prudence and Collins. Well, I didn't blame *her*, of course – I mean, she's an innocent, really – Collins took advantage of her. No, I just handled it my own way.

GEORGE: Really?

HARRY: Oh yes. Collins wouldn't be showing his face around the fair sex for quite a while to come . . . and a real smiler, he was. It was the craftiness I didn't like. He was seducing her right under my nose and he thought I couldn't see. An insult to my intelligence – that was it.

GEORGE: What did you –?

(HARRY *has turned round, holding a syringe.*)

What's that?

HARRY: No point in causing unnecessary suffering, is there?

(GEORGE *opens his mouth to protest.*)

That's it. (*He puts in the needle.*) We'll just give it a minute . . . Yes, well, I didn't go to law, if that's what you mean. I *could* have done – oh yes, an open and shut case – I could have sued him for thousands. But of course there was no point – I mean, he wasn't a man of substance. If he'd been a man of substance, I wouldn't have hesitated. Thousands. And the scandal. It would have ruined a man of substance. How's business?

GEORGE: What?

HARRY: Doing well? I always said to Prudence, George is a man with a big future. Barring accidents. Oh yes.

GEORGE: Well, it's all go. No time to myself for weeks.

HARRY: Of course it is. How's the rowing?

GEORGE: The what?

HARRY: I thought you were a rowing man.

GEORGE: No, I wouldn't say that.

HARRY: Oh, I thought you were a great one for the sculls on the Serpentine.

GEORGE: Not me.

HARRY: Umm. Well . . . getting numb?

GEORGE: What? Oh – yes, I think so.

HARRY: Let's have a look – (*Probes.*) Yes, funny business. I mean, I had no reason to disbelieve it, because I know that with Tuesday being Prudence's free afternoon – (GEORGE *jerks.*)

Sorry!

(HARRY *withdraws.*)

Better leave it a minute, then. (*Sighs.*) Who can one believe, then?

GEORGE: Oh – of course – I'm with you – you mean on the Serpentine with Prudence.

HARRY: That's right.

GEORGE: *Rowing!*

HARRY: That's what I said.

GEORGE: Yes – quite. I mean, it wasn't actually *rowing*.

HARRY: No?

GEORGE: No – it was more in the nature of paddling.

HARRY: Ah.

GEORGE: Yes, I was in the Park, and you don't often get a chance to have a bit of a paddle – yes, I was just fixing up a boat for myself – it was more a canoe, really – and lo! – there was Prudence – 'Hello,' I said, 'what are you doing here?' 'Hello,' she said, 'fancy seeing you.' 'Fancy a paddle,' I said . . . Yes, she mentioned seeing me, did she?

HARRY: No, she didn't mention it. It was Archie Sullivan.

GEORGE: Who?

HARRY: Archie Sullivan. Do you know him?

GEORGE: No, I don't believe I do.

HARRY: Oh. He knows *you*.

GEORGE: Oh.

HARRY: Yes, he told me he saw you and Prudence having a bit of a row on the Serpentine on her afternoon off work. I can't think what she was doing in the Park – though of course she does have her activities as I told you.

GEORGE: Yes, it was the flowers, I think. Picking flowers. To arrange.

HARRY: That's funny.

GEORGE: Well, I suppose you have to bring your own – you won't find the local authorities lashing out the rates on floral composition.

HARRY: No, but Tuesday is old people.

GEORGE: Oh – yes – She did have some old people with her. Three or four. Very decent lot, I thought. Very clean and well behaved.

HARRY: Did you have them in the boat?

GEORGE: No, they didn't fancy it.

HARRY: Very nice.

GEORGE: What?

HARRY: Very nice, if you can get it. I don't know how you do it. Still getting your bit, then? On the job?

GEORGE: Now, Harry –

HARRY: No, I envy you – what a job! Lovely.

GEORGE: Oh, the job – Well, it's very varied work, of course –

HARRY: Yes, you should have been on 'What's My Line?' They'd never have guessed you, would they, not with your mime. There you'd be rowing your boat – they'd never guess Salesman in a million years. You'd have got a diploma. (*He has wandered off and has suddenly turned round with a mallet and chisel.* GEORGE *sits bolt upright and squawks* –)

GEORGE: Harr!

(HARRY *puts the chisel against the head-rest bracket and gives it a good thump with the mallet.*)

HARRY: Must get that seen to. (*He puts down the mallet and chisel.*) Open up now. (*Probes.*) Yes, you won't feel a thing.
(*The drill;* GEORGE's *eyes.*)
Mmmm . . . (*Whistles softly for a moment.*) Incidentally, when you and Mary come round could you bring Prudence's shoes with you.
(GEORGE's *eyes.*)
Steady now. (*Withdraws.*)

GEORGE: What?

HARRY: Apparently she left them at your place after she fell in.

GEORGE: What are you talking about?

HARRY: Shoes. She left them behind. At your place after she fell in. Of course, that's my deduction, I may be wrong.

GEORGE: You are wrong, Harry. What are you trying to say? – Prudence never came home without her shoes, did she?

HARRY: No, she was wearing Mary's. Lucky thing you live so close to the Park – she might have got pneumonia with her shoes wet.

GEORGE: Mary's shoes?

HARRY: Got Mary's name in them. Same kind of shoes, only with Mary's name in them. Lucky they take the same size. Must remember to thank her. Rinse please.
(GEORGE *rinses and thinks*.)

GEORGE: Oh – yes. Of course. Yes, it was when she was getting out of the boat, she sort of –

HARRY: Fell in.

GEORGE: Well, no – I mean – she certainly got her feet wet, yes. 'Tell you what,' I said – 'My place is very handy – I'll just nip up for a pair of Mary's shoes for you to go home in, don't want to get pneumonia –'

HARRY: But she went with you, didn't she?

GEORGE: Well, it seemed simpler, yes – cup of tea to warm her up – footbath – Yes, you asked her about it, did you?

HARRY: No, I've hardly had a chance to speak to her. It was Archie Sullivan who told me.

GEORGE: Oh? I must say, he gets about, doesn't he? (*Laugh*.) *He* ought to have been on 'What's My Line?' if anyone – with *his* mime – just following people about, they'd never guess him in a million years.

HARRY: Oh, I don't know. I mean, he's a private enquiry agent, isn't he?

GEORGE: Is he?

HARRY: Well, he says he is. I don't see why he should lie about it. (*Up*.) Mary!
(*The door opens and the* WIFE *enters*.)
Ah, Mary – this husband of yours is having a bit of trouble after all –

WIFE: Not serious is it, Harry?

GEORGE: I meant to tell you, lover – you'd never guess who I met in the Park –

(*He finds his mouth full of drill*.)

HARRY: (*Drilling*) Well, it's not too good at all. He hasn't been taking care. I'm trying to save what I can.

But . . . (*Withdraws*.)

(GEORGE *starts to speak*.)

Spit.

(GEORGE *rinses*.)

GEORGE: Yes – I couldn't get a taxi – traffic jams as far as you could see – and I had to meet this big client – so I thought, I know – I'll cut through the Park – and of course I forgot about the lake – bang in the way – so what do you think I did? I'll tell you –

(HARRY *has returned with brush and liquid*.)

HARRY: Now whatever you do, don't move your head while I'm doing this.

GEORGE: What does it do?

HARRY: Stains green – we don't want to get it on your teeth, but it's very good for your gum condition, so I'm giving it a try. Ready?

(GEORGE *freezes with mouth open*. HARRY *administers. The* WIFE *mixes paste*.)

. . . I was just saying, Mary – old George has a very interesting job. Takes him into all sorts of places.

WIFE: Mostly pubs.

HARRY: Yes – and the lake.

WIFE: What lake?

HARRY: The Serpentine. You'll never guess what he was doing yesterday.

WIFE: Demonstrating a new line, he said.

HARRY: Ha-ha – that's a new line – eh, George?

(GEORGE *frozen*.)

(MARY *comes round to the front and notices the extractors. She picks them up*.)

MARY: Harry, you don't mean –?

HARRY: Don't worry – you won't know the difference.

MARY: (*Upset*) It's not the same, though, is it?

HARRY: Well, he should have thought of that in all these months of neglect.

MARY: But he's always brushing his teeth. He's a maniac about them.

HARRY: It's the gums, Mary, it's the gums. Oh – you moved, George!

(*He withdraws.*)

Yes, he was on the lake, demonstrating –

GEORGE: Life-jackets. Have you got green on my teeth?

MARY: Life-jackets?

GEORGE: The new line. I was demonstrating it, rowing a boat – the client was worried about it causing restriction – He was going to order a thousand as long as it didn't interfere with the rowing – that's what he said – so I went out and –

MARY: Life-jackets. It was my birthday, too. He let me down, you know.

HARRY: Tsk, tsk. You don't know when you're well off, George – a beautiful wife –

MARY: Oh really, Harry –

HARRY: Beautiful, I said – and on her birthday – if I was in your shoes, George – oh, that reminds me – Ah! – you moved again? Where was I?

MARY: Do you think I'm beautiful, really, Harry?

HARRY: I say it in front of George. A man would be proud to have you for a wife.

MARY: Oh, Harry – isn't he sweet, George? You see I've got them on? [*Earrings.*]

HARRY: You do something for those earrings. They're nothing by themselves.

MARY: You're flirting!

HARRY: Oh, I wouldn't do it behind George's back.

MARY: No, you don't say much, Harry – but I did wonder – (*She touches her earrings.*)

HARRY: He's a lucky fellow. Yes, I was telling you – he took Prudence for a boat-ride on the Serpentine yesterday.

MARY: He what?

GEORGE: (*Free but strangled*) Yes, I was demonstrating the life-

41

jacket and it all went very well, and suddenly I saw Prudence. Well, I took her for a paddle, just for a minute, and when she was getting out of the boat she slipped and fell in – I mean, got her shoes wet – so as it was cold, I suggested that she borrowed a pair of yours so she wouldn't get pneumonia, and we nipped back to the flat and she borrowed your shoes, I knew you wouldn't mind, of course –

HARRY: They all had a cup of tea.

MARY: All?

HARRY: She had some old people with her, according to George.

GEORGE: Yes – three or four, very nice old people – we all had a brew-up while Prudence was changing her shoes – cup of tea and a piece of cake – me and Prudence and some old folks, in the flat yesterday . . . I forgot to tell you.

HARRY: Old Pru certainly gets about. She's never at home. Just like George.

GEORGE: I meant to tell you – I say, Harry – you haven't got green on my teeth, have you?

HARRY: Only one of them – I told you not to move –

MARY: George –

HARRY: Don't you worry – it's lucky it's that one –

GEORGE: Why? – what's lucky about it?

(HARRY *inserts a clamp: this is a fitting like a tiny girder – the top and bottom hold apart the upper and lower jaw, preventing* GEORGE *from closing his mouth, which is wide open.*)

HARRY: I'm afraid he won't be needing it anyway.

MARY: Not that I care. Life-jackets.

HARRY: Fascinating job. Of course I'm very dull.

MARY: No, you're not, Harry.

HARRY: Nothing very romantic about dentistry.

MARY: But you're romantic at heart, Harry – that's what counts. You're a gentleman.

HARRY: I'm glad you liked the earrings.

MARY: Did you choose them, Harry?

HARRY: Yes – I really looked around for those. Actually, I didn't get around to mentioning it to Prudence – didn't want her to get any ideas –

MARY: What ideas would she get, Harry?

42

(HARRY *withdraws from* GEORGE's *mouth. They go out of his vision and their voices are off screen. We are left with* GEORGE's *eyes and gaping mouth.*)

HARRY: Oh . . . ideas . . .

MARY: You don't have ideas, do you Harry?

HARRY: Well, I'm only human. Aren't we all? George and Prudence and you are . . .

MARY: I'm only human –

HARRY: Of course you are, Mary . . . Are you sure those earrings aren't too tight –

MARY: Well, of course, being new . . .

HARRY: I was worried about that – there, does that pinch a bit –

MARY: It's slipped a bit, that's what it is –

HARRY: This way?

MARY: No, the other way, Harry . . . if you just push my hair back a little –

HARRY: Like this . . .?

MARY: Can you see . . .?

HARRY: Just turn your head a little –

MARY: Yes, Harry . . . that's better . . . that's nice . . .

(*The dialogue runs down to silence while we stay on* GEORGE's *face. His eyes move right and left. He tries to twist but he can't see behind the head-rest.*

Six or seven seconds of silence.

They come back into GEORGE's *view. Harry's tie is almost under his ear. Mary's little white dental receptionist's cap is cock-eyed.* HARRY, *humming softly, fits the oxygen mask over* GEORGE's *face. Dissolve into* FLORA *and* AGNES *in the waiting room. There are two or three new people in the waiting room: old ill-kept faces.* FLORA *and* AGNES *are sitting together as before.*)

FLORA: Oh, I could have had him – just like that – (*She snaps her fingers*) – he was begging me.

AGNES: I can see it now . . . On his knees.

FLORA: On his knees. I told him.

AGNES: You did.

FLORA: Straight out. I want a man who's all there.

AGNES: A whole man –

FLORA: I'm not interested in half a man, I said –

43

AGNES: You're right.

FLORA: Or three-quarters – a complete man is what I want. I want the lot and I can get it. I said to him – I don't care about how you *look* without them – though he did look horrible – that's not the point, it's the principle –

AGNES: That's it, I wouldn't have a man without them on principle –

FLORA: Because if *they*'ve gone already, what'll go next, I said.

AGNES: That's the point.

FLORA: (*Pause; sighs*) Mind you, I was sorry. Six months later mine turned black. I would've had *any*body.

(*They sigh.*

The door to Mary's office opens. MARY *is there. Behind her* GEORGE *comes out of the surgery into the office, followed by* HARRY. GEORGE *is a stricken man.*)

MARY: Er . . . who was next?

(AGNES *and* FLORA *start telling each other to go first.*

We move through to GEORGE *and* HARRY.

GEORGE *moves.* MARY *turns to let him go by, but in the doorway –*)

(*Cool*) Did you say you'd be late again tonight?

HARRY: Same boat – It's dressmaking tonight . . . I wonder what she does with all the dresses she makes . . .

(GEORGE *is going.*)

Oh – by the way – I was going to catch up on the paperwork today – I was wondering if I could ask Mary to stay behind a while – as she knows the ropes . . . Would you mind, Mary – ?

MARY: Oh no, that'll be all right – George is out tonight, he's tied up.

HARRY: Well, take care, George – and don't forget – daily massage, get in there with the woodpoints.

(GEORGE *turns to face the patients, who all stare at him with blank faces.* GEORGE *lets out a thin smile which is more like a wince. His middle tooth is missing. At this, all the patients smile at him, as one of their own. All around there are smiles like broken-down brooms.*)

ANOTHER MOON
CALLED EARTH

CHARACTERS

PENELOPE
BONE
ALBERT
CROUCH
TV COMMENTATOR

Another Moon Called Earth was first transmitted in June 1967 by the BBC. The cast included:

PENELOPE	Diane Cilento
BONE	John Wood
ALBERT	John Bennett
CROUCH	Donald Eccles
PRODUCER	Graeme McDonald
DIRECTOR	Alan Gibson

1. INT. BONE'S STUDY. DAY

BONE *is working.*

PENELOPE: (*Off-camera, distant*) Dah-ling!
    (BONE *takes no notice.*)
    Dah-ling. . . .
    (*He has heard but won't respond.*)
    Help! Fire! Murder!

BONE: (*Murmurs*) Wolf . . .

PENELOPE: Wolves! Look out!! Rape! Rape! Rape!

BONE: Not the most logical of misfortunes.

PENELOPE: Go away, you brute! Don't force me! My husband
    will kill us both!

BONE: I do not insist on plausibility –

PENELOPE: Because I love him.

BONE: Logic is all I ask.

PENELOPE: Oooooh . . . aaaah . . . I can't fight you any more –
    It's too lovely – oh – don't stop – ah – I don't care if he comes
    in –
    (BONE *weakens, cracks and breaks. He slams down his pen,*
    marches to her room.)

2. INT. PENELOPE'S ROOM. DAY

TV set shows ceremonial parade.

PENELOPE: I think you owe me an apology.

BONE: Penelope, you know I can't have my work interrupted –

PENELOPE: Here you are, at the gallop – not bearing buckets of
    water – by no means with a poker raised to my defence –

BONE: Where's Pinkerton?

PENELOPE: – not a trace of aniseed dusted on your trousers to
    lure away the pack – oh no –

BONE: For God's sake –

PENELOPE: As far as you're concerned, credibility begins with
    the thought of my unfaithfulness –

49

BONE: Penelope –

PENELOPE: How dare you?

BONE: I'm sorry –

PENELOPE: If that's what you think of me –

BONE: I don't – not for a moment did I think –

(*They have been competing with the television music.* BONE *turns it off. The music continues, fainter, but more real.*)

PENELOPE: Do you mind? there's going to be a commentary –

(BONE *goes to the window. The music drifts up.* BONE *stares down.*)

BONE: A parade . . .

PENELOPE: A parade . . .! Where've you been for the last ten days?

BONE: Oh yes . . . the moon man. He's come back . . .

PENELOPE: The moon man? You make him sound like a piece of cheese. Don't you see he was the first? He's changed everything.

BONE: Well, he didn't discover it, after all. We all knew it was there. Nor did he have to navigate. He just – sat, really. And somebody had to be first. One thing leads to another; the last thing led to the moon. Logic. (*Peering out*) I can't see him . . . He must come near the end . . .

PENELOPE: You're such a fool – you should be down there cheering with all the rest. Can't you see he's smashed through?

(BONE *closes the window. He turns back from the window.*)

BONE: A cargo. He might have been a piece of cheese. He used to be a monkey. Before that he was a television camera. Now he is a man – but still a cargo. He sat. What else did he do?

PENELOPE: Isn't that enough? He stood off the world with his feet on solid ground, and brought everything into question – because up till then the world was all there was – and always had been – it was us and we were it – and every assumption was part of the world which was all there was, and is no longer –

(*He stares at her, uncomprehending.*)

BONE: What did you want me for?

PENELOPE: I can't remember.

BONE: Well, I'll . . .

PENELOPE: I can't remember.

BONE: Well, I'll . . .

(PENELOPE *remembers*.)

PENELOPE: The window . . .

(BONE *goes to the window and opens it*.)

I wanted you to close the window . . .

(BONE *goes back and closes it*.)

BONE: Penelope, I've go to get on with my work.

PENELOPE: History! Do you think history matters now?

BONE: I do not write history, I dissect it – lay bare the logic which other men have taken to be an arbitrary sequence of accidents.

PENELOPE: Read me what you've done today.

BONE: You think in quantities. I am not a typist.

PENELOPE: You don't care that I'm ill.

BONE: Where's Pinkerton?

PENELOPE: I don't know.

BONE: It's her job to look after you.

PENELOPE: I let her go out to watch the parade.

BONE: She would have had a better view from the window. (*He moves*.)

PENELOPE: Play with me – just till Albert comes.

BONE: Is he coming again?

PENELOPE: Why shouldn't he come?

BONE: Why should he?

PENELOPE: You resent me having visitors?

BONE: You don't have visitors. You have Albert. He never comes to see me.

PENELOPE: There's nothing the matter with you.

BONE: I don't like him.

PENELOPE: You don't know him.

BONE: So you entertain a man I don't even know?

PENELOPE: Entertain?

BONE: What am I supposed to think?

PENELOPE: What do you think?

BONE: I make no judgements. I'm asking you.

PENELOPE: Asking me what?

51

BONE: What would you think in my position?

PENELOPE: I don't think I like your tone. Albert is a very dear friend, and it is natural that I should ask him to come and see me. You have never bothered to emerge from your cave to introduce yourself and now you ask why you don't know him.

BONE: I can put two and two together, you know. Do not think you are dealing with a man who has lost his grapes. Putting two and two together is my speciality. I did not fail to notice it when you began to receive visits from a handsome stranger who arrived once or twice a week with an air of quiet expectation, to leave an hour later looking more than a little complacent –

PENELOPE: Albert's been coming to see me for months.

BONE: I did not leap to any hasty conclusion – I do not deal in appearances, suspicions or wild surmise. I bide my time and examine the evidence. But ten days ago you took to your bed and remained there for no reason that has declared itself, while at the same time, the stranger, Albert by name, began calling every day. So I think it's time we had this out. There is no doubt a logical explanation. (*Starts to pace.*) We have on the one hand, that is to say in bed, an attractive married lady whose relations with her husband are, at their highest, polite, and have been for some time. We have, on the other hand, daily visits by a not unhandsome stranger who rings the doorbell, is admitted by Pinkerton and shown into the lady's bedroom, whence he emerges an hour or so later and lets himself out. Now let's see, does anything suggest itself? Wife in bed, daily visits by stranger. What inference may one draw?

PENELOPE: Sounds to me that he's the doctor.

BONE: Doctor?

PENELOPE: What the hell did you think he was?

BONE: You mean you're ill?

PENELOPE: Good grief . . .

BONE: But he came before and you weren't ill then.

PENELOPE: How do you know? Perhaps I was being brave. You don't care! All you can do is accuse me –

BONE: Really, Penelope, I never –

PENELOPE: How could you – ?

BONE: I made no accusations – I merely –

PENELOPE: You don't care that I'm not well –

BONE: How was I supposed to know you weren't well! I didn't know he was a *doctor*.

(*She turns on the TV*.)

TV COMMENTATOR: . . . and what a magnificent occasion it is! Not even the rain can dampen the spirit here today as the people of London pay their homage to the lunanaut . . . and here comes the second rank of the Household Cavalry – I can see the glint of their brass as they come up out of Whitehall into the square, followed by the massed bands of the Royal Air Force – Well, we still have some way to go before the high point of the procession, the golden capsule itself, reaches us here at – And here comes the fly-past of – (*Jets roar in and whine away.*

BONE *heads for the door*. PENELOPE *switches off the set.*)

PENELOPE: Darling . . . play with me . . .

BONE: I can't . . . I'm so behind . . .

PENELOPE: Oh, play with me.

(*The jets reach the house, roar overhead and whine away.*)

BONE: You don't mean –? Do you mean? – Oh, Penelope . . .

(*He reaches for her. She disengages herself peevishly.*)

PENELOPE: Oh, stop it! I meant play *games*.

BONE: Games.

PENELOPE: Amuse me. Jolly me along.

BONE: That's what Pinkerton's for.

PENELOPE: I got rid of her. Actually.

BONE: What do you mean?

PENELOPE: Gave her the push.

BONE: You didn't.

PENELOPE: This morning.

BONE: Why?

PENELOPE: Sudden impulse.

BONE: You can't.

PENELOPE: Did.

BONE: You must have had a reason.

PENELOPE: Felt like it.

BONE: A reason –

PENELOPE: Thirty-four years – suddenly it was quite enough.

BONE: She was your nanny – part of the family –

PENELOPE: Serve her right.

BONE: You can't just throw your old nanny into the street!

PENELOPE: Did. Well, she always won.

BONE: Won what?

PENELOPE: Everything! Every damn thing. Cards, noughts and crosses, charades – she had a mean winning streak, old Pinkers, so out she went.

BONE: I'm shocked.

PENELOPE: You'd think she'd have known something about the psychology of being a patient – but oh no! 'Oh, Penny, look at me, I've won again!'

BONE: What was behind it? – No such thing as pure impulse – Yes, I'm shocked. And you need someone – I can't stop to – If you're going to stay in bed there's got to be someone –

PENELOPE: Albert will get me somebody. Albert would do anything for me.

BONE: Why, what do you do for him?

PENELOPE: Play with me.

BONE: What exactly is the matter with you?

PENELOPE: It hasn't got a name yet. I'm the first person to have it.

BONE: Measles? Yellow fever? Gastroenteritis? – what's the matter with you?

PENELOPE: Nothing, in here. I'm all right in bed.

BONE: I've got to work.

PENELOPE: Tell me about it!

BONE: Tell you . . . ?

PENELOPE: Entrance me! What are you on now?

BONE: I'm still on the Greeks.

PENELOPE: The Greeks! Warriors and poets! Lovers! Philosophers! Extending knowledge and empire – the rule of law and democracy! – sculptors in marble and gods in the image of man!

BONE: Yes, those Greeks.

PENELOPE: How far have you got?

BONE: The third century.

PENELOPE: You're catching up!

BONE: BC.

PENELOPE: Oh. But you've done the Etruscans.

BONE: Yes.

PENELOPE: The Etruscans! Mysterious shadows in the warm Italian stones that guard the secret of a vanished culture – a civilization under the olive hills!

BONE: (*Rises*) Which explains nothing.

PENELOPE: Play! Here then – just one go. [*Pencils and paper.*] I'll be crosses, you be noughts.

BONE: Are you better today?

PENELOPE: I'm keeping my spirits up. Albert says that's the main thing.

BONE: Do you like him?

PENELOPE: He's all right in his way.

BONE: What way is that?

PENELOPE: Oh, you know.

BONE: No. What does he do?

PENELOPE: He's a doctor.

BONE: I mean –

PENELOPE: Three crosses! I won. You're better than Pinkerton.

BONE: I thought –

PENELOPE: At losing. Keep it up – remember what happened to her. (BONE *looks at her.*)

Only teasing, darling. Again!

BONE: Why does he bring you flowers?

PENELOPE: I'm a private patient.

BONE: You must be paying him a fortune.

PENELOPE: I've got a fortune.

BONE: Well, you never earned it, any more than me!

PENELOPE: Never said I did. But my daddy earned it more than your daddy earned it. Your go.

BONE: What does he do to you, Albert?

PENELOPE: He keeps my spirits up. My trouble is psychosomatic, you see.

BONE: Is it?

55

PENELOPE: Yes. I haven't actually got it, you see.

BONE: Got what!

PENELOPE: I've just got the symptoms.

BONE: Hysterical.

PENELOPE: Hilarious.

BONE: I meant –

PENELOPE: I've won again! Let's play battleships. Pinkerton sank my entire fleet in three minutes. That's really what did it, you know.

BONE: I think you should get up.

PENELOPE: I can't. I've lost the use of my legs.

(*She is preparing battleship papers.*)

BONE: That was very sudden.

PENELOPE: No it wasn't. It was very gradual. There, that's yours. Mark it one to eight down and A to H across. You're allowed four submarines, three destroyers, two cruisers and an aircraft-carrier. Put them anywhere you like.

BONE: I know how to play. (*He marks his paper.*) If you're not going to get any better we'll have to change your doctor.

PENELOPE: There's no question of my getting better. I can only hope to hold my own.

BONE: Does he ever mention me?

PENELOPE: Mmmmmm, he says you're only half a man.

BONE: That's a filthy lie and you know it! – I am constantly repulsed –

PENELOPE: . . . because every time he comes, he sees half of you, peering through the door. C-four.

BONE: What?

PENELOPE: C-four. Have I hit anything?

BONE: Oh. No.

PENELOPE: Your go.

BONE: B-six.

PENELOPE: No. G-two.

BONE: Submarine.

PENELOPE: Pow! Starboard torpedo away, sir! . . . Boom!

(*Distant gun booms.*)

We've got her! By George, we've got her! The sea is boiling and here she comes up like a great wounded whale, and the

56

conning tower flies open and little men are jumping into the
sea! Depth charges! Let go number one! Let go number two!
– Boom!
(*Distant gun again.*
BONE *rises.*
Third gun.)

BONE: What was that?

PENELOPE: The salute . . . Now they're saluting him . . .
(*Music in.*)

BONE: Are they going round the block?

PENELOPE: No! – the procession is miles long. They've got
eighteen different military bands and then there's the tanks
and everything, and the rocket-carrier with the capsule and
the lunanaut . . . I want to see him – his face – I want to see if
it shows, what he has seen.

BONE: What?

PENELOPE: God, is it only me? I tell you, he has stood outside
and seen us whole, all in one go, little. And suddenly
everything we live by – our rules – our good, our evil – our
ideas of love, duty – all the things we've counted on as being
absolute truths – because we filled all existence – they're all
suddenly exposed as nothing more than local customs –
nothing more – because he has seen the edges where we stop,
and we never stopped anywhere before –

BONE: Penelope –

PENELOPE: I'm telling you – when that thought drips through to
the bottom, people won't just carry on. The things they've
taken on trust, they've never had edges before.
(*Jets scream over the house and whine away into the distance.*)

BONE: Oh come on now . . . Er, G-five.

PENELOPE: Nothing. H-three.

BONE: Nothing. A-four.

PENELOPE: Nothing. B-seven.

BONE: Nothing. E-six.

PENELOPE: Nothing. C-two.

BONE: Nothing. D-four.
(*He has scored, it's on her face. Horror.*
The doorbell rings.)

57

PENELOPE: Ding-ding-ding!

Alarm stations, alarm stations! We've been hit – We're blowing up – Don't jump! – don't jump – the sea's on fire. (*She throws herself back on the bed, hiding her face.*

The doorbell rings again.

She lifts her face, smiling.)

That was close! Don't let him in till I'm ready.

3 · INT. HALL. DAY

BONE *opens the front door*. ALBERT *is there, carrying an expensive bunch of flowers*.

ALBERT: Good morning.

BONE: Good morning. Miss Pinkerton isn't here today.

ALBERT: I've come to see Mrs Bone.

BONE: Yes, I know. I was just saying Miss Pinkerton isn't here today, that's all. I thought you might have been wondering why she didn't open the door today.

ALBERT: Yes, I was wondering.

BONE: Well, she isn't here today.

ALBERT: Ah.

BONE: Well, this way! She won't keep you a moment.

4 · INT. BONE'S STUDY. DAY

BONE: I'm Mrs Bone's husband.

ALBERT: Mr Bone.

BONE: Yes . . . Yes, I'm something of a logician myself.

ALBERT: Really? Sawing ladies in half – that kind of thing?

BONE: Logician. Well, sit down, sit down! My wife speaks very highly of you.

ALBERT: And I'm very fond of her.

ALBERT *and* BONE: (*Together*) How is she?

BONE: Well, you're the doctor – how am I supposed to know how she is? She doesn't tell me anything. The first day she stayed in bed I thought she'd had a bad night, and the next day I thought – lazy old thing! – and – well, it's just gone on and on and there's no end to it. All she'll say is, she's all right in bed.

ALBERT: Yes, well, there's something in that.

BONE: You think so? I understand you're a good friend of hers.

ALBERT: Thank you. Is this where you do your work?

BONE: What? – Oh . . . yes. Yes, this is where I'm getting it all down. It's an immense undertaking of course –

(ALBERT *is regarding the unkempt bed, turning over the blanket with his stick.*)

Yes – I bunk down in here – the midnight oil, you know – I've been bunking down in here since – well, it's my life's work of course.

ALBERT: Your life's work!

BONE: Yes. How long would you say I've got?

ALBERT: Are you inviting tenders?

BONE: No – just a professional estimate.

ALBERT: Well, I'd say as long as you've had.

BONE: (*Appalled*) Is that all? But I'm not half-way yet – not nearly.

ALBERT: What do you write?

BONE: It's sort of history.

ALBERT: What of?

BONE: The world.

ALBERT: The history of the world! How far have you got?

BONE: I'm doing the Greeks at the moment, third century.

ALBERT: Broken the back of them.

BONE: BC. But I've done the Etruscans.

ALBERT: Found plenty of new stuff, have you?

BONE: Well no, I mean practically nothing is known about the Etruscans. You see, I'm not exactly a *historian* – the actual history has all been written up by other people – but I'm discovering the patterns – exposing the fallacy of chance – there are no impulsive acts – nothing random – everything is logical and connects into the grand design.

ALBERT: Is there one?

BONE: There's got to be something going on beside a lot of accidents. If it's all random, then what's the point?

ALBERT: What's the point if it's all logical?

BONE: I hadn't meant to do a history of the world, only of myself . . . but the thing keep spreading, making connections back,

wider and deeper all the time, the real causes, and suddenly I
knew that everything I did was the culminating act of a
sequence going back to Babylon . . .

PENELOPE: (*Off-camera*) Dah-ling . . .

ALBERT: Ah! (*Moves.*) Mind you, this lunanaut – he'd make a
good end to your book.

BONE: The lunanaut?

ALBERT: The logical place to stop, I would have thought. The day
man bridged the cosmic gap. That was the day she took to
her bed, you know.

(BONE *reacts.*)

PENELOPE: (*Off-camera*) Dah-ling!

ALBERT: Well, if you'll excuse me –

BONE: (*Blocking his way*) What exactly do you do in there?

ALBERT: Well, I . . . examine her.

BONE: She won't let me examine her! You must have a good time,
examining people.

ALBERT: Well, it's different for us medical men, you know. You
think that when I'm examining Penelope –

BONE: Penelope?

ALBERT: Her name is Penelope, isn't it?

BONE: Yes.

ALBERT: She told me it was. You think that when I'm examining
Penelope I see her eyes as cornflowers, her lips as rubies, her
skin so soft and warm as milk . . . you think that when I run
my hands over her back I am carried away by the delicate
contours that flow like a sea shore from shoulder to heel –
Oh, I know, dear fellow! – you think my mind turns to ripe
pears as soon as I press those firm pink –

BONE: No, I don't!

ALBERT: But it's misconception. To us medical men the human
body is an imperfect machine constructed from cells, tissues,
organs . . .

PENELOPE: (*Off-camera*) Help! Fire, murder!

ALBERT: Funny thing, I knew a fellow called Bone once – I
wonder if he was a relation? Yes, he wanted to be an
osteopath but he couldn't face the pleasantries –

ALBERT: – which every patient would have felt obliged to make, so he took his wife's maiden name of Foot and now practises in Frinton as a chiropodist. My name is Pearce. Albert Pearce.

PENELOPE: (*Off-camera*) Rape! Rape! Rape!

ALBERT: I believe she's ready for me.
(*The doorbell rings.*
ALBERT *enters the bedroom, closing the door.*
BONE *answers the front door.* CROUCH *is standing there.*)

BONE: Yes?

CROUCH: Crouch, sir. Hall porter downstairs.

BONE: Is the lift out of order?

CROUCH: No sir, it's another matter I've come about.

BONE: You look as if you could do with a sit-down.

CROUCH: You're right sir, thank you sir – it's a long haul.

BONE: Come this way. Did you want to see me?

CROUCH: Well, I'm seeing everybody, sir, making enquiries. You know what happened out there?

BONE: The parade?

6. INT. BONE'S STUDY. DAY

CROUCH: The incident. There's been a bit of an incident. (*He sags into a chair.*) Woman, middle-aged to elderly, five foot one, grey hair in a bun, blue dress, starched apron, fell in the street. Dead.

BONE: Oh . . . yes?

CROUCH: I've seen her coming in and out, but I've drawn a blank at the other flats. No one missing of that description here, sir?

BONE: Pinkerton . . .

CROUCH: Ah.

BONE: Oh dear . . . A small old-looking grey-haired lady in a white apron?

CROUCH: (*Takes off his peaked cap*) Relative, sir?

BONE: My wife's nanny.

CROUCH: I've got to make a bit of a report, you see.

BONE: Yes . . . I'd better go and break the news . . . she'll be most upset.

CROUCH: Right, sir. I'll wait here.

(BONE *goes out*.)

7. INT. HALL. DAY

BONE *crosses hall, goes into bedroom.*

8. INT. PENELOPE'S ROOM. DAY

PENELOPE *is sitting up in bed.* ALBERT *is kneeling on the bed, kissing her chastely. He releases her and kneels back. They take no notice of* BONE.

PENELOPE: Do that last bit again.

(*He kisses her.*)

Pray-kiss?

ALBERT: No.

PENELOPE: Start again, from the beginning.

Tip-toe?

Slow?

ALBERT: (*A clue*) Ssssh!

PENELOPE: Quiet? Soft?

(ALBERT *nods*.)

Soft?

(ALBERT *grabs her*.)

Grab?

ALBERT: As if you were running away.

PENELOPE: Catch!

ALBERT: Y!

PENELOPE: Catchy?

(*He prays*.)

Priest? Pray? Monk?

(*He nods*.)

Monk!

(ALBERT *kisses her*.)

BONE: Softly softly catchee monkey.

62

ALBERT: Correct!
PENELOPE: Shut up! He spoilt it! What do you want?
BONE: Pinkerton's dead.
ALBERT: Dead!
BONE: There's a man come to make a report.
PENELOPE: What does he want to know?
BONE: I don't know.
PENELOPE: Well, it's a fat lot of good asking me, then, isn't it?
BONE: Monk-key. In the singular. Softly softly catchee monkey. Not monkiss.
ALBERT: Mr Bone, this is intolerable! I will not be interrupted in this frivolous manner while I'm bringing aid and comfort to a patient!

(BONE *retreats, closing the door.*)

9. INT. BONE'S STUDY. DAY

In the study CROUCH *is looking at one of Bone's notebooks.*
CROUCH: The Etruscans soon fizzled out, didn't they? I mean, there wasn't much *to* them. I never thought much of Eye-talians, mind you . . .
BONE: (*Briskly*) Mr Crouch, how exactly can we help you regarding this matter of Pinkerton's death? She was an old lady, rather frail. She fell down, fractured something perhaps – and died. It's very sad, but she had a splendid life in the best houses – what else can one say?
CROUCH: I thought you might know how it happened.
BONE: I thought she fell in the street?
CROUCH: From the window. We were all watching the parade and suddenly, behind us – thump . . . Amazing to think where he's been, the lunatic . . .

(*But* BONE *is already marching back to the bedroom.*)

10. INT. HALL. DAY

BONE *crosses hall to bedroom.*

11. INT. PENELOPE'S ROOM. DAY

BONE *storms in and stops dead.*
No one is in sight. The drapes are drawn round the bed. Albert's shoes,
stick, hat and cape are lying neatly outside, on chair.
PENELOPE: (*Inside*) Who is it?
BONE: Me. How is she?
   (PENELOPE's *head and bare shoulder appears.*)
PENELOPE: What?
BONE: I was asking how you were.
PENELOPE: What do you want?
BONE: He says Pinkerton fell from the window.
PENELOPE: Who does?
BONE: He says –
PENELOPE: I wish you'd shut up about Pinkerton! Go away!
   (*She ducks back inside.*)
BONE: Well, it must have been your window – it's the only one
   overlooking . . . You can't hide!
PENELOPE: Hee hee hee, can't see me!
BONE: Who gave Pinkerton the push?
ALBERT: (*Within*) Say ninety-nine.
PENELOPE: Ninety-nine, doctor.
ALBERT: Feel any pain . . . there?
PENELOPE: No . . . no . . .
ALBERT: There?
PENELOPE: That's closer . . . down a bit . . . Yes, yes . . . Oh yes,
   that's it . . . yes, yes . . . yes . . . oh yes . . .
   (BONE *retires.*)

12. INT. HALL. DAY

BONE *crosses.*

13. INT. BONE'S STUDY. DAY

BONE: My wife's in bed with the doctor at the moment, Mr . . .
CROUCH: Crouch, sir. I see you're a historical man. I've got a
   historical turn of mind myself. Have you read *The Last of the
   Wine?*

BONE: Mr Crouch, let us not draw any hasty conclusions, let us be logical. Firstly, you say Miss Pinkerton fell from the window. Secondly, there is only one window overlooking the parade. Therefore – thirdly, my wife has lost the use of her legs, so – fourthly – Why didn't you take the lift, as a matter of interest?

CROUCH: Ah, well, I was calling at every floor, you see, and it was always a case of just one more – but you're right, sir, it does build up on you.

BONE: You could have taken the lift to the top and worked your way down.

CROUCH: By God, that's a brainwave you've got there.

BONE: Thank you. As you can see, I'm a cerebral man. I – fifthly, Miss Pinkerton was in service with my wife's family for thirty-four years and well loved – a second mother almost, certainly third or fourth – fifthly – sixthly – it's unthinkable.

CROUCH: Yes, it's a truly wonderful era, sir, for brains – they get you right to the top – take the loony – he's put us out of date –

BONE: Therefore –

CROUCH: Ah!

(ALBERT *has appeared, perfectly dressed once more*.)

ALBERT: Is this the fellow?

CROUCH: Good morning, sir.

ALBERT: Splendid. You examined the body?

(*He takes out a pad of certificates and starts scribbling*.)

CROUCH: I did have a look.

ALBERT: Well done. Eyes dilated?

CROUCH: Could well have been.

ALBERT: Excellent. Heart stoppage?

CROUCH: Not a flutter.

ALBERT: Adds up. Any signs of vertigo?

CROUCH: Well, she fell a long way.

ALBERT: Quite agree.

(*He tears off certificate, hands it to* CROUCH.)

Put yourself in my hands. No point in casting a shadow over a day of triumph.

CROUCH: Oh yes, sir – we better hurry if we want to see him.

65

They move towards front door.

BONE: Just a minute –

ALBERT: Ah – yes, I think she's out of danger now. The main thing is – keep her amused. Humour her – plenty of fruit drinks – that kind of thing –

BONE: You think I'm a fool, don't you?

ALBERT: Mr Bone, medicine has many forms not given to the layman to understand – but we medical men have given up our youth to learn its mysteries and you must put your trust in us.

BONE: There's nothing wrong with her. When's she going to get up?

ALBERT: Get up? My dear fellow, Penelope can't get up. She's unable to leave her bed. I'm sorry, there's nothing I can do. She'll never walk again.

(*Briskly to* CROUCH:) Come along, let's get this matter tidied up.

(*They leave.*

BONE *walks to bedroom door.*)

15. INT. PENELOPE'S ROOM. DAY

Sound of parade, cheering.

PENELOPE *is standing by the window, watching the parade. She does not look round.*

PENELOPE: There he goes . . . standing so straight and handsome in his yellow uniform . . . There goes God in his golden capsule. You'd think that he was sane, to look at him, but he doesn't smile because he has seen the whole thing for what it is – not the be-all and end-all any more, but just another moon called Earth – part of the works and no rights to say what really goes – he's made it all random.

BONE: She was your nanny.

PENELOPE: Poor Pinkers. You think I'm just a bad loser – but no one is safe now.

BONE: You can't hush it up, you know. And what about me?

There's the law – accessory after the fact. You can't flout the
laws – and nor can Albert.

PENELOPE: (*Fondly*) Huh – him and his ripe pears . . .

BONE: And don't think I don't know what's going on!

PENELOPE: Nobody knows except me, and him; so far. Albert
almost knows. You'll never know. There he goes . . . (*She
smiles. Waves her hand slightly at the lunanaut below.*)
Hello . . .

(*The parade fades into the distance.*)

NEUTRAL GROUND

MAIN CHARACTERS

PHILO
a native of Eastern Europe; aged around fifty, but looking older
and more ravaged, especially in the later Montebiancan scenes

ACHERSON
a young, clean-cut Englishman, as they say; about thirty, well
educated

CAROL
about the same age; a competent, good-looking type

OTIS
American, ten years older, and ten years harder; conservative in
appearance

LAUREL and HARDY
killers but fairly relaxed about it: they don't go around with grim
poker-faces all the time

SANDERS
an up-and-coming Acherson

BOY
about ten years old, bright; simply dressed

And

COMISKY	an American salesman
'LOCALS'	four travellers, including a pretty girl
TRAIN POLICE	
FRONTIER GUARDS	
ASSASSIN	
WAITER	
NURSE	
VET (WOLENSK)	
MAID	
MRS BUCHNER	a beautiful and rich lady
BORIS	the boy's father
VILLAGERS	
BOYFRIEND	for NURSE
BRIDE and GROOM	
BOUNCERS	in discotheque
DESK CLERK	in hotel
MIDDLE-AGED WOMAN	in hotel
FOSTER	a diplomat
BARBER	
PORTER	

Montebianca is assumed to be a small country on the borders of Yugoslavia, consisting of a capital (also called Montebianca) and some outlying villages.

The village is very small, a few houses around a church and a bar.

Neutral Ground was first transmitted in December 1968 by Thames Television. The cast included:

PHILO	Patrick Magee
ACHERSON	Nicholas Pennell
CAROL	Polly Adams
OTIS	Alan Webb
PRODUCER	Margaret Morris
DIRECTOR	Piers Haggard

1. EXT. OPEN COUNTRY. DAY. WINTER

An establishing shot of a passenger train.

2. INT. TRAIN. DAY

The compartment is full, six passengers. Four of them are 'LOCALS', including one pretty GIRL. The fifth is COMISKY, an American salesman. The sixth is PHILO, who is distinguished from the others by his air of slightly nervous reserve; by his clothes, which suggest a bureaucratic correctness despite being offset by a fur hat; and by his tiny pet monkey, which peeps from his overcoat pocket.
It seems like a party, and COMISKY is the life and soul of it. The chatter of the LOCALS is in a foreign tongue. A bottle is passed round. Fruit and bread rolls are being shared. Only PHILO abstains.
COMISKY *concentrates on the* GIRL, *who is wearing a fur hat much like Philo's.*
COMISKY *takes her hat and puts it on his head. He prevents her from snatching it back.*
COMISKY: I will take you home to America. I love you. Mrs
    Comisky will learn to love you, give her time. (*He brushes
    aside interruptions and defends the hat.*) I love you. Is this man
    your husband? Forget him. (*He kisses her hand gallantly. She
    snatches her hat back. He takes a swig from a proffered bottle.*)
    OK, at least let me take your hat to America. I want to buy
    the hat. I always wanted a fur hat.
    (*He takes out his wallet and from the wallet a note. The gesture is
    misunderstood. Ribald laughter and protest. The* GIRL *slaps him
    lightly.*
    PHILO *interrupts for the first time – tells the girl briefly, in her
    language, that the man just wants the hat. At this point two
    uniformed officials,* TRAIN POLICE, *enter and the* LOCALS
    *obviously know them well. Tickets and travel documents are
    offered. The cramped compartment is alive with chatter, the*
    TRAIN POLICE *joining in. The* GIRL *puts up with the flirting.*

73

Philo's document is obviously 'special' – it consists of several items, passport, letter, photo, identity card. The attitude of the TRAIN POLICE *changes into one of nervous respect, which rapidly infects the other people, except* COMISKY, *who remains oblivious until he is the only person left talking.* COMISKY *falls silent and looks round blankly.*)

Whassamatter . . . ?

(*The* OFFICIALS *salute* PHILO *and leave.* PHILO *strokes his monkey, and looks embarrassed.*)

3. EXT. FRONTIER STATION. DAY

A small frontier post, not even a village.
At one platform a train is waiting to leave, just beyond a guarded gate.
A few people in view, several in uniform.
In the distance our first train is approaching.

4. INT. TRAIN. SAME TIME

Only COMISKY AND PHILO *are left in the compartment.* PHILO *drinks from a small bottle of spirits, emptying it.*

COMISKY: You're coming all the way?

PHILO: Yes.

COMISKY: Sam Comisky – the New Jersey Comiskys, capitalists – except the laundromat failed. You been in there on a trip?

PHILO: Yes.

COMISKY: It's a tight country for a salesman. I'm in and out.
      (*The train brakes and slows.*)
      The frontier. All change. I'll be glad to get back into Austria. How long was your visit?

PHILO: Fifteen years. Do you have by any chance some Austrian money – a coin for the public telephone?
      (COMISKY *looks at him in surprise but fishes a fistful of coins out of his pocket.*)

COMISKY: Probably. There, how's that?
      (*He gives* PHILO *a coin.*)

PHILO: Thank you. May I also make you a gift?

74

(PHILO *takes off his fur hat and offers it to* COMISKY.)
COMISKY: Really? . . . Well, gee thanks.

5. EXT. FRONTIER STATION. DAY

PHILO, *with no luggage except a briefcase, hatless now, gets off the train and walks rapidly towards the guarded gate, towards the waiting train. Amid the other passengers* COMISKY *follows, carrying a suitcase and the hat. He stops and puts the hat on.*
The monkey climbs out of Philo's pocket, up his coat.
An ASSASSIN *is scanning the passengers, uncertainly, not sure of himself.*
PHILO *is at the gate.*
The monkey with a little squeal jumps off PHILO *and scampers up* COMISKY, *comically-angrily pulling at his hat.* COMISKY *laughs. The monkey sits on* COMISKY's *shoulder. The* ASSASSIN *sees* COMISKY *and the monkey now.*
The ASSASSIN *produces a machine-pistol and starts shooting from close range. It takes one long burst and then* COMISKY *and the monkey are dead on the platform.*
PHILO *takes that in at a glance and turns swiftly through the gate, unnoticed. The passengers and* GUARDS, *etc. scatter, some towards the corpse.*
PHILO *pulls himself up into the waiting train.*

6. INT. STATION OFFICE. SAME TIME

Two GUARDS *stand nervously, holding guns, watching the* ASSASSIN. *The* ASSASSIN *holds the phone to his ear and waits, drumming his fingers on a piece of paper on the table. The paper is a snapshot, a long-range blow-up of* PHILO *with the monkey on his shoulder. Behind the* ASSASSIN, *the train with* PHILO *on it can be seen leaving the station.*

7. INT. RAILWAY STATION. DAY

Establish Vienna Station. Philo's train arriving.

8. INT. VIENNA STATION. SAME TIME

PHILO *disembarks from the train.*
He is being covertly watched by two or three men. One of the men is
SANDERS; *another,* OTIS.

9. INT. VIENNA STATION. SAME TIME

PHILO *studies the phone, etc., reading the instructions, holding*
Comisky's coin.
Cutaway: SANDERS *and* OTIS *watching.*
PHILO *dials.*
TELEPHONE: Toytown International.
PHILO: Toytown? Thank you. I want the Sales Director in charge
    of train sets.
    (*A hand comes over* PHILO's *shoulder and cuts off the call.*
    PHILO *turns and sees* SANDERS.)
SANDERS: I'm out.
    (OTIS's *head joins him in the frame.*)
    This is Mr Otis of Model Aeroplanes. He's taken over
    Exports.

10. CREDITS

11. EXT. SMALL RAILWAY STATION. DAY

A third railway station. (The film is to end on a railway station, and
this plethora of stations is intended to top and tail the whole; thus it is
hoped that a virtue is made of the repetition.) This station is
Montebianca, clearly not much of a place.
A train has just arrived. Two men get off it: they will be referred to as
LAUREL *and* HARDY, *whom they resemble in shape though not in*
amiability.
LAUREL *and* HARDY *each carry a small suitcase. They move slowly*
and deliberately, taking in the station as though it were a hotel room.

12. EXT. STATION BOOKSTALL. SAME TIME

LAUREL *picks up a* Guide to Montebianca.

13. EXT. PAVEMENT CAFE. DAY

LAUREL *and* HARDY *sit at a table.* LAUREL *reads the guidebook.*
HARDY *sits with his fingers on a closed file lying in front of him on the*
table. They are in the same clothes as before – town suits, town shoes,
collars and ties, but slightly shabby. No suitcase now.

LAUREL: (*Reading*) 'The population of Montebianca is sixteen
thousand, five hundred.'
(*He looks around the café, where a handful of people are sitting.*)
Sixteen thousand, four hundred and ninety-two to go.
(*The* WAITER *comes with their order of drinks, which he places*
on top of the file. HARDY *carefully puts the drinks to one side.*)

HARDY: My friend, perhaps you can help me a little.
(HARDY *turns over the cover of the file, revealing a formal photo*
of PHILO, *and a banknote.*)   I will be quite frank with you.
It is a little matter of a runaway husband. An old story.
Maybe he is a customer here?
(*The* WAITER *examines the photo.*)
It is not recent. He's missing for two years.

WAITER: Yes. Maybe I can help you a little.
(HARDY *gives him the banknote. The* WAITER *puts it in his*
jacket pocket.)
Yes, I can help you. Here he is definitely not a customer.
(*The* WAITER *smiles and goes about his business.* LAUREL
shakes his head.)

LAUREL: Sixteen thousand . . . Well, sooner or later they will all
walk past this table.

HARDY: Our orders are forty-eight hours.

LAUREL: Orders.
(*A couple stroll past the table.*)
Sixteen thousand, four hundred and ninety.

HARDY: Does it say how many bars?

LAUREL: (*Looking through the guidebook*) Probably a hundred.
(HARDY *downs his drink, closes the file and stands up.*)

HARDY: You see? The odds improve.

(LAUREL *also finishes his drink.* HARDY *moves out, having dropped some money on the table.* LAUREL *makes a small detour towards the* WAITER, *who is balancing a laden tray on the tips of his fingers.* HARDY *approaches him smiling, dips his hand into the waiter's pocket and retrieves the banknote. With his other hand he delicately flicks the tray, sending it crashing to the floor.*)

LAUREL: Don't play games.

(*He turns and follows* HARDY *away.*)

14. MONTAGE OF THREE BAR INTERIORS

LAUREL *and* HARDY *are having no success in their search for* PHILO. *Barmen and serving girls, etc. are shown the photo but it means nothing to them.*

15. INT. BAR

LAUREL: Why would he come here anyway?

HARDY: To drink.

LAUREL: No, to Montebianca. It's nothing, it's too small, it's not a country, it's a joke.

HARDY: Yes, it's a funny place.

LAUREL: It's a joke with postage stamps. Who wants it?

HARDY: Tourists. The mountains . . . very beautiful, they say.

LAUREL: Let's go. Maybe he's stopped drinking. Two years is a long time – many things about him must have changed.

HARDY: No, he drinks. I know them. Besides, what else do we know of him? Did you read the file? Half a sheet. How can we work from half a sheet on a whole man?

(HARDY *looks around absently and notices at an adjoining table an oldish man playing with a white kitten.* HARDY *pauses on that.*)

Zut!

16. INT. VETERINARY SURGERY. DAY

A cat in a cage. Then a line of cages containing puppies, birds, mice, etc., with which LAUREL *is trying to ingratiate himself.*

LAUREL *and* HARDY *are alone in the room. The door opens and a* NURSE *in white enters.*

NURSE: No, I'm sorry, Doctor Wolensk is operating just now.

HARDY: I just want the vet.

NURSE: Doctor Wolensk is the animal doctor.

HARDY: Oh. The *animal* doctor . . . Well, I'll just go and talk to him a minute. (*He moves to the door.*)

NURSE: I'm sorry, it is not permitted –
  (LAUREL *catches her by the arm, quite pleasantly.*)

LAUREL: He's an animal lover.
  (HARDY *goes through the door. The* NURSE *tries to get free of* LAUREL, *who pulls her up, not quite so pleasantly.*)
  People he don't like so much.

17. INT. OPERATING ROOM. SAME TIME

WOLENSK *is working over an unconscious dog. He looks up and sees* HARDY.

WOLENSK: Who are you?

HARDY: I'm looking for a friend.

WOLENSK: There is no one here. Please leave.

HARDY: (*Sympathetically*) Oh! . . . A broken leg?

WOLENSK: That's right. A car accident.

HARDY: I would shoot him.

WOLENSK: (*Shocked*) Shoot the dog?

HARDY: No, the driver.

WOLENSK: : (*Shouts*) Nurse! (*To* HARDY) Who gave you permission – ?
  (HARDY *takes out an automatic and examines it casually.*)

HARDY: No, I mean I'd really shoot him, I get so angry.
  (WOLENSK *pauses and looks fearfully at* HARDY.)
  This friend of mine has a monkey.

WOLENSK: What's his name?

HARDY: I don't know.

WOLENSK: You don't know your friend's name?

HARDY: Oh – I thought you meant the monkey.

WOLENSK: Look – what is this?

HARDY: Where do monkeys come from?

WOLENSK: Africa . . . South America . . .

HARDY: Yes. They are not native to Central Europe. There are no Austrian monkeys or Serbian, Bulgarian, no Montebiancan monkeys. Naturally. It gets too cold for them. And of course we do not have the jungle. Altogether, a monkey needs special attention here. Injections and so on. They would come to you; of course. You are the only vet. The only animal doctor, that is to say. My friend had another monkey but it died. A shooting accident. I think probably there is another monkey now. Very very probably. If so, no doubt you have done injections, and you can tell me where my friend lives.

WOLENSK: Oh . . .

HARDY: By the way, this gun is a toy, I do not really shoot motorists.

(HARDY *puts the gun back in his pocket, rendering it harmless at the psychological moment.*

WOLENSK *laughs his relief, laughs away his own foolishness for being so frightened.*)

WOLENSK: Yes . . . Your friend lives in the Sondra Apartments, top floor.

HARDY: Thank you, Doctor. By the way, what is my friend's name?

WOLENSK: Buchner.

(*The illogicality of the question catches up on him, but* HARDY *has gone.*)

18. INT. SONDRA APARTMENT BLOCK. DAY

It is obviously fashionable and expensive. LAUREL *and* HARDY *approach it and glance dubiously at each other, but they go in.*

19. INT. SONDRA APARTMENTS. DAY

The lift arrives at the top floor. LAUREL *and* HARDY *come out of the lift. They are in a carpeted hall.*
HARDY *takes out his automatic and holds it down by his side.*
LAUREL *rings the doorbell of the penthouse.*
The door is opened by a uniformed MAID. LAUREL *and* HARDY *don't like this.*
LAUREL: Mr Buchner at home?
MAID: Mrs Buchner?
LAUREL: Mr Buchner.
MAID: No Mr Buchner.
    (HARDY *pushes past her and goes in.*)

20. INT. PENTHOUSE. SAME TIME

As though he owns the place HARDY *throws open every door he sees. Behind the third one is* MRS BUCHNER *in bed, sitting up and looking very beautiful in a negligee, eating breakfast off a tray and offering a spoonful of soft-boiled egg to her monkey.*

21. EXT. SONDRA APARTMENT BLOCK. DAY

LAUREL *and* HARDY *walk out of the building.* HARDY *pauses on the pavement and furiously thumps his fist against the wall, and wonders what to do next.*
Down the road comes a car, a smallish saloon, say a Fiat. It just goes past, but the occupants are featured – ACHERSON *and* CAROL.

22. EXT. MONTEBIANCA. DAY

The Fiat drives out of the town.

23. EXT. COUNTRY ROAD. DAY

The Fiat in the distance, in bare, hilly country. Its approach is being watched by a BOY. *The* BOY *is with the camera on a hilltop. Down the opposite slope, in the valley, is the village. The car is heading towards the village.*

24. INT. CAR. SAME TIME

CAROL *is looking at the guidebook.*
The road is a very bad one, narrow and rutted. The car bumps all the time and has to go quite slowly.
CAROL: Nice to get off the beaten track.
  (ACHERSON *is silent.*)
  It says the views are unexampled by the largest traveller.
ACHERSON: Views of what?
CAROL: I don't know. Do you want to stop for a while?
ACHERSON: Why?
CAROL: *Why?* We're supposed to be on holiday. What's the matter?
ACHERSON: Nothing's the matter. I'm not in a holiday mood. Besides, I'm combining it with business, aren't I? I'm taking the little woman on a sales trip. Nice hotel, exotic food, unexampled views, all on the firm. A perk.
CAROL: Who'd send a salesman to Montebianca?
ACHERSON: We would. It's off the beaten track. Tell me, do you *fancy* Giles Foster?
CAROL: Yes, I do rather.
ACHERSON: I thought you did.
CAROL: I thought you thought I did. (*Pause.*) Were you really at school with him?
ACHERSON: Yes.
CAROL: Well, he's doing quite well. I hope you're not going to spoil my holiday.

25. EXT. THE ROAD. SAME TIME

The BOY, *in the same position, watches the car, which is too far away to be audible. Then he turns and starts making his way quickly down the opposite slope, descending towards the village.*

26. EXT. THE VILLAGE. SAME TIME

The BOY *runs into the village. He goes into the bar.*

82

27. INT. BAR. SAME TIME

The bar is almost empty. The boy's father (BORIS) is the barman. He is talking to the only customer. The BOY goes past them, through a door and then up the back stairs.

28. INT. PHILO'S ROOM. SAME TIME

PHILO is asleep on an unkempt bed in an unkempt room. He obviously has few possessions; but one of them is a monkey. The boy's knock is heard. The monkey wakes PHILO. The BOY opens the door and comes in.

BOY: Captain! Somebody comes.

PHILO: (*Waking*) Hah?

BOY: A car comes. You said to wake you any time –

PHILO: Yes. Who comes?

BOY: A car. A Fiat, I think.

PHILO: So?

BOY: You told me –

PHILO: Yes. How many people?

BOY: I don't know. I was on the hill. I ran here.

PHILO: Of course. My good scout.

BOY: Maybe only a tourist. They get lost.

PHILO: Of course. They will drive through to Zlens. Tell me if they stop, eh? If it's children in the car it's all right. Tell me if it's just men. Anything funny, you tell me, eh?

BOY: Yes, Captain. Who do we wait for?

PHILO: I tell you, it could be a bishop and his grandmother, or the last man in the Tour de Monte bicycle race. But probably there is no need for play-acting. Probably he will look like a debt collector. A debt collector can be any man in a suit and a car. Tell me if it stops.

BOY: He wishes you to pay a debt?

PHILO: Yes.

BOY: But you do not wish to pay it?

PHILO: If it can be avoided. I do not owe it. Do you see?

BOY: Of course. Will you buy me a gun?

PHILO: What do you want a gun for? This is not cowboys. (*He picks up the monkey.*) Oh no, it is not cowboys.

29. INT. HOTEL ROOM. IN THE TOWN. DAY

Laurel's and Hardy's room.
LAUREL *lies on his back on one of the twin beds.* HARDY *paces up and down.*

LAUREL: Books. The library.

HARDY: For me it's still the monkey. For ten years in Moscow he keeps a monkey. Maybe the monkey is the only friend he trusted, a man in his position. Now he is alone somewhere. I see him with a monkey. We'll try the pets' doctor again. Show him the photo.

LAUREL: *Now* you show him the photo . . . (*He laughs shortly.*)

HARDY: Who would expect two people with monkeys in a place like this?

LAUREL: Not me. A monkey is a risk for him. 'Look at that man, he has a monkey' . . . no.

HARDY: After a while a man takes risks. Two years now. He thinks he is well hidden. Maybe even forgotten. He needs a friend who asks no questions. I think we visit the animal doctor.

LAUREL: No, the animal nurse. You spoiled the doctor. Next time if he has any more friends with monkeys he will say nothing and then telephone.

30. EXT. VILLAGE. DAY

ACHERSON *and* CAROL *walk into the village. They are objects of great curiosity. It is not the kind of village which is used to tourists.*
VILLAGERS, *mainly children and old people, emerge and watch them.*

31. INT. PHILO'S ROOM. SAME TIME

PHILO *sees this from the window.* ACHERSON *starts talking to one of the* VILLAGERS.
The BOY *enters the room urgently.*

PHILO: Yes – I see them. I don't like this walking.
(*Cutaway to* ACHERSON.)

ACHERSON: It's very simple. I want – to buy – money – look, I

have money – I want to buy *petrol*. Auto er no go, halt.
(*Nobody understands him.* BORIS *shows up and gestures*
ACHERSON *and* CAROL *to enter the bar.*
Finish cutaway.)

BOY: Tourists. English.

PHILO: Yes. I suppose so.

BOY: My father is bringing them. What shall I do, Captain?

PHILO: Nothing. Yes – take Mimi. In your room.
(*He gives the* BOY *the monkey, and the* BOY *goes out.* PHILO
*takes a big drink, pouring from a bottle into a dirty glass. There is
a knock on the door, and* BORIS *shows in* ACHERSON *and*
CAROL, *with a flourish.*)

BORIS: Anglitch!

ACHERSON: I say, do you speak English?

PHILO: Yes.

ACHERSON: Thank the Lord for that. We've run out of petrol,
about a mile down the road, if you can call it a road.

PHILO: You were coming here?

ACHERSON: No. Well, we weren't going anywhere in particular.
Just having an afternoon off . . . a bit of a tour . . . the views,
and all that.

PHILO: An afternoon off?

ACHERSON: We're in Montebianca, for the week; business and
pleasure, sales and marketing – last year was Majorca,
frightful place, but it gets you away –

CAROL: Charles . . .

ACHERSON: Oh yes – getting off the point. My name's Acherson
. . . My wife, Carol.

CAROL: How do you do? – We'd be awfully grateful if you . . .

PHILO: You ran out of petrol just from Montebianca?

ACHERSON: We hired the car there, paid for it to be topped up –
they're all such thieves. They took me for just another stupid
tourist. Well, they won't get away with it. I've got
connections at the Consulate. Look – is there any petrol in
the village?

PHILO: No, no cars, no tractors. The fields are too rocky, they
use horses.
(*He speaks briefly to* BORIS, *who replies.*)

Yes, there's a pump four miles back where you turned off
the main road. He'll send someone to get a can for you.

ACHERSON: Thank you. Can you tell him we'll pay f-- --
trouble.

PHILO: He knows that.

(BORIS *leaves the room.*)

ACHERSON: Well, we mustn't impose on you.

CAROL: No. Is there a bathroom? – I could do with

PHILO: (*Suddenly deciding to accept them*) There's cle
the jug. Please avail yourself. The towel's clean
you're lucky; I count the weeks by clean towels

ACHERSON: Have you been here long?

PHILO: Yes.

ACHERSON: Well, the simple life. I must say I quite

CAROL: (*Pouring water*) At the hotel he made a fuss
claret wasn't château-bottled.

ACHERSON: Well, one must draw the line. . . . You'
English, are you?

PHILO: No.

ACHERSON: It's our first time here. Always been curious to see
the place. Beautiful country, charming people –

CAROL: He can't stand it –

ACHERSON: Now hold on, Carol . . .

PHILO: I can't stand it either.

ACHERSON: Frightful hole, isn't it? Why don't you leave?

PHILO: I have a problem with papers.

ACHERSON: Oh yes . . . they're very keen on papers. Well –
(*He turns to* CAROL, *who is drying her hands.*)

PHILO: Did you find soap?

CAROL: Yes, thank you. Where should I empty the water?

PHILO: It's all right.

CAROL: Well, thank you.

ACHERSON: We'll be in the bar. Might see you there. Perhaps
we could buy you a drink before the fellow comes back with
the petrol.

PHILO: Yes. Thank you. I usually have a glass or two around
this time.

ACHERSON: Fine.

86

(PHILO *closes the door after them, and sits down on the bed. He laughs to himself, at himself, and has a drink on himself.*)

32. EXT. MONTEBIANCA TOWN. SHOPS CLOSING. LATE AFTERNOON

LAUREL *and* HARDY *are watching the vet's door. One or two cars are parked around there.* LAUREL, *bored, is glancing at the guidebook. He starts to laugh.*

LAUREL: Hey, it mentions you. The views are unexampled by the largest traveller.

(HARDY *glowers at him.*

Up the road, the NURSE *comes out of the vet's. She walks away from them, and they start to move. But after three paces she stops and gets into the front passenger seat of a waiting car.* LAUREL *and* HARDY *look round helplessly but this is not a taxi-laden place. The* NURSE *is seen to kiss the* BOYFRIEND *as the car moves.* HARDY *throws his hat on the ground.*)

33. INT. VILLAGE BAR. LATE AFTERNOON

BORIS *behind the bar. Some* LOCALS. PHILO, ACHERSON *and* CAROL *share a table and a bottle. The* BOY *enters, carrying a two-gallon can with some difficulty. He stops when he sees the three of them together.*

PHILO: Here! – S'okay.

(*It is apparent that* PHILO *is looser through drink. The* BOY *sees now that* CAROL *is holding Mimi the monkey.*)

They are friends. (*To* CAROL.) Here is my other friend – in fact he is my scout.

CAROL: He's a scout?

(*The* BOY *smiles but is disappointed by* PHILO. ACHERSON *gives the* BOY *money, which the* BOY *gives to* BORIS. PHILO *explains this* –)

PHILO: His father.

ACHERSON: Oh. Well, are you ready, Carol?

CAROL: I'll wait for you here, darling. You'll be back in half an hour.

87

ACHERSON: Well, come for the walk.

CAROL: No, I've walked enough. You've got to drive past this
way so you might as well pick me up.

(*He's not sure about it.*)

Honestly, I'll be perfectly all right.

ACHERSON: Fine. Well, see you both later.

CAROL: Bye-bye, darling.

(CAROL *gives Mimi to* PHILO *and gets up to see* ACHERSON *to
the door.* ACHERSON *goes.* Mimi *sits on* PHILO's *shoulder.*
PHILO *pours a drink.*

There is a flash. CAROL *has taken his picture. The camera was in
her shoulder bag.*)

PHILO: (*Sharply*) What are you doing?

CAROL: What's the matter?

(*Everybody in the bar looks at* CAROL.)

I like to take pictures. Is it all right?

PHILO: (*Subsiding*) Yes . . . of course.

CAROL: I'd like to take some in the village.

PHILO: Yes. Why not?

34. EXT. THE CHURCH. LATE AFTERNOON

A wedding is taking place.

A BRIDE *and* GROOM *and wedding guests come out of the church with
much gaiety.*

CAROL *takes a picture.*

CAROL *moves around the village looking for and finding picturesque
subjects. She is watched by not particularly friendly faces of women.*

CAROL *see* PHILO *watching her from his upstairs window. She waves
at him cheerfully. She raises the camera to her eye, but through the lens
she sees his window empty.*

The shadows lengthen.

35. EXT. ROAD. SAME TIME

ACHERSON *walks along the road. There is no one in sight. Then*
ACHERSON *gets the feeling he is being watched. He looks around.*
Perhaps he hears a sound. The surroundings begin to look sinister to

*him. He hurries on towards the car. Then he definitely sees something
move, off the road, behind rocks. He puts the can down quietly and
moves off the road and waits. After a moment he moves aside quietly
and then changes direction back towards the road. Ahead of him, his
back to* ACHERSON, *the* BOY *reveals himself.*

ACHERSON: (*Relieved*) Hey! – You scouting?

    (*The* BOY *looks at him, embarrassed.*)

    Come on, then.

    (*The car is only yards away.* ACHERSON *gets the can. The boy
takes the cap off the tank, and* ACHERSON *pours the petrol.
When the can is empty,* ACHERSON *puts it into the car. The* BOY
screws the cap on the tank.

    There is the sound of petrol trickling. ACHERSON *sees petrol on
the road and realizes the tank is holed.*

    The BOY *is paying no attention. On the back window-ledge of the
car, among boxes and odds and ends, he sees part of a rifle.*)

36. INT. VILLAGE BAR. LATE AFTERNOON

PHILO, *without Mimi, is drinking.* CAROL *comes in and puts the
camera on the table in front of him.*

CAROL: Hello.

PHILO: Mrs . . . I've forgotten your name.

CAROL: Acherson.

PHILO: Mrs Acherson . . . It's very nice for me that you ran out of
    petrol. I don't see many people . . .

CAROL: You didn't seem very pleased at first.

PHILO: I didn't know who you were . . . You could have been . . .
    anybody.

CAROL: Well we were. (*She smiles at him.*)

PHILO: What does your husband do?

CAROL: He's a sales executive.

PHILO: What does that mean? A salesman?

CAROL: I suppose so. He never discusses work at home. I suppose
    he's just a salesman.

PHILO: He said he had connections. At the Consulate.

CAROL: Oh that. A school friend. Charles was just bad-tempered
    about the car. He isn't frightfully good about Abroad. Last

year the Spaniards were dirty, the year before the French were grasping and the year before that the Italians were impertinent. Now the Montebiancans are all thieves – oh, I say, you're not – ?

PHILO: No, I'm not.

CAROL: Well, what are you?

PHILO: We're not on the maps any more. The Russians, you know . . . They saved us in the war, that's how it started, and now they have saved us out of existence. I'd like to go back while my own language is still being spoken. But I can't leave here.

CAROL: Did you choose to come?

PHILO: Choose? I don't know. It's neutral ground. They let me in and they let me stay.

CAROL: What do you do?

PHILO: Drink. I have some savings, in the bank in town. I write Boris a cheque once a month.

CAROL: And when the money's gone?

PHILO: When the money's gone I'll be dead, if I time it right. What does your husband sell?

CAROL: Toys.

(*This naturally brings* PHILO *up short.*)

PHILO: Toys?

CAROL: Yes, that's right. Toytown International. He's on the export side.

(PHILO *stares at her.*)

37. MIX TO REPRISE, SCENE 9

Telephone: Toytown International.

PHILO: Toytown? Thank you. I want the Sales Director in charge of train sets.

(SANDERS *cuts off the call.*)

SANDERS: I'm out.

(OTIS *joins him in the frame.*)

This is Mr Otis of Model Aeroplanes. He's taken over Exports.

OTIS: Welcome to Vienna, Mr Marin.

SANDERS: Mr Otis is an American. I'm afraid.

OTIS: I'm attached to London. Just happened to be visiting. Kind of lucky.

38. EXT. VIENNA STATION. SAME TIME

PHILO, SANDERS *and* OTIS *walk out of the station and into a waiting car, all three men getting into the back.*

39. INT. CAR. SAME TIME

The car moves off through the city.

SANDERS: My name is Sanders. A friend of a friend called from the frontier. Pity about the trouble. Who was it?

PHILO: An American salesman. Comisky, I think. Poor man. They killed my monkey, too.

OTIS: Your monkey, Mr Marin?

PHILO: I couldn't leave Nana behind – I'd had her for years.

OTIS: That's an exotic sort of pet, Mr Marin. You must have felt pretty secure.

PHILO: Why not?

OTIS: But at the frontier . . .

PHILO: I don't understand it.

SANDERS: They must have known you were doing a bunk. They were waiting for you.

PHILO: I don't know – I've been thinking, perhaps it *was* Comisky they wanted – perhaps he was – somebody in the game – a bizarre coincidence . . .

OTIS: (*Coldly*) They were waiting for you. Think about it, Marin. Just stay quiet and think about it.

PHILO: (*To* SANDERS) Who is this man? I want to see Brigadier Payne in London. I work for *him*. And him I trust.

SANDERS: He's Major-General Payne, Retired. Retired to his club, where he reads *The Times* through a magnifying glass, I'm told. The old soldiers have gone, and the professionals are in charge.

OTIS: You've been away a long time, Marin, and for the last four years you've been working for me. And at the moment I don't even know if you are who you are supposed to be, because you're supposed to be dead, you and your monkey. (*The car stops outside an old nondescript building.*)

40. EXT. CAR. SAME TIME

The three of them get out of the car and enter the building. Outside the main door there is a brass plate: Toytown International.

41. INT. TOYTOWN OFFICE. DAY

A simple room. Sanders's office.
SANDERS *sits behind the desk.* PHILO *stands.* OTIS *is not there.*
PHILO: You take your orders from an American?
SANDERS: I wouldn't put it like that. It's liaison, common interest. There's been a merger. None of us likes it. Otis reports to a committee of three, one of whom is a German. Funny old world. I can tell you that because the German's mistress ran off to Moscow with the Naval Attaché. But I suppose you'd heard.
PHILO: No, I hadn't. Brigadier Payne was kicked out?
SANDERS: : Decent sort, Payne. Trouble was he bumped off a couple of Washington's lads in East Berlin – the Americans' own fault, in my view, since they never told us what they were about, but the result was this idiotic combined ops, and I have to take orders from Otis. Though I wouldn't put it like that. He's top man for the toy factory now as far as Clearance goes. I'm told he's decent sort when you get to know him, but no one ever has, so his decency is a sort of secret.
PHILO: Have you got a drink in here?
SANDERS: Heavens, no.
PHILO: Well, what happens now?
SANDERS: What did you want?
PHILO: I want to go back to England.
SANDERS: To the office?
PHILO: I don't know.

SANDERS: Nor me. It's not like it was with Payne.

PHILO: I had a right to leave, Sanders.

SANDERS: You were working for us.

PHILO: I'm not a British agent. I don't belong to anybody.
>   (OTIS *enters, carrying a file*.)
>   I don't owe you people a thing.

OTIS: An explanation, Philo.

PHILO: Oh – so I'm not dead?

OTIS: Your prints came through for you. (*He tosses a fingerprint card on the desk*.) Well, now. What brings you to Vienna?

PHILO: (*Shrugs*) You had a friend inside. One day he had enough.

OTIS: Why?

PHILO: That would take a lot of explaining.

OTIS: Well, I'd like to take your explanation back to London, and I'm leaving tonight.

PHILO: Without me?

OTIS: That depends. Why did you have enough?

PHILO: Look, I wasn't in it for your country. I had my own.

OTIS: Common interest.

PHILO: That may have been so in the old days. Now my country doesn't even show on *your* maps. The tanks have been followed by the map-makers, and in the schools the children are only taught Russian. I wasn't doing any good in there. I was doing more before.

OTIS: (*Angrily*) What – with that sad little group of émigrés keeping the flag flying from a maisonette in Notting Hill? That's where Payne took you from, Marin, and it's a lot sadder now with their photographs of dead generals and their middle-aged amateurs getting picked up in Leningrad with their coat linings stuffed with leaflets. Leaflets! Don't tell me you came back for that?

PHILO: No.

OTIS: What, then?

PHILO: Listen, Otis. They've got away with it. My war is lost. It was probably lost before I joined it. And I'm tired of fighting in yours.

OTIS: That's why you got out?

PHILO: Yes.

OTIS: Just like that? Catch a train in Moscow, change here and there, across borders, everything smooth, no questions, all the way to the frontier. And then they shoot the wrong man.

PHILO: That's right.

OTIS: Most people have more trouble.

PHILO: Most people would. Listen, Otis, back in the East you can't do much without the right papers, but *with* the right papers you can do *anything*. They *believe* in papers. Papers are power. And my job was papers.

OTIS: And the shooting?

PHILO: I don't know – I'll never know.

OTIS: What do you want, Marin?

PHILO: I want a home. A country. I think you owe me that.

OTIS: I don't owe you a thing except your gratuity, and that's in the bank.

PHILO: I don't want it. I want nationality, Otis.

(OTIS *regards him coolly.*)

OTIS: We've got papers too, you know.

42. EXT. DISCOTHEQUE. NIGHT

LAUREL *and* HARDY *have found the car. Parked. Empty.*

43. INT. DISCOTHEQUE. SAME TIME

LAUREL *and* HARDY *find the* NURSE *dancing with her boyfriend, two rockers in a room jammed with rockers.* LAUREL, *with old-world courtesy, 'cuts in', a custom clearly new to the* BOYFRIEND, *who would resist but* HARDY *gathers him in a friendly embrace with a hearty cry of recognition. The* BOYFRIEND *protests.* HARDY *kisses him on each cheek, and lifts him an inch off the floor and moves him like a shop-window dummy behind a pillar and puts him down. The* BOYFRIEND *hits* HARDY, *who starts a casual sort of fight which quickly achieves Hardy's intention: two* BOUNDERS *converge on* HARDY *and the* BOYFRIEND *and expel them from the premises.* HARDY *plays it soft.*

44. EXT. DISCOTHEQUE. SAME TIME

HARDY *and the* BOYFRIEND *are shoved out by the* BOUNCERS. HARDY *shakes himself loose and lights a cigar, offering one to the* BOYFRIEND. *The* BOYFRIEND *swings at* HARDY, *who massacres him in a few seconds.* HARDY *settles against the wall to wait for* LAUREL.

45. INT. DISCOTHEQUE. SAME TIME

Everybody is dancing appropriately to the rock music except LAUREL, *who is firmly foxtrotting with the helpless and bewildered* NURSE.

NURSE: What do you *want*?

LAUREL: I have a message from a friend. He asked me to give you this. (*In his 'leading hand', the one holding her hand, he is clutching the photo of Philo. He turns the photo towards her.*)

NURSE: What's that?

LAUREL: You know him. Think back.
(*The gamble pays off.*)

NURSE: Oh yes. What do I want with a picture of Mr Kramer?

LAUREL: Kramer. Exactly. He brought his monkey to the animal doctor and instantly he was in love.

NURSE: Monkey? What monkey? I knew him when I worked in the library. That was a year ago.

LAUREL: The library, by all the saints. (*Pause*) He lived near the library?

NURSE: In the Olympia Hotel. I was always sending him reminders.

LAUREL: Reminders?

NURSE: For the books. Where is my friend? Will you stop making this stupid dance, you make me ridiculous.

LAUREL: Listen, you're dancing with a genius. (*He shakes his head scornfully.*) Monkey . . .

46. INT. FOYER OF OLYMPIA HOTEL. NIGHT

LAUREL *and* HARDY *arrive. It's a small hotel, and there is only a* DESK CLERK *around.* LAUREL *is still smirking and laughing to himself.* HARDY *looks grim. They arrive at the desk.*

CLERK: Good evening.

HARDY: What room is Mr Kramer?

CLERK: Kramer? There is no Mr Kramer.

> (HARDY *reaches out for the* CLERK's *throat, drags him over the counter and stands him up.*)

HARDY: Do not tell me there is no Mr Kramer.

LAUREL: (*Amused*) The one with the monkey.

CLERK: Oh – him.

> (*The smile drops off* LAUREL's *face.* HARDY *turns to look at him expressionlessly.*)

HARDY: Yes. Him.

47. INT. THE BAR. EVENING

Some kind of bar game going on. Skittles perhaps. CAROL *is watching it.* LOCALS *playing and drinking. She reaches for her camera to take a picture, starts to check that she's turned the film on, pauses, frowns at the camera. She opens the camera. There is no film in it now.*

48. EXT. COUNTRYSIDE. EVENING

PHILO *is moving rapidly towards the car, short-cutting across rocks. From behind a rock, a rifle pokes at him.*

Close-up of trigger being squeezed.

It's a cap-rifle. The BOY *stands up gleefully. He's got a cowboy hat on, too.* PHILO *turns the other way and sees* ACHERSON.

ACHERSON: Hello, old man. Bad news.

PHILO: The car will not take you away after all.

ACHERSON: Right. Tank's holed.

PHILO: Of course. You're bad news for me, Acherson.

ACHERSON: How's that, old man?

> (PHILO *goes up to the car and looks in. He takes out one of the boxes lying on the back seat. The box has a picture of a train set and some writing.* PHILO *looks at the box and tosses it back.*)

PHILO: So you're in the toy business.

ACHERSON: That's it. Santa Claus.

PHILO: You might as well go home.

ACHERSON: Old man, I don't understand you at all. How far is
that garage?
PHILO: (*Pause*) It's not a garage. It's a pump.
ACHERSON: This is a welding job. It seems we're here for the
night. (*He moves to walk back.*)
PHILO: Acherson! – you're wasting your time! I don't owe you
people a thing!
ACHERSON: Anything you say, old man. (*He strides off.*)
BOY: Is he the debt collector?
PHILO: No – not the one I feared. This one I despise.

49. INT. CONTINUATION OF FLASHBACK

Two locomotives race past each other.
*It's a toy train set, or rather several of them combined into an extensive
layout, on the floor of a store room which contains many boxes of toys,
including boxes identical to the one seen in Acherson's car in the last
scene.*
PHILO *is playing trains.*
The door is audibly unlocked and opened.
PHILO: (*Without turning round*) I'm not hungry, take it away.
(*But it's* OTIS, *accompanied by* SANDERS.)
OTIS: Well, you've managed to pass the time, I see. I'm glad
somebody plays with the window-dressing.
PHILO: Where've you been?
OTIS: Taking a personal interest, in London.
(OTIS *gets interested in the train set and squats down to mess with
it. Pretty soon trains are whizzing round, with* OTIS *working the
points as he talks.*)
PHILO: I could have come with you.
OTIS: On your papers?
PHILO: Next time I'll come out with a British passport and a
working permit. Look, can't we just go and discuss it over a
drink somewhere?
OTIS: As of now you're free. Sorry it took so long.
PHILO: Free? Free to do what? go where?
OTIS: Home.
PHILO: London?

(OTIS *looks at him.*)

OTIS: Home.

PHILO: What are you talking about? You know what would happen to me if I went back there . . . God, I need a drink . . .

OTIS: What made you hit the bottle?

PHILO: Hit the bottle?

OTIS: You made a fool of yourself at a public dinner on the seventh; you were drunk at a reception for the Polish delegation the week you came out, and at another for the Bulgarians the week before that. It seems you even drank in your office. Why was that?

PHILO: Well, I congratulate you. I also drank in bed. Did no one tell you?

OTIS: Why?

(SANDERS *has squatted down and is messing with the trains but he gets the points switched wrong and there is a minor derailment.*) (*Irritably*) Sanders, what the hell do you think you're doing? (*To* PHILO) Why?

PHILO: Nerves.

OTIS: What did you have to be nervous about?

PHILO: That's a damn silly question.

OTIS: *What were you nervous about?* (*Pause.*) You were all right. A comrade. Good record. Impeccable behaviour. Regular promotion. Suddenly you had nerves.

PHILO: I had decided to get out.

OTIS: Why?

PHILO: I told you.

OTIS: Speeches. Speeches about maps and schoolchildren. Why did you get out?

PHILO: Otis, I'm not talking to you any more.

OTIS: And *how* did you get out? (*For this he abandons the train set and looks straight into* PHILO'*s eyes.*) Think before you reply. The right answer might get you where you want to go.

PHILO: I'm telling you the truth. I told you why and I told you how.

OTIS: You gave yourself false papers.

PHILO: Not false. The real thing, falsely obtained. That's a trick

98

which perhaps only one man in the country could have played, and only once, but I was the man.

OTIS: It sounds plausible. It might even have been possible. (*He spells it out now.*) Only you were already blown.

PHILO: (*Total disbelief*) No.

OTIS: You were blown.

PHILO: I tell you I wasn't.

OTIS: How long had they been on to you?

PHILO: If they were on to me I didn't know it.

OTIS: You knew it because they told you.

PHILO: *No!* They had nothing on me! For God's sake, I was sending you stuff almost to the week I left.

OTIS: Fakes.

PHILO: Don't be stupid – the stuff was from my own department.

OTIS: They were fakes, Marin. The Reschev Memorandum was a fake, and so was the Geller business. Blinds, both of them, and that takes us back four months.

PHILO: You're wrong –

OTIS: I'm not wrong, because Geller's dead. What do you think I was doing in Vienna when you showed up?

PHILO: (*Shaken*) I didn't know. I swear I didn't know. If they were using me I didn't know it.

OTIS: Then how did you get out?

(PHILO *now understands the implication.*)

PHILO: You think I made a deal with them?

OTIS: I think you might have. A man working from inside my operation . . .

PHILO: You're mad. And they're not stupid. If I had made a deal they'd expect you to think of it.

OTIS: So they shot that poor bastard Comisky.

(PHILO *is shaken by that.*)

PHILO: Oh . . . Otis, if you think that, there's no talking to you.

OTIS: I don't like that shooting. It makes you look too clean for words, it's like a diploma. I don't like it at all. Those babies don't shoot the wrong man, and they don't shoot anybody on a frontier railroad track like it was their nomination for an Oscar. If they wanted you they could have taken you any time you stepped outside your front door. Why didn't they?

99

PHILO: If you want to know what I think, I think now that they *were* on to me, they found out I'd gone; but they didn't know where I was till I showed my papers on that last train, and then there was no time to do things properly, just a quick bullet at the frontier for the man with the monkey.

OTIS: You'd never have got so far.

PHILO: I was careful, and I had the right papers.

OTIS: You would have been followed for weeks, everywhere. They would have known everything you were doing.

PHILO: How do you know? Maybe I had a tail, maybe not. Maybe I lost him or he lost me. Maybe I was luckier than I knew. I don't know, and you don't know.

OTIS: I didn't know. But there's a doubt, and that's enough. The British don't want you. Do you, Sanders?

(SANDERS *says nothing.*)

PHILO: Now wait a minute – I'm not asking you for a job. But a home is one thing you owe me. (*He turns to* SANDERS.) I was your man, I played your game for fifteen years, and now I want to come *home*.

SANDERS: I'm sorry . . . You're a bad risk, that's all. I really am sorry, Marin . . . you know what they're like.

OTIS: They didn't like the Reschev thing going wrong. It cost a lot of money. And they didn't like Geller being dead. I don't like it either. In fact if I had my way, I wouldn't let you walk away quite so fast and easy.

(OTIS *turns to leave the room. On his turn,* PHILO *moves forward in anger to grab him, but* SANDERS *restrains* PHILO; *which saves* PHILO*'s life, because* OTIS *has turned back with a gun in his hand. This tableau slowly relaxes.*)

PHILO: Yes . . . you really believe it, don't you? You think I came over to work from your factory.

OTIS: I doubt they were hoping for the jackpot, not in the factory but maybe somewhere on the road . . . I guess they'd know I wouldn't employ a Russian national in the factory, however clean he was.

PHILO: (*His worst moment*) *I'm not Russian!*

(*Even* OTIS *is taken aback by that.*)

OTIS: Like you said, look at the maps. (*He goes out.*)

From a zip-bag, SANDERS *is taking out the possessions which had been taken from* PHILO *on his arrival.*

PHILO *watches him from the chair, his energy gone.*

SANDERS: Wallet . . . money. . . diary . . . lighter.

    (*The lighter is in pieces.* SANDERS *reassembles it.*)

PHILO: You're making a mistake.

SANDERS: It's like this, Marin. There are two kinds of mistake Otis can make. He can let a bad apple in or keep a good apple out. If he makes the first mistake things could go very badly for Otis. If he makes the second mistake – well, who's going to ever know? (*Hands over the lighter.*) Lighter. (*Opens a cigarette case.*) How many cigarettes did you have in here?

PHILO: I don't know.

    (SANDERS *reaches into his pocket for his own case and feeds a few of his cigarettes into Philo's case.*)

SANDERS: The Americans are so touching. They still expect to find something inside a cigarette.

PHILO: Where am I supposed to go?

SANDERS: That's up to you. Anywhere they'll have you. Shop around.

PHILO: Shop? I can't even move. I've got to have papers – you know that.

SANDERS: I could mention a couple of embassies to you. It's most unfortunate. There used to be quite a few places, but nowadays it's all one big place, underneath.

    (PHILO *stares out of the window.*)

PHILO: They'll be looking for me. I think you know that, Sanders.

SANDERS: (*Evenly*) If they find you I'll know it. It really isn't my show, you know.

PHILO: Sanders, I'll tell you this now. Otis is going to be looking for me himself. Perhaps next month, perhaps next year – it could be longer; but that Reschev paper was the real thing, and when Otis realizes that, he's going to need me badly. He's going to need me to save his little war, *and* his career. But you tell him not to waste his time, because now I wouldn't *spit* on him, not if he was on *fire*.

51. INT. PHILO'S ROOM. NIGHT

PHILO , *drinking, alone, lying on the bed.*
He hears sounds outside the window and goes to look. In the yard, a
horse is pulling the Fiat in, with the BOY *at the horse's head, and*
ACHERSON *at the wheel.* ACHERSON *gets out of the car, and looks up*
steadily at PHILO *while* PHILO *stares back.*

52. INT. SECOND (ACHERSONS') ROOM. SAME TIME

CAROL *also watching from the window.*
This room is bare . . . two beds, a couple of chairs, a washstand.

53. INT. HOTEL CORRIDOR. NIGHT

The DESK CLERK *leads* LAUREL *and* HARDY *to one of the bedroom*
doors. He knocks. The door is opened by a wild-looking middle-aged
woman with a parrot on her shoulder.
WOMAN: What is it, Joseph?
JOSEPH: There are some men, they wish to speak with you.
    (LAUREL *and* HARDY *move in politely but firmly.*)

54. INT. WOMAN'S ROOM. SAME TIME

The room is a menagerie of pets of all kinds, and consequently squalid.
WOMAN: The maid refuses to clean my room, Joseph. Will you
    speak to her?
HARDY: We are friends of Mr Kramer.
CLERK: You remember Mr Kramer? With the monkey?
WOMAN: Of course. I have not seen him since he left here.
CLERK: These men were wondering if you knew . . . if he told you
    where he was going.
WOMAN: He was my friend.
HARDY: Naturally.
WOMAN: As you see I have many friends, but he was unique, you
    understand.
LAUREL: I understand. He talked to you.
WOMAN: All my friends talk to me.

LAUREL: Oh yes. (*To parrot*) Where's Kramer? (*He tries to ruffle the parrot's neck and gets nipped. He looks around.*) Which is your best friend?

WOMAN: (*Indicating parrot*) My oldest friend is Tamburlaine. He is very old.

LAUREL: Yes . . . well . . . here's a friend. (*He strokes a puppy, making friends.*)

HARDY: About Mr Kramer. Is he in town?

WOMAN: No, in the country.

HARDY: In the country? Where?

WOMAN: It's a secret.

HARDY: A secret? We're his friends.

WOMAN: That's what he said. He said you'll come and say you are his friends.
(LAUREL *produces a wicked looking flick-knife and snaps the blade out, with his other hand holding up the puppy by the scruff of its neck. The* WOMAN *and the* CLERK *stare at him in disbelief.* LAUREL *smiles.*)

HARDY: I'm sorry about my friend. Now, for one dog – where is Mr Kramer?

55. INT. ACHERSONS' ROOM. NIGHT

ACHERSON *and* CAROL *are lying on their backs on separate beds, not talking, perhaps smoking. Faint music is heard – a local band.*

ACHERSON: Well, here we are.

CAROL: Here we are.

ACHERSON: Boris says that Stanislavsky the welder will be brought from Zlens in the morning.

CAROL: How big is that hole?
(ACHERSON *makes a small hole with his finger and thumb.*)
Did nobody think of chewing-gum?

ACHERSON: Stanislavsky works with nothing else. It's his method.

CAROL: (*Amiably*) Oh, shut up.

ACHERSON: (*Pause*) Well, I think I'll get drunk, then.
(*A knock at the door.*)

CAROL: Yes, why don't you? Come in!

(PHILO *enters*.)

PHILO: Excuse me.

CAROL: Hello, Mr Kramer. Thank you for arranging the room.

PHILO: I'm afraid it is not very nice, but of course they are not used to . . .

CAROL: Of course.

PHILO: (*Pause*) I've been thinking about . . . about you being here.

CAROL: Oh yes?

PHILO: (*To* ACHERSON) I see you do not wish to talk to me. I am sorry I was rude to you.

ACHERSON: Not at all. But thank you anyway for the thought.

CAROL: What were you thinking about?

PHILO: About coincidence. I think this is the first time any tourist has spent the night in this village, in this house. Why you? – why now?

CAROL: Funnily enough, my mind was going on the same lines. In fact I was wondering whether Charles had arranged the whole thing.

(ACHERSON *looks at her in sharp surprise.* PHILO *is also taken aback.*)

PHILO: Why should you think that?

CAROL: We were supposed to be having dinner with some people tonight. He doesn't like them.

ACHERSON: (*Relapsing*) Oh, don't be ridiculous.

CAROL: The Fosters will think we've stood them up. They'll be disappointed.

ACHERSON: Giles Foster will be *very* disappointed.

CAROL: And *I'm* disappointed –

(ACHERSON *gets suddenly to his feet.*)

ACHERSON: (*To* PHILO) Come on – I'll buy you a drink. What's that music?

PHILO: The wedding feast. The whole village is there.

ACHERSON: Can we go?

PHILO: You will be welcomed. There is a tradition of hospitality here.

ACHERSON: Good. (*To* CAROL) Coming?

CAROL: No, thanks.

(ACHERSON *hesitates and then leaves with* PHILO.)

104

56. INT. OUTSIDE ACHERSONS' ROOM. SAME TIME

As they go . . .

PHILO: The Fosters?

ACHERSON: Friends of ours in Monte.

PHILO: The British Consul?

ACHERSON: Yes. I was at school with him. Always was a little toady. Do you know him?

PHILO: No. Is that why you came here?

ACHERSON: No – I told you. A sales trip.

PHILO: Oh yes. Another coincidence. Where did you go last year?

ACHERSON: Majorca. I think I mentioned that too.

PHILO: And before that?

ACHERSON: Italy. No – that was the year before. Paris last year. Wonderful town but the French are awful, the waiters and so on, they're tip mad. No place like home, is there?

PHILO: When do you go back?

ACHERSON: Tomorrow night. Last train to Trieste then the sleeper to Paris, and the boat train from there . . . Ever been to England?

PHILO: Yes. Years ago.

ACHERSON: Well, if you ever think of going back I hope you'll look us up. We're in the book. Acherson. Will you remember?

PHILO: I'll remember Toytown International.

ACHERSON: I doubt that you'll find me there, between you and me. Carol doesn't know it yet but I'm sort of due for the push.

PHILO: Oh. I'm sorry. Why?

ACHERSON: Long story. I'm not really their type.

57. INT/EXT. WEDDING FEAST. NIGHT

Whatever this involves, it involves music, dancing and drinking not to say drunkenness.
Judging by Acherson's state, a good lot of drinking time has elapsed.
PHILO, *also drunker but joylessly, finds* ACHERSON, *among new friends. They are able to speak English,* ACHERSON *and* PHILO,

105

without being understood by those around them.

ACHERSON: Frightfully good party, old man. I wish Carol would come down.

PHILO: Yes – she could take pictures.

ACHERSON: (*Hush-hush*) Natives don't like it – ruined her last film, she says. I say, you don't happen to have a ladies' nightie and some perfumed soap . . . ?

PHILO: I'm afraid not.

ACHERSON: She wanted to get away from the tourists. Now she wants perfumed soap. Never mind, let's have a drink.

PHILO: I like your wife very much. You don't mind me saying that?

ACHERSON: Not at all, old man.

PHILO: How long have you been married?

ACHERSON: Four years. It's the only life, you know. Splendid girl, Carol. Didn't want to marry me at first.

PHILO: No?

ACHERSON: No, stuck on a tennis champion. Thick as two planks.

PHILO: Do you play tennis?

ACHERSON: Golf. Handicap of eighty-one. Play much golf?

PHILO: Not much.

ACHERSON: You should. If you played golf you'd know people. (*Pauses.*) Still, I don't suppose there's a lot of golf around here.

PHILO: Not a lot.

ACHERSON: (*Nodding wisely*) They haven't got the grass.

PHILO: What else do you do?

ACHERSON: How do you mean – ?

PHILO: I want to know about your life.

ACHERSON: Oh, it's a good life, on the whole – lots of friends, bridge friends, golf friends . . . I don't know . . . I mow the lawn and help with the dishes. Quiet life, really, I don't ask for more. Of course, England is the place, isn't it? I mean, if you're English. God, I must sound – sorry, sorry, old man, where was I? – No, the thing about England is the *trees*. Don't you agree?

PHILO: The trees?

ACHERSON: You don't get nice trees in other places, not the variety. Nice trees are taken for granted in England. Yes, awfully fond of trees, damned fond, I don't mind telling you. I say, I'm not drunk, you know, not entirely. Carol's got a tree, you know – her own. I actually *bought* her a tree for her birthday. You can do that – phone them up and tell them to send round a tree, and round it comes, on a lorry, not a sapling, a *tree*. They dig a hole and in it goes, bingo. Cherry tree. No cherries, it's the blossom she likes. I'd do almost anything for Carol. (*He wipes away a tear.*)

PHILO: Yes. I hope you will be happy, and find a job where you – where you are their type. It's not good, is it, if you're not really interested in the things.

ACHERSON: What things?

PHILO: Well, the toys, of course.

ACHERSON: Oh ah. The toys. (*He starts to giggle.*)

PHILO: What's the matter?

ACHERSON: Oh, the whole thing's so frightful, old man. I'm glad I'm going really.

PHILO: Why are they throwing you out?

ACHERSON: I stopped a few black marks, that's all. That's what the factory is all about. The actual job is merely the surface activity. Underneath that runs the main current of preoccupation, which is keeping one's nose clean at all times. This means that when things go wrong you have to pass the blame along the line, like pass-the-parcel, till the music stops – and you don't know the half of it.

PHILO: No?

ACHERSON: No. I have the title of Co-ordinator. The lowest rank of technical responsibility. Do you see the hideous subtlety of that position? All the black marks at the bottom rise like damp till they reach me. And those that start at the top are deflected down. I am a sort of elephants' graveyard for every black mark somewhere in motion in the Department. (*He looks earnestly at* PHILO, *caution apparently gone.*) They're making a scapegoat out of me, old man. Acherson pays so that honour is satisfied, and the big chief can carry on. Well, he's probably right. And furthermore I don't care, because it

was making me sick – the callous abstraction of human lives:
the pin moved across the map, the card removed from the
index . . . it's a trick, old man, a sleight of mind which allows
the occasional squalid alliance for the necessary end, the
exceptional act of injustice for the overall good, the regrettable
sacrifice for the majority's health – yes, he's probably right
and he's certainly got the cleanest nose in Christendom, but if
there's a God above it will all catch up on him one day and
perhaps even he will see himself as the cold-blooded zombie
he really is, and I wish to God I could be there.

(*It is evident that, in his cups,* ACHERSON *has gone beyond the
physical presence of* PHILO; *but seeing* PHILO *staring at him,*
ACHERSON *registers the shock of self-awareness – and tries to
smile, but* PHILO *can't resist it now – he comes clean.*)

PHILO: Otis . . .

(ACHERSON's *brain takes this. He tries to say something but his
instinct is to get away from his own indiscretion. He staggers away,
starts to run, with* PHILO *going after him, leaving the party music,
etc.*)

58. EXT. VILLAGE. NIGHT/DAWN. SAME TIME

The street is deserted. ACHERSON *stumbles and runs into an open space,
where there is a fountain pool or a horse trough; at which point* PHILO
catches up with him, grabs him and pushes him under the water.
ACHERSON *comes up fighting and spluttering, and goes down again
under the water.* PHILO *drags him up and shakes him, and lets him go.
The whole experience – and the water – have done something to sober
both of them.*

PHILO: Now you tell me why you are in Montebianca.

ACHERSON: Who are you?

PHILO: Marin.

ACHERSON: Marin?

PHILO: Philo.

ACHERSON: Philo Marin?

PHILO: No. My code name was Philo.

ACHERSON: Code name? I'm afraid I don't know what you're
talking about.

PHILO: Well, I'm not talking about toy trains.
    (*After a pause* ACHERSON *gives up*.)
ACHERSON: You see how I'm not their type.
PHILO: You remember Philo?
ACHERSON: Yes . . . I remember when you came out. There was a fuss, wasn't there? – at the frontier . . . Small world.
PHILO: Is it? What's this so-called sales trip you've told your wife about?
ACHERSON: It's just a security leak at the Consulate. They think the place has sprung a leak.
PHILO: A coincidence, you mean?
ACHERSON: That's right . . . What the hell would I want with you? (*He picks himself up, his clothes dripping*.)
PHILO: What do they say about me? Or am I forgotten?
ACHERSON: No, you're remembered.
PHILO: What is remembered? What do they say? That I was a traitor?
ACHERSON: (*Uncomfortably*) Well, I wouldn't call it that. You were one of them, weren't you? Doesn't that make you a patriot?
PHILO: Acherson, you're a *pig*.
ACHERSON: (*Turning to go*) Well, there's no point in discussing it. It was a long time ago – and I'm getting pneumonia.
PHILO: No – I want you to know what happened.
ACHERSON: You were blown, weren't you?
PHILO: I don't know if I was or not. But Otis thought they'd let me out on a long string.
ACHERSON: Otis would.
PHILO: Yes, of course he would, he'd be in the wrong job if he didn't – but you're as bad as Otis, Acherson – worse because you're not even honest. You get a little drunk and you start moralizing and you think because you have seen through the dirt, that makes you clean. But you didn't have the morality to get out before you were kicked out, and to tell Otis why.
ACHERSON: Point taken. Now if you'd excuse me . . .
PHILO: I'm sorry Acherson, but I won't excuse you. You talk about Otis making lives into abstract bits of his game – but I stand in front of you and my life means nothing. Otis knows

what he did to me, but you don't know, Acherson. You think I'm lucky not to be in a British gaol or a Russian cemetery, so on the whole I'm OK.

ACHERSON: No . . . that's not . . .

PHILO: You don't know what it is to be an outlaw. There are only two sides in Europe now and I'm tainted to both. Well, I found a place, and here I rot – in this no man's land among people who don't speak my language, where the landscape, the smells, the architecture, the very air, is foreign to me. You come here for a few days and you think it's charming till you have to spend one night too close to it, and then you'll go back home and tell your golf friends about your little adventure. Well, tell them about me. Acherson. Tell them what they did to me.

(PHILO *has followed* ACHERSON *towards the bar, which is dark and empty.* ACHERSON *turns before going in.*)

ACHERSON: Look, I'll talk to Otis –

PHILO: Don't waste your time.

ACHERSON: No, no, I'll tell him . . .

PHILO: You don't understand, Acherson. He had his chance. I'd rather die in this prison.

59. INT. ACHERSONS' ROOM. SAME TIME

Dawn. CAROL *is asleep.* ACHERSON *comes in quietly. He starts to strip off his wet clothes, and to dry himself.* CAROL *wakes.*

CAROL: Charles . . .!

ACHERSON: It's all right. Go back to sleep.

CAROL: What happened to you?

ACHERSON: Our friend pushed me in the fountain.

(CAROL *lies back and chuckles.*)

CAROL: Good party?

ACHERSON: What do you think of him?

CAROL: He doesn't know whether to be friendly or suspicious. What did he have to say?

ACHERSON: Quite a bit. People like that . . . what does one do about them?

(*The note in his voice brings her up.*)

CAROL: He upset you.

ACHERSON: He did a bit.

CAROL: You're sorry for him?

ACHERSON: I suppose so.

CAROL: You can't afford to be sorry for people. Not if there's nothing you can do about it.

ACHERSON: He'd like to leave. I offered to put in a word for him at home, but he didn't go for that.

CAROL: Oh . . . perhaps he'll change his mind.

ACHERSON: He doesn't like us.

CAROL: He likes me. Let's not talk about him. (*She comes over to his bed, wearing only underwear, and kisses him tamely.*) It's better than the hotel now.

ACHERSON: Is it?

CAROL: More sordid. (*She kisses him again.*) Much better.
(*He starts to respond.*)

60. EXT. THE ROAD. EARLY MORNING

Along the unmade road, out of sight of the village a handful of children are walking, fooling around as they go. They are dressed for school and carry books. The BOY *is among them.*
Their road is approaching a more important metalled road. There are still no houses in view.
The group reaches the junction. A car is heard approaching.
The car arrives, slows down.
HARDY *is driving,* LAUREL *is looking at a map. They are going to turn into the village road but they are not certain about it. The car stops some way from the children.*
    The BOY *looks at the car, at* LAUREL *and* HARDY, *and he feels that these are the 'debt collectors'. He goes up to the car.*

LAUREL: Ah . . . Ask him.

HARDY: (*To* BOY) Vlastok? (*He points.*)
    (*The* BOY *shakes his head. He points down the main road, and signifies a turn further along.*)

BOY: Vlastok – that way – the next road.
    (LAUREL *squints at his map, but* HARDY *is already reversing the car. They drive off in the direction indicated by the* BOY.
    A tattered old bus that serves as a school bus arrives. The other

children climb aboard, but the BOY *breaks away and starts to trot back towards the village.*)

61. EXT. BAR. THE YARD. MORNING

STANISLAVSKY *the welder is busy welding under the Fiat.* ACHERSON *stands by.*

62. INT. ACHERSONS' ROOM. SAME TIME

The door is open. CAROL, *dressed, is repairing her face and hair.*
PHILO *comes to the door.*

CAROL: Hello. Charles has just gone down.

PHILO: Is the car all right?

CAROL: Pretty well. He's just checking it. You look a bit rough.

PHILO: Yes. I'm sorry I kept your husband up so late . . . I think he's a good man.

CAROL: Well, why shouldn't he be a good man?
  (CAROL *takes some Alka Seltzer out of her handbag.*)
  Here's something for you. Charles had some.
  (*There is water in a jug, and a glass.*)
  I suppose the water's all right?

PHILO: Oh yes – much better than you drink in London.

CAROL: Sorry. (*She gives him the drink.*)

PHILO: Thank you.

CAROL: Who looks after you?

PHILO: I don't need much looking after. I eat downstairs on credit. I've got a bank account in town.

CAROL: Do you go?

PHILO: No. It's a three-mile walk to the bus. Boris usually goes in for me, if I need anything.

CAROL: You're a bit of a mystery, aren't you?

PHILO: I do not think so. A refugee drinking up his savings. There must be many. Do you mind if I ask you a pointless question?

CAROL: No, go ahead. I don't promise to answer.

PHILO: What kind of trees do you have in your garden at home?

CAROL: Trees?

PHILO: Yes.

CAROL: (*Amused*) Well, let's see – there are only three I think, a couple of elms or something like that, and a cherry.
PHILO: Thank you.
CAROL: Is that all?
PHILO: Yes. Do you like cherries?
CAROL: Yes, but there's no fruit on it, just flowers.
PHILO: Ah. Does your husband look after the garden?
CAROL: What, him? Golf most weekends.
PHILO: Do you play?
CAROL: No.
PHILO: What do you play?
CAROL: Nothing.
PHILO: You never did?
CAROL: I played some tennis – look, what is this?
PHILO: I'm sorry. Mrs Acherson, I'm very glad you came this way. You are an innocent person.
CAROL: That sounds rather dull.
PHILO: Oh no, innocence is rare.
CAROL: Mr Kramer . . . are you in some kind of trouble?
PHILO: (*Pause*) I'd like to ask your husband a favour.
CAROL: Oh. You won't get *him* into trouble, will you?
PHILO: No.
CAROL: All right. I'll be down in a couple of minutes.

63. EXT. THE YARD. MORNING

ACHERSON *is coming out from under the car.* BORIS *finishes pouring in petrol from a can. He screws on the cap.* STANISLAVSKY *has a tiny Citroën, battered. He packs his tools.*
PHILO *helps* ACHERSON *to his feet.*
PHILO: Is it all right?
ACHERSON: Yes.
PHILO: Leaving now?
ACHERSON: In a few minutes.
PHILO: About last night.
ACHERSON: I behaved stupidly.
PHILO: Yes. But you're all right. (*Pause.*) You said you might help me.

113

ACHERSON: If I can.

PHILO: You can. I'd like to come with you. Give me a few
minutes – I haven't got much I want to take.

ACHERSON: Hold on, old man – go where?

PHILO: I want to come with you, when you leave the country.

ACHERSON: What do you mean?

PHILO: I want to travel with you. Party of three. Tourists.
Friends.

ACHERSON: To England?

PHILO: No, only as far as Trieste.

ACHERSON: (*Bewildered*) You want to go to Trieste?

PHILO: I want to go home. I can make my own way from Trieste.

ACHERSON: I don't understand – what do you want?

PHILO: (*Climbing*) Papers, Acherson. I'm asking you for papers.
And for your company over the border. Three English
tourists. They aren't going to pick me out.

ACHERSON: (*Up*) What the hell are you talking about?

PHILO: *Papers*, Acherson! British papers! I've earned them. I'm
owed them. Now I'm asking you to give them to me.

ACHERSON: How on earth do you expect me to –

PHILO: Don't lie to me, Acherson. Refuse if you're afraid of Otis,
but don't lie to me. I know you've got the rank, and I know
Foster has got the blank documents. Every season some
British tourist loses his passport, and I know what papers
Foster has got. They just need his stamp. (*Pause.*) Look, I
can't leave the country in my own identity because the West
doesn't want me, I tried before. And I can't go East because
the Russians *do* want me. But as a British subject I can get
into Trieste, and from Trieste I can disappear. I've still got
friends, and I want to go home.

ACHERSON: You don't know what you're asking.

PHILO: Yes, I do. I'm asking you to deny the Otises. I'm a
used-up spy without a country, and I'm asking you to
recognize me.

ACHERSON: Look, I can probably fix a British visa, given time,
but that's for England, Marin. You can't use it like a free
pass to the world.

PHILO: I don't want to go to England. I'm dying, Acherson, I'm

114

slowly killing myself, bottle by bottle. Well, it doesn't matter very much, but I don't want to die here, I want to die where I was born. I might last years, or only weeks, or I could get caught on my first day, but I want that day, Acherson.

(CAROL *comes prettily towards the car*.)

CAROL: Have you paid?

ACHERSON: Yes.

CAROL: Well, I suppose we should . . . (*To* PHILO) Thank you for everything.

ACHERSON: (*Like a sudden decision*) Mr Kramer is coming with us.

CAROL: Oh – fine. Into town?

PHILO: I hope to travel with you when you leave.

CAROL: Oh really? A holiday in England?

PHILO: Just as far as Trieste. Your friend Mr Foster is going to help with the papers. That was the favour.

CAROL: I'm sure Giles will do all he can to help. If he won't do it for Charles, he'll do it for me. (*She glances at* ACHERSON.) He thinks I fancy him, but I don't. (*She gives* ACHERSON *a brief kiss*.)

ACHERSON: All right, let's get a move on.

64. EXT. THE ROAD. DAY

Long shot.
The Fiat is going back along the road.
The BOY *is short-cutting to the village, over the hill. He sees the car in the distance, and pauses to watch it, then continues to hurry.*

65. INT. FIAT. DAY

ACHERSON *driving,* CAROL *in front,* PHILO *at the back amid luggage and boxes of toys – guns, cars, etc.* PHILO *holds the monkey.*

PHILO: Will you do something for me?

ACHERSON: What's that?

PHILO: We go through Pilz – the next village on the main road. Can you stop at the school there. I want to say goodbye to the boy. It won't take a minute.

ACHERSON: Yes, all right.
> (*Another car is coming towards them – the* LAUREL *and* HARDY
> *car, say a Mercedes. The road is narrow and the Mercedes is
> travelling fast. An accident is avoided.*)
> Who's that?

PHILO: (*Worried*) I don't know.

66. EXT. VILLAGE. SAME TIME

The BOY *runs into the village, worried and scared.*
The Mercedes is already there, parked, empty.
The BOY *runs straight into the bar.*

67. INT. PHILO'S ROOM. SAME TIME

LAUREL *and* HARDY *are quietly looking at the room. They realize
that the bird has flown.*
The BOY *is heard running. He arrives in the room.*
The BOY *stops dead.* LAUREL *and* HARDY *recognize him.* HARDY
sighs and looks at LAUREL.
The BOY *backs away, but* LAUREL *closes the door. The* BOY *is really
frightened and starts to cry.* HARDY *opens the door with a sudden
movement and goes.* LAUREL *follows him.*

68. EXT. VILLAGE. SAME TIME

The Mercedes drives away at speed.

69. EXT. THE METALLED ROAD. DAY

The Mercedes at speed.

70. EXT. THE METALLED ROAD. DAY

The Fiat is being driven sedately.

71. EXT. THE METALLED ROAD. DAY

The Mercedes at speed drives through Pilz and out of frame, leaving the Fiat in frame parked by the school.
PHILO *comes out of the school looking disappointed and puzzled.*

72. EXT. MONTEBIANCA TOWN. DAY

The Fiat drives into town.

73. EXT. MONTEBIANCA HOTEL. SAME TIME

The Fiat stops to drop CAROL *and* PHILO. *They go into the hotel. The Fiat moves on.*

74. EXT. BRITISH CONSULATE. SAME TIME

The Fiat stops round the corner. ACHERSON *gets out and walks into the Consulate.*

75. INT. CONSULATE. SAME TIME

ACHERSON *climbs the rather fine staircase.*

76. INT. CONSULATE OFFICE. SAME TIME

GILES FOSTER *in one chair.*
ACHERSON *enters.*
OTIS *is standing by the window.*
OTIS: Hello, Charles . . . How did it go?
    (ACHERSON *sits tiredly in a chair.*)
ACHERSON: He's at the hotel. I think we've got him all right. But I don't think he'll play when he finds out. God, what a pantomime, eh, Giles?

77. INT. HOTEL BATHROOM. DAY

PHILO *enjoying a bath. The monkey is there.*

78. INT. HOTEL BATHROOM. DAY

PHILO *shaving, taking off much of his beard.*

79. INT. BARBERSHOP. DAY

PHILO *getting a haircut.*
CAROL *waits for him.*
The Mercedes cruises by slowly. LAUREL *and* HARDY *looking for the Fiat.*

80. EXT. CLOTHES SHOP. DAY

PHILO *in new clothes, emerging with* CAROL.

81. INT. PHOTOGRAPHER'S. DAY

Flash! PHILO *has his picture taken.*

82. INT. CONSULATE OFFICE. DAY

Close-up of Philo's new photo on document. The document is held by OTIS. ACHERSON *is the other person in the room.*
OTIS: There you are, Charles. With this he'll be almost as British as you are. And that's awfully British . . . old man.
  (ACHERSON, *it is at once clear, is in no mood for jokes, especially jokes about Philo.*)
ACHERSON: He really does want to go his own way, you know.
OTIS: That's all right. Just get him on that train.
ACHERSON: What happens when he gets to Trieste?
OTIS: Charles, just get him on the train. The rest is taken care of.
ACHERSON: Have you got a legal hold on him?
OTIS: (*Smiles*) Well, he'll have British papers, won't he?
ACHERSON: All this to get one old man through one gate. Why are you here? Why do you want him so badly?
OTIS: You were briefed. You were told enough to operate on. What the hell did you expect?
ACHERSON: I expected to be told the truth. He's not *working*. I

know he isn't. He's got *nothing*. He's drunk a lot of the time and he sees nobody. And what on earth could anyone pick up in this place?

OTIS: Look, you've done your job. So far he trusts you. So just finish it.

ACHERSON: (*Heedless*) But he was clean when he came out . . . You know that now, don't you?

(*It's an accusation.* OTIS *hesitates, but nods, and tells the truth.*)

OTIS: Yes. And he's not working. All right, I dropped him and now we need him. I made a mistake.

ACHERSON: (*Laughs shortly*) Black mark . . . So here you are, taking an interest.

OTIS: Are you trying to tell me I'm here to save my own skin?

ACHERSON: Are you trying to tell me you aren't?

OTIS: (*Sharply*) Don't push it, Charles. They might junk me yet but they'd still need Marin. And badly. We've got a new pipeline on Reschev. It looked all wrong but now it could make a lot of important sense and we need Marin to read it. *That's* why I'm here, so get off your white horse. It never bothered you much while you sat behind your desk in London – you've got people like Marin walking tightropes all over Eastern Europe and some of them fall off; it never bothered you, and now suddenly it's all become a nice old drunk dreaming of the old country. Well, forget it. (*Pause.*) (*Forgiving*) Look, you and I – we've worked pretty well together. I thought we understood each other.

ACHERSON: I'm beginning to understand you, Otis. Do you know I surprised myself a little, talking to Marin. When I got to the bit about you, what a bastard you were and all that, I surprised myself. I found I was quite articulate on the subject.

OTIS: Feel free. Just deliver.

ACHERSON: Oh yes, I'll deliver. But it won't do you any good. He hates you and he hates us.

OTIS: Yes, he's full of poison. It's had time to build up, and I'll need time to release it. He wants a change of scene, someone to talk to. He'll come round, I know him. Just get him on the train.

ACHERSON: No. He doesn't want to go to England.

OTIS: He thinks he doesn't, but it's just his hurt feelings. England was what he was holding out for.

ACHERSON: It's gone sour on him. You turned it sour. Look, he's not a professional, and you're playing by professional rules. He's a sick old man who probably shortened his life by the number of years he's worked for us and then got kicked out for his pains. You can't make it *good* now.

OTIS: (*Losing patience*) I'm not here to make things good. And nor are you. What the hell do you think I'm running – a compensations board? He was the victim of an accident and he wasn't insured, and it was a pity for him, and you don't like it. Well, *I* don't like it. But he can't go home now because the first time he gets drunk, or the third, or the fortieth, he's going to confide in someone again; and if they find out what it is we've got, then what we've got is no *good* any more. Do you understand *that*?

ACHERSON: Yes. Yes, I suppose I do.

OTIS: Good. Well, that's why we spent two months looking for him before we got lucky. The Russians have been looking for him for two years. Let's see if we can keep ahead for one more day.

83. EXT. STREET. DAY

The Fiat is where ACHERSON *parked it.*
LAUREL *and* HARDY *have found it.*
LAUREL *stands on the pavement, keeping a watch.*
HARDY *is half in the car.*

84. INT. CAR. SAME TIME

HARDY *is rummaging around, puzzled at finding boxes of toys. He tosses cars, six-shooters and dolls aside; shakes his head. Must be the wrong Fiat. He opens the glove locker, looks behind the sun-visors, in the door pockets. He gets out of the car.*

85. EXT. STREET. SAME TIME

HARDY *walks to* LAUREL.
HARDY: I don't know. Toys.
LAUREL: We're wasting time.
HARDY: No . . . It smells right. We'll see.

86. EXT. STREET. DAY

The Fiat waits. LAUREL *and* HARDY *sit in the front seats.*

87. INT. CAR. SAME TIME

LAUREL *looks straight ahead – cross-cut Laurel's point-of-view.*
HARDY *watches the mirror – cross-cut Hardy's point-of-view. A few
people approach and pass from each direction.* LAUREL *and* HARDY
are looking for someone, who hesitates on seeing them.
HARDY *sees* ACHERSON *in the mirror.* ACHERSON *hesitates, and walks
on.*
HARDY: Here he is.
(ACHERSON *walks past the Fiat, disowning it.*
LAUREL *and* HARDY *glance at each other and watch as*
ACHERSON *walks on ahead.*
HARDY *starts the car.*
Insert ACHERSON's *tense face.*)

88. EXT. STREET. SAME TIME

The Fiat moves forward slowly. When it is a few yards behind
ACHERSON, LAUREL *gets out of the Fiat while it is still moving at
walking pace. The Fiat overtakes* ACHERSON, *stops.* HARDY *gets out,
turns to* ACHERSON *and moves to meet him.*
ACHERSON *looks over his shoulder to see* LAUREL *walking towards
him. They move up to* ACHERSON, *and without comment, ignoring
Acherson's protest, frisk him, taking out his wallet and an envelope first.*
ACHERSON: What the devil – ? Who are you?
(*There is nothing in Acherson's pockets to enlighten* LAUREL *and*
HARDY. HARDY *goes through Acherson's wallet.*)

I don't want any trouble. There's money in there – take it.
(HARDY *drops the money and bits of paper on the ground. He
hesitates.* LAUREL *is disgusted.*)
LAUREL: Toy salesman . . .
ACHERSON: That's right.
(HARDY *rips open the envelope. It contains Philo's documents,
with the photo.*)

89. EXT. TOWN/COUNTRY. DAY

HARDY *drives the Fiat.* ACHERSON *sits next to him. Behind*
ACHERSON *is* LAUREL *with a gun to* ACHERSON'S *neck.*

90. EXT. COUNTRY DAY

The Fiat draws up off the road at a lonely spot. HARDY *gets out and
looks around. He nods at* LAUREL.
LAUREL *gets out from the back, opens Acherson's door and stands a
few paces back.* LAUREL *beckons. He holds his gun down, relaxed.*
ACHERSON, *without hurrying, picks up a shiny Lone Ranger six-
shooter from the floor between the seats. He levels it at* LAUREL, *cocks
the hammer.* LAUREL *blinks in surprise and starts to laugh. He brings
his gun hand up, but* ACHERSON *fires and the bullet knocks* LAUREL
over backwards.
HARDY *starts getting his own gun out but* ACHERSON *kills him with
his second shot.*

91. INT. RAILWAY STATION. EVENING

This is the station where we saw LAUREL *and* HARDY *arrive. A*
PORTER *trundles the Achersons' luggage.* CAROL *is there. She tips the*
PORTER. *The* PORTER *puts the luggage on the platform. The train is
arriving.*

92. EXT. STATION BAR. SAME TIME

ACHERSON *and* PHILO *at a table with drinks. The monkey is in
Philo's pocket.* ACHERSON *takes the (ripped) envelope out of his*

pocket and gives it to PHILO.

OTIS: Marin . . . are you listening to me?

PHILO: What?

ACHERSON: Change your mind. Come all the way.

(PHILO *looks up from examining the papers.*)

PHILO: Why? Why does it matter to you?

ACHERSON: They'll find you and kill you.

PHILO: If they want to kill me badly enough they'll find me in England. I'd rather go home.

ACHERSON: England was your home once.

PHILO: I thought so too but I was wrong.

ACHERSON: (*Almost angry*) Marin – will you listen –

PHILO: What's the matter? – You haven't changed your mind?

ACHERSON: No . . .

PHILO: You don't have to worry about me. Everything's going to be all right.

ACHERSON: That's bloody nonsense! – you're as good as dead if you don't come with me. Please stop thinking about going home – will you, Marin?

PHILO: You don't understand, Acherson . . . I'm old . . . I accept things . . . I think differently. My memories are good ones now. I don't think about the commissars, the fear, the system, all the things that changed when the Russians came. The things I remember don't change. I was born in a small town. I lived in a street which led into a small square and twice a week there was a market in the square. And round about six o'clock in the evening, when the market was packing up, the ground would be littered with vegetables which hadn't sold and were too cheap to save – cabbage leaves, carrots, some peppers. I particularly remember the peppers lying around the edges of the square – red, orange, yellow, green, and all shades in between, all sunset and forest colours, lying about the square. What mattered to us then was that they were edible, and free, but what I remember now is the way the square looked on a summer evening after the market. (*Pause.*) That's what you are giving back to me. (*The train is heard arriving in the station. The few people in the bar get up to leave.* PHILO *stands up.* ACHERSON *sits tense and anguished.*

123

CAROL *comes into the bar.*

CAROL: Come on, we must get on the train. The porter's taken the luggage.

(*She turns to leave again and* PHILO *follows her. The door closes behind them.* ACHERSON *stands up and with a sudden decision moves briskly out, on to the platform, where* PHILO *and* CAROL *are moving away from him.*)

93. THE PLATFORM. SAME TIME

ACHERSON: (*Shouts*) Marin!

(PHILO *and* CAROL *turn to him.*)

You're not going home!

PHILO: What?

ACHERSON: Forget all that! Otis is on that train.

(PHILO *moves towards him.* CAROL *stares at* ACHERSON, *then turns and starts running towards the train, out of the scene.* PHILO *reaches* ACHERSON.)

The whole thing is his operation. I'm sorry . . .

(PHILO *spits in his face.*)

Marin – please understand –

PHILO: You Judas! I spit on you. I am ashamed of the stupid old man I am – but on you I *spit*!

ACHERSON: I'm sorry.

PHILO: – because you cheat so much for such a small prize. Well, I will not go with you to England.

ACHERSON: Yes, I know that.

PHILO: You can take away my hope but you will not take my honour.

(PHILO *is raving.* ACHERSON *seems stunned, but now he's suddenly had enough and he turns angrily on* PHILO.)

ACHERSON: Honour? – what *honour*? You're a stubborn, bitter old man. I don't blame you – it's understandable, you have been ill-used. Otis made a mistake and you paid for it because in the game we're playing his skin is worth more than yours and there's never enough justice to go round. But you carry your grievance around like a badge – that's all your bloody honour is and you've got to like it.

PHILO: I trusted you after I'd forgotten how to trust.
(*The steam goes out of* ACHERSON.)
ACHERSON: It's not such a significant betrayal, judged by the scale of the world's duplicity.
(PHILO *pushes the papers back to* ACHERSON.)
PHILO: I thought you were my friend.
ACHERSON: Well, as it turns out, you were right. (*He pushes the papers back again.*) I should hang on to these, because you can't stay here. We got to you only just in time, one move ahead of your other friends. If I were you I should take the morning train and see how far you can get.
PHILO: You're lying. Where are they?
ACHERSON: I had to kill them, but there'll be others.
PHILO: (*Incredulous*) You? (*Laughs.*) You can't stop trying, Acherson.
(PHILO *turns to go.*
OTIS *enters the scene.* CAROL *is behind him.* OTIS *greets* PHILO *like an old friend.*)
PHILO: I am very much as you last saw me. Please do not waste time in persuasion. Use force or let me go.
OTIS: Marin, I need you.
PHILO: I am the same man, the same risk.
OTIS: Marin . . .
PHILO: No. You had no time for me then and you will not make use of me now.
OTIS: You need me.
PHILO: No. You cheated me, Otis.
OTIS: (*Getting angry*) You're cheating yourself. You want freedom – I'm giving it to you. You want a country – you can have it. You want apologies – you'll get them. But you won't forgive and you won't accept, and I knew you wouldn't so we had to go through this whole bloody charade. And now you want to go home. All right – but first ask yourself to which side you really belong.
PHILO: Not yours, Otis. Not anyone's.
OTIS: Look, there are no neutral corners in this world, not for you. I made a mistake and I'm sorry, but in this world, you are with *us*.

PHILO: Words.

OTIS: You'd rather wait till their triggermen find you?

PHILO: Yes, I would.

(OTIS *pauses, then nods with finality. He turns to* ACHERSON *expressionlessly.*)

OTIS: Are you coming?

ACHERSON: Yes.

OTIS: Think about it, Acherson.

ACHERSON: You can do what you like with me. I've just had enough of this picnic. And at bottom I think you're wrong.

OTIS: You had a duty.

ACHERSON: Duty! He's been conned all down the line. The Russians conned him out of his country, and the British conned him into working for them, and you conned him out of his due at the end of that, and now you're conning him to get what's left and cover up your mistakes. So don't preach at me about duty.

(CAROL *is frightened by this outburst.*)

CAROL: (*Coming forward*) Charles –

ACHERSON: You go ahead. I'll be coming.

CAROL: It's stupid. It may be right but it's stupid.

ACHERSON: Yes, that's about it.

(*The train makes sounds of getting ready to go.*)

OTIS: Come on, let's forget it.

(OTIS *turns to go to the train.* CAROL *turns to follow him.* PHILO *grabs her sleeve.*)

PHILO: You're his wife!

(*She looks at him with stone eyes.*)

CAROL: No. No, I'm not, actually.

(*She follows* OTIS. PHILO *is stunned.*)

PHILO: So much deception. Was it all necessary?

ACHERSON: Why not? It was Carol who got through your distrust, wasn't it? (*He moves.*)

PHILO: Are you really going back?

ACHERSON: Yes.

PHILO: What will they do to you?

ACHERSON: I don't know.

PHILO: Are you frightened?

ACHERSON: No, I'm just tired. Goodbye, Marin.

PHILO: Do you think I'm worth it, Acherson?

ACHERSON: Yes, I think so.

PHILO: (*A curse*) Otis . . . I'll kill him!

(ACHERSON *smiles helplessly and moves.* PHILO *moves with him.*)

You touched me, Acherson. Yes, I am a stubborn, bitter man, and you *are* stupid, but we are holding out for something. Aren't we? Stay.

ACHERSON: How can I? What for?

PHILO: They'll break you for this.

ACHERSON: One of those things.

PHILO: (*Bursts out*) You think I'll go with you, don't you? – to save your neck.

ACHERSON: No. Goodbye.

PHILO: You're blackmailing me! (*Desperate*) Otis set this up, didn't he?

ACHERSON: No.

PHILO: Tell me he set it up!

ACHERSON: (*Rounds on him*) That's what you want to think so you can forget all about it. Well, think it.

PHILO: No – just tell me the truth.

ACHERSON: Otis didn't set it up.

(ACHERSON *starts running towards the train.* PHILO *stands still for a moment.*)

PHILO: (*Screams*) Acherson!

(PHILO *runs after* ACHERSON *as the train starts to move.*)

94. EXT. TRAIN AT SPEED. NIGHT

95. INT. TRAIN. NIGHT

ACHERSON *stands in the corridor looking out at the night. Behind him are the closed doors of the sleeping compartment.*
The nearest door opens and OTIS *comes to* ACHERSON's *shoulder.*
PHILO *can be seen sitting inside the compartment, on the bunk.*
The adjacent compartment is seen, CAROL *in the doorway.*

OTIS *pats* ACHERSON *on the shoulder.*

OTIS: Very nice. Very nice. (*Pause*) You need a holiday, Charles.

(OTIS *goes back into the sleeper he shares with* PHILO *and closes the door.*

CAROL *looks at* ACHERSON, *troubled and sympathetic.*)

CAROL: Are you coming in?

(ACHERSON *does not respond, but continues to stare at the black country rushing by.*

Fade to black.)

PROFESSIONAL FOUL

To Vaclav Havel

CHARACTERS

ANDERSON
MCKENDRICK
CHETWYN
HOLLAR
BROADBENT
CRISP
STONE
CAPTAIN (MAN 6)
POLICEMAN (MAN 1)
POLICEMAN (MAN 2)
POLICEMAN (MAN 3)
POLICEMAN (MAN 4)
POLICEMAN (MAN 5)
POLICEMAN (MAN 6)
MRS HOLLAR
SACHA (ten years old)
GRAYSON
CHAMBERLAIN
FRENCHMAN
CHAIRMAN
CLERK, LIFT OPERATORS, CONCIERGES,
INTERPRETERS, CUSTOMS, POLICE, etc.

Professional Foul was first shown on BBC TV in September 1977.
The cast was as follows:

ANDERSON	Peter Barkworth
MCKENDRICK	John Shrapnel
CHETWYN	Richard O'Callaghan
HOLLAR	Stephen Rea
BROADBENT	Bernard Hill
CRISP	Billy Hamon
STONE	Shane Rimmer
CAPTAIN	David de Keyser
MAN 1	Ludwig Lang
MAN 2	Milos Kirek
MAN 3	Arnoft Kopecky
MAN 4	Paul Moritz
MRS HOLLAR	Susan Strawson
SACHA	Stefan Ceba
GRAYSON	Sam Kelly
CHAMBERLAIN	Victor Longley
FRENCHMAN	Graeme Eton
CHAIRMAN	Ivan Jelinek
CLERK	Patrick Monckton
INTERPRETER	Sandra Frieze
SCRIPT EDITOR	Richard Broke
DESIGNER	Don Taylor
PRODUCER	Mark Shivas
DIRECTOR	Michael Lindsay-Hogg

I. INT. AEROPLANE. IN FLIGHT

The tourist class cabin of a passenger jet.
We are mainly concerned with two passengers. ANDERSON *is an Oxbridge don, a professor. He is middle-aged, or more. He is sitting in an aisle seat, on the left as we look down the gangway towards the tail.* MCKENDRICK *is also in an aisle seat, but across the gangway and one row nearer the tail.* MCKENDRICK *is about forty. He is also a don, but where* ANDERSON *gives a somewhat fastidious impression,* MCKENDRICK *is a rougher sort of diamond.*
MCKENDRICK *is sitting in the first row of smokers' seats, and* ANDERSON *in the last row of the non-smokers' seats, looking aft. The plane is by no means full. The three seats across the aisle from* ANDERSON *are vacant. The seat next to* ANDERSON *on his right is also vacant but the seat beyond that, by the window, accommodates a* SLEEPING MAN.
On the vacant seat between ANDERSON *and the* SLEEPING MAN *is lying a sex magazine of the* Penthouse *type. The magazine, however, is as yet face down.*
The passengers are coming to the end of a meal. They have trays of aeroplane food in front of them.
MCKENDRICK *puts down his fork and lights a cigarette.*
ANDERSON *dabs at his mouth with his napkin and puts it down. He glances around casually and notes the magazine next to him. He notes the* SLEEPING MAN.
MCKENDRICK *has a briefcase on the seat next to him, and from this he takes a glossy brochure. In fact, this is quite an elaborate publication associated with a philosophical congress. The cover of this programme is seen to read: 'Colloquium Philosophicum Prague 77'.*
ANDERSON *slides out from under his lunch tray a brochure identical to McKendrick's. He glances at it for a mere moment and loses interest. He turns his attention back to the magazine on the seat. He turns the magazine over and notes the naked woman on its cover. He picks the magazine up, with a further glance at the* SLEEPING MAN, *and opens it to a spread of colour photographs. Consciously or unconsciously, he*

133

is holding the brochure in such a way as to provide a shield for the magazine.

MCKENDRICK, *casually glancing round, sees the twin to his own brochure.*

MCKENDRICK: Snap.

(ANDERSON *looks up guiltily.*)

ANDERSON: Ah . . .

(ANDERSON *closes the magazine and slides it face-up under his lunch tray.*

McKendrick's manner is extrovert. Almost breezy.

Anderson's manner is a little vague.)

MCKENDRICK: I wasn't sure it was you. Not a very good likeness.

ANDERSON: I assure you this is how I look.

MCKENDRICK: I mean your photograph. (*He flips his brochure open. It contains small photographs and pen portraits of various men and women who are in fact to be speakers at the colloquium.*) The photograph is younger.

ANDERSON: It must be an old photograph.

(MCKENDRICK *gets up and comes to sit in the empty seat across the aisle from* ANDERSON.)

MCKENDRICK: (*Changing seats*) Bill McKendrick.

ANDERSON: How odd.

MCKENDRICK: Is it?

ANDERSON: Young therefore old. Old therefore young. Only odd at first glance.

MCKENDRICK: Oh yes.

(ANDERSON *takes a notebook, with pencil attached, from his pocket and writes in it as he speaks.*)

ANDERSON: The second glance is known as linguistic analysis. A lot of chaps pointing out that we don't always mean what we say, even when we manage to say what we mean. Personally I'm quite prepared to believe it. (*He finishes writing and closes the notebook. He glances uneasily out of the window.*) Have you noticed the way the wings keep *wagging*? I try to look away and think of something else but I am drawn back irresistibly . . . I wouldn't be nervous about flying if the wings didn't wag. Solid steel. Thick as a bank safe. Flexing like tree branches. It's not natural. There is a

coldness around my heart as though I'd seen your cigarette
smoke knock against the ceiling and break in two like a
bread stick. By the way, that is a non-smoking seat.
MCKENDRICK: Sorry.
    (MCKENDRICK *stubs out his cigarette.* ANDERSON *puts his
notebook back into his pocket.*)
ANDERSON: Yes, I like to collect little curiosities for the
language chaps. It's like handing round a bag of liquorice
allsorts. They're terribly grateful. (*A thought strikes him.*)
Oh, you're not a language chap yourself?
    (*The question seems to surprise* MCKENDRICK, *and amuse him.*)
MCKENDRICK: No. I'm McKendrick.
ANDERSON: You'll be giving a paper?
MCKENDRICK: Yes. Nothing new, actually. More of a summing
up of my corner. My usual thing, you know . . .
    (MCKENDRICK *is fishing but* ANDERSON *doesn't seem to notice.*)
ANDERSON: Jolly good.
MCKENDRICK: Perhaps you've come across some of my
stuff . . .?
    (ANDERSON *now wakes up to the situation and is contrite.*)
ANDERSON: Clearly that is a reasonable expectation. I *am* sorry.
I'm sure I know your name. I don't read the philosophical
journals as much as I should, and hardly ever go to these
international bunfights. No time nowadays. They shouldn't
call us professors. It's more like being the faculty almoner.
MCKENDRICK: At least my paper will be new to you. We are the
only English, actually singing for our supper, I mean. I
expect there'll be a few others going for the free trip and the
social life. In fact, I see we've got one on board. At the
back.
    (MCKENDRICK *jerks his head towards the back of the plane.*
ANDERSON *turns round to look. The object of attention is*
CHETWYN, *asleep in the back row, on the aisle.* CHETWYN *is
younger than* MCKENDRICK *and altogether frailer and neater.*
ANDERSON *squints down the plane at* CHETWYN.)
Do you know Prague?
ANDERSON: (*Warily*) Not personally. I know the name. (*Then he
wakes up to that.*) Oh, *Prague.* Sorry. No, I've never been

there. (*Small pause.*) Or have I? I got an honorary degree at Bratislava once. We changed planes in Prague. (*Pause.*) It might have been Vienna actually. (*Pause. He looks at the window.*) Wag, wag.

MCKENDRICK: It's Andrew Chetwyn. Do you know him?

ANDERSON: (*Warily*) Not personally.

MCKENDRICK: I don't know him *personally*. Do you know his line at all?

ANDERSON: Not as such.

MCKENDRICK: (*Suspiciously*) Have you *heard* of him?

ANDERSON: No. In a word.

MCKENDRICK: Oh. He's been quite public recently.

ANDERSON: He's an ethics chap, is he?

MCKENDRICK: His line is that Aristotle got it more or less right, and St Augustine brought it up to date.

ANDERSON: I can see that that might make him conspicuous.

MCKENDRICK: Oh, it's not *that*. I mean politics. Letters to *The Times* about persecuted professors with unpronounceable names. I'm surprised the Czechs gave him a visa.

ANDERSON: There are some rather dubious things happening in Czechoslovakia. Ethically.

MCKENDRICK: Oh yes. No doubt.

ANDERSON: We must not try to pretend otherwise.

MCKENDRICK: Oh quite. I mean I don't. My work is pretty political. I mean by implication, of course. As yours is. I'm looking forward to hearing you.

ANDERSON: Thank you. I'm sure your paper will be very interesting too.

MCKENDRICK: As a matter of fact I think there's a lot of juice left in the fictions problem.

ANDERSON: Is that what you're speaking on?

MCKENDRICK: No – you are.

ANDERSON: Oh, am I? (*He looks in his brochure briefly.*) So I am.

MCKENDRICK: 'Ethical Fictions as Ethical Foundations'.

ANDERSON: Yes. To tell you the truth I have an ulterior motive for coming to Czechoslovakia at this time. I'm being a tiny bit naughty.

136

MCKENDRICK: Naughty?

ANDERSON: Unethical. Well, I am being paid for by the Czech government, after all.

MCKENDRICK: And what . . .?

ANDERSON: I don't think I'm going to tell you. You see, if I tell you I make you a co-conspirator whether or not you would have wished to be one. Ethically I should give you the opportunity of choosing to be one or not.

MCKENDRICK: Then why don't you give me the opportunity?

ANDERSON: I can't without telling you. An impasse.

(MCKENDRICK *is already putting two and two together and cannot hide his curiosity*.)

MCKENDRICK: Look . . . Professor Anderson . . . if it's political in any way I'd really be very interested.

ANDERSON: Why, are you a politics chap?

MCKENDRICK: One is naturally interested in what is happening in these places. And I have an academic interest – my field is the philosophical assumptions of social science.

ANDERSON: How fascinating. What is that exactly?

MCKENDRICK: (*Slightly hurt*) Perhaps my paper tomorrow afternoon will give you a fair idea.

ANDERSON: (*Mortified*) Tomorrow afternoon? I say, what rotten luck. That's exactly when I have to play truant. I *am* sorry.

MCKENDRICK: (*Coldly*) That's all right.

ANDERSON: I expect they'll have copies.

MCKENDRICK: I expect so.

ANDERSON: The science of social philosophy, eh?

MCKENDRICK: (*Brusquely*) More or less.

ANDERSON: (*With polite interest*) McCarthy.

MCKENDRICK: McKendrick.

ANDERSON: And how are things at . . . er . . .

MCKENDRICK: Stoke.

ANDERSON: (*Enthusiastically*) *Stoke!* An excellent university, I believe.

MCKENDRICK: You know perfectly well you wouldn't be seen dead in it.

(ANDERSON *considers this*.)

ANDERSON: Even if that were true, my being seen dead in a place

137

has never so far as I know been thought a condition of its excellence.

(MCKENDRICK *despite himself laughs, though somewhat bitterly*.)

MCKENDRICK: Very good.

(*An air hostess is walking down the aisle, removing people's lunch trays. She removes Anderson's tray, revealing the cover of the sexy magazine, in the middle of McKendrick's next speech, and passes down the aisle*.)

Wit and paradox. Verbal felicity. An occupation for gentlemen. A higher civilization alive and well in the older universities. I see you like tits and bums, by the way.

ANDERSON: (*Embarrassed*) Ah . . .

(*The turning of tables cheers* MCKENDRICK *up considerably*.)

MCKENDRICK: They won't let you in with that, you know. You'll have to hide it.

ANDERSON: As a matter of fact it doesn't belong to me.

MCKENDRICK: Western decadence, you see. Marxists are a terrible lot of prudes. I can say that because I'm a bit that way myself.

ANDERSON: You surprise me.

MCKENDRICK: Mind you, when I say I'm a Marxist . . .

ANDERSON: Oh, I see.

MCKENDRICK: . . . I don't mean I'm an apologist for everything done in the name of Marxism.

ANDERSON: No, no quite. There's nothing anti-socialist about it. Quite the reverse. The rich have always had it to themselves.

MCKENDRICK: On the contrary. That's why I'd be really very interested in any extra-curricular activities which might be going. I have an open mind about it.

ANDERSON: (*His wires crossed*) Oh, yes, indeed, so have I.

MCKENDRICK: I sail pretty close to the wind, Marx-wise.

ANDERSON: Mind you, it's an odd thing but travel broadens the mind in a way that the proverbialist didn't quite intend. It's only at airports and railway stations that one finds in oneself a curiosity about er – er – erotica, um, girlie magazines.

(MCKENDRICK *realizes that they've had their wires crossed*.)

MCKENDRICK: Perhaps you've come across some of my articles.

138

ANDERSON: (*Amazed and fascinated*) You mean you write for –?
(*He pulls himself up and together.*) Oh – your – er articles – I'm
afraid as I explained I'm not very good at keeping up with the
philosophical. . . .
(MCKENDRICK *has gone back to his former seat to fish about in his
briefcase. He emerges with another girlie magazine and hands it
along the aisle to* ANDERSON.)
MCKENDRICK: I've got one here. Page sixty-one. The science fiction
short story. Not a bad life. Science fiction and sex. And, of
course, the philosophical assumptions of social science.
ANDERSON: (*Faintly*) Thank you very much.
MCKENDRICK: Keep it by all means.
(ANDERSON *cautiously thumbs through pages of naked women.*)
I wonder if there'll be any decent women?

2. INT. HOTEL LOBBY. PRAGUE

We are near the reception desk. ANDERSON, MCKENDRICK *and*
CHETWYN *have just arrived together. Perhaps with other people. Their
luggage consists only of small overnight suitcases and briefcases.*
MCKENDRICK *is at the desk, half-way through his negotiations. The
lobby ought to be rather large, with lifts, etc. It should be large enough to
make inconspicuous a man who is carefully watching the three
Englishmen. This man is aged thirty-five or younger. He is poorly
dressed, but not tramp-like. His name is* PAVEL HOLLAR. *The lobby
contains other people and a poorly equipped news-stand.*
We catch up with ANDERSON *talking to* CHETWYN.
ANDERSON: (*Enthusiastically*) *Birmingham!* Excellent university.
Some very good people.
(*The* DESK CLERK *comes to the counter, where* MCKENDRICK *is
first in the queue. The* CLERK *and other Czech people in this script
obviously speak with an accent, but there is no attempt here to
reproduce it.*)
CLERK: Third floor. Dr McKendrick.
MCKENDRICK: Only of philosophy.
CLERK: Your baggage is there?
MCKENDRICK: (*Hastily*) Oh, I'll see to that. Can I have the key,
please?

CLERK: Third floor. Dr Anderson. Ninth floor. A letter for you.

(*The* CLERK *gives* ANDERSON *a sealed envelope and also a key.* ANDERSON *seems to have been expecting the letter. He thanks the* CLERK *and takes it.*)

Dr Chetwyn. Ninth floor.

(*The three philosophers walk towards the lifts.* PAVEL *watches them go. When they reach the lift* ANDERSON *glances round and sees two men some way off across the lobby, perhaps at the news-stand. These men are called* CRISP *and* BROADBENT. CRISP *looks very young; he is twenty-two. He wears a very smart, slightly flashy suit and tie.* BROADBENT, *balding but young, is in his thirties. He wears flannels and a blazer.* CRISP *is quite small.* BROADBENT *is big and heavy. But both look fit.*)

ANDERSON: I say, look who's over there . . . Broadbent and Crisp.

(*The lift now opens before them.* ANDERSON *goes in showing his key to the middle-aged woman in charge of the lift.*

MCKENDRICK *and* CHETWYN *do likewise. Over this:*)

CHETWYN: Who? (*He sees them and recognizes them.*) Oh yes.

MCKENDRICK: (*Sees them*) Who?

CHETWYN: Crisp and Broadbent. They must be staying here too.

MCKENDRICK: Crisp? Broadbent? That kid over by the news-stand?

ANDERSON: That's Crisp.

MCKENDRICK: My God, they get younger all the time.

(*The lift doors close.*

Inside the lift.)

ANDERSON: Crisp is twenty-two. Broadbent is past his peak but Crisp is the next genius in my opinion.

MCKENDRICK: Do you know him?

ANDERSON: Not personally. I've been watching him for a couple of years.

CHETWYN: He's Newcastle, isn't he?

ANDERSON: Yes.

MCKENDRICK: I've never heard of him. What's his role there?

ANDERSON: He's what used to be called left wing. Broadbent's in the centre. He's an opportunist more than anything.

(*The lift has stopped at the third floor.*)

(*To* MCKENDRICK) This is you – see you later.

(MCKENDRICK *steps out of the lift and looks round*.)

MCKENDRICK: Do you think the rooms are bugged?

(*The lift doors shut him off.*

Inside the lift. ANDERSON *and* CHETWYN *ride up in silence for a few moments.*)

ANDERSON: What was it Aristotle said about the higher you go the further you fall . . .?

CHETWYN: He was talking about tragic heroes.

(*The lift stops at the ninth floor.* ANDERSON *and* CHETWYN *leave the lift.*)

I'm this way. There's a restaurant downstairs. The menu is very limited but it's all right.

ANDERSON: You've been here before?

CHETWYN: Yes. Perhaps see you later then, sir.

(CHETWYN *goes down a corridor, away from Anderson's corridor.*)

ANDERSON: (*To himself*) Sir?

(ANDERSON *follows the arrow towards his own room number.*)

3. INT. ANDERSON'S HOTEL ROOM

The room contains a bed, a wardrobe, a chest. A telephone. A bathroom containing a bath leads off through a door.

ANDERSON *is unpacking. He puts some clothes into a drawer and closes it. His suitcase is open on the bed.* ANDERSON *turns his attention to his briefcase and brings out McKendrick's magazine. He looks round, wondering what to do with it. There is a knock on the door.* ANDERSON *tosses the girlie magazine into his suitcase and closes the case. He goes to open the door. The caller is* PAVEL HOLLAR.

ANDERSON: Yes?

HOLLAR: I am Pavel Hollar.

ANDERSON: Yes?

HOLLAR: Professor Anderson.

(HOLLAR *is Czech and speaks with an accent.*)

ANDERSON: Hollar? Oh, heavens, yes. How extraordinary. Come in.

HOLLAR: Thank you. I'm sorry to –

ANDERSON: No, no – what a pleasant surprise. I've only just arrived, as you can see. Sit where you can. How are you? What are you doing? You live in Prague?

HOLLAR: Oh yes.

(ANDERSON *closes the door*.)

ANDERSON: Well, well. Well, well, well, well. How are you? Must be ten years.

HOLLAR: Yes. It is ten. I took my degree in sixty-seven.

ANDERSON: You got a decent degree, too, didn't you?

HOLLAR: Yes, I got a first.

ANDERSON: Of course you did. Well done, well done. Are you still in philosophy?

HOLLAR: No, unfortunately.

ANDERSON: Ah. What are you doing now?

HOLLAR: I am a, what do you say – a cleaner.

ANDERSON: (*With intelligent interest*) A cleaner? What is that?

HOLLAR: (*Surprised*) Cleaning. Washing. With a brush and a bucket. I am a cleaner at the bus station.

ANDERSON: You wash buses?

HOLLAR: No, not buses – the lavatories, the floors where people walk and so on.

ANDERSON: Oh. I see. You're a *cleaner*.

HOLLAR: Yes.

(*Pause*.)

ANDERSON: Are you married now, or anything?

HOLLAR: Yes. I married. She was almost my fiancée when I went to England. Irma. She is a country girl. No English. No philosophy. We have a son who is Sacha. That is Alexander.

ANDERSON: I see.

HOLLAR: And Mrs Anderson?

ANDERSON: She died. Did you meet her ever?

HOLLAR: No.

ANDERSON: (*Pause*) I don't know what to say.

HOLLAR: Did she die recently?

ANDERSON: No, I mean – a cleaner.

HOLLAR: I had one year graduate research. My doctorate studies were on certain connections with Thomas Paine and Locke. But then, since sixty-nine . . .

142

ANDERSON: Cleaning lavatories.

HOLLAR: First I was in a bakery. Later on construction, building houses. Many other things. It is the way it is for many people.

ANDERSON: Is it all right for you to be here talking to me?

HOLLAR: Of course. Why not? You are my old professor.

(HOLLAR *is carrying a bag or briefcase. He puts this down and opens it.*)

I have something here.

(*From the bag he takes out of the sort of envelope which would contain about thirty type-written foolscap pages. He also takes out a child's 'magic eraser' pad, the sort of pad on which one scratches a message and then slides it out to erase it.*)

You understand these things of course?

ANDERSON: (*Nonplussed*) Er . . .

HOLLAR: (*Smiling*) Of course.

(HOLLAR *demonstrates the pad briefly, then writes on the pad while Anderson watches.*)

ANDERSON: (*Stares at him*) To England?

(HOLLAR *abandons the use of the pad, and whispers in* ANDERSON's *ear.*)

HOLLAR: Excuse me.

(HOLLAR *goes to the door and opens it for* ANDERSON. HOLLAR *carries his envelope but leaves his bag in the room.* ANDERSON *goes out of the door baffled.* HOLLAR *follows him. They walk a few paces down the corridor.*)

Thank you. It is better to be careful.

ANDERSON: Why? You don't seriously suggest that my room is bugged?

HOLLAR: It is better to assume it.

ANDERSON: Why?

(*Just then the door of the room next to Anderson's opens and a man comes out. He is about forty and wears a dark rather shapeless suit. He glances at* ANDERSON *and* HOLLAR. *And then walks off in the opposite direction towards the lift and passes out of sight.* HOLLAR *and* ANDERSON *instinctively pause until the man has gone.*)

I hope you're not getting me into trouble.

HOLLAR: I hope not. I don't think so. I have friends in trouble.

ANDERSON: I know, it's dreadful – but . . . well, what is it?

(HOLLAR *indicates his envelope*.)

HOLLAR: My doctoral thesis. It is mainly theoretical. Only ten thousand words, but very formally arranged.

ANDERSON: My goodness . . . ten years in the writing.

HOLLAR: No. I wrote it this month – when I heard of this congress here and you coming. I decided. Every day in the night.

ANDERSON: Of course. I'd be very happy to read it.

HOLLAR: It is in Czech.

ANDERSON: Oh . . . well . . . ?

HOLLAR: I'm afraid so. But Peter Volkansky – he was with me, you remember – we came together in sixty-three –

ANDERSON: Oh yes – Volkansky – yes, I do remember him. He never came back here.

HOLLAR: No. He didn't come back. He was a realist.

ANDERSON: He's at Reading or somewhere like that.

HOLLAR: Lyster.

ANDERSON: Leicester. Exactly. Are you in touch with him?

HOLLAR: A little. He will translate it and try to have it published in English. If it's good. I think it is good.

ANDERSON: But can't you publish it in Czech? . . . (*This catches up on him and he shakes his head*.) Oh, Hollar . . . now, you know, really, I'm a guest of the government here.

HOLLAR: They would not search you.

ANDERSON: That's not the point. I'm sorry . . . I mean it would be bad manners, wouldn't it?

HOLLAR: Bad manners?

ANDERSON: I know it sounds rather lame. But ethics and manners are interestingly related. The history of human calumny is largely a series of breaches of good manners. . . . (*Pause*.) Perhaps if I said correct behaviour it wouldn't sound so ridiculous. You do see what I mean. I am sorry. . . . Look, can we go back . . . I ought to unpack.

HOLLAR: My thesis is about correct behaviour.

ANDERSON: Oh yes?

HOLLAR: Here, you know, individual correctness is defined by what is correct for the state.

ANDERSON: Yes, I know.

HOLLAR: I ask how collective right can have meaning by itself. I ask where it comes from, the idea of a collective ethic.

ANDERSON: Yes.

HOLLAR: I reply, it comes from the individual. One man's dealings with another man.

ANDERSON: Yes.

HOLLAR: The collective ethic can only be the individual ethic writ big.

ANDERSON: Writ large.

HOLLAR: Writ large, precisely. The ethics of the state must be judged against the fundamental ethic of the individual. The human being, not the citizen. I conclude there is an obligation, a human responsibility, to fight against the state correctness. Unfortunately that is not a safe conclusion.

ANDERSON: Quite. The difficulty arises when one asks oneself how the *individual* ethic can have any meaning by itself. Where does *that* come from? In what sense is it intelligible, for example, to say that a man has certain inherent, individual rights? It is much easier to understand how a community of individuals can decide to give each other certain rights. These rights may or may not include, for example, the right to publish something. In that situation, the individual ethic would flow from the collective ethic, just as the state says it does. (*Pause.*) I only mean it is a question you would have to deal with.

HOLLAR: I mean, it is not safe for me.

ANDERSON: (*Still misunderstanding*) Well yes, but for example, you could say that such an arrangement between a man and the state is a sort of contract, and it is the essence of a contract that both parties enter into it freely. And you have not entered into it freely. I mean, that would be one line of attack.

HOLLAR: It is not the main line. You see, to me the idea of an inherent right is intelligible. I believe that we have such rights, and they are paramount.

ANDERSON: Yes, I see you do, but how do you justify the assertion?

145

HOLLAR: I observe. I observe my son for example.

ANDERSON: Your son?

HOLLAR: For example.

(*Pause.*)

ANDERSON: Look, there's no need to stand out here. There's . . . no point. I was going to have a bath and change . . . meeting some of my colleagues later . . .

(ANDERSON *moves to go but* HOLLAR *stops him with a touch on the arm.*)

HOLLAR: I am not a famous dissident. A writer, a scientist . . .

ANDERSON: No.

HOLLAR: If I am picked up – on the way home, let us say – there is no fuss. A cleaner. I will be one of hundreds. It's all right. In the end it must change. But I have something to say – that is all. If I leave my statement behind, then it's OK. You understand?

ANDERSON: Perhaps the correct thing for me to have done is not to have accepted their invitation to speak here. But I did accept it. It is a contract, as it were, freely entered into. And having accepted their hospitality I cannot in all conscience start smuggling . . . It's just not ethical.

HOLLAR: But if you didn't know you were smuggling it –

ANDERSON: Smuggling entails knowledge.

HOLLAR: If I hid my thesis in your luggage, for instance.

ANDERSON: That's childish. Also, you could be getting me into trouble, and your quarrel is not with me. Your action would be unethical on your own terms – one man's dealings with another man. I am sorry.

(ANDERSON *goes back towards his door, which* HOLLAR *had left ajar.* HOLLAR *follows him.*)

HOLLAR: No, it is I who must apologize. The man next door, is he one of your group?

ANDERSON: No. I don't know him. (ANDERSON *opens his bedroom door. He turns as if to say goodbye.*)

HOLLAR: My bag.

ANDERSON: Oh yes.

(HOLLAR *follows* ANDERSON *into the room.*)

HOLLAR: You will have a bath . . .?

146

ANDERSON: I thought I would.

(HOLLAR *turns into the bathroom.* ANDERSON *stays in the bedroom, surprised. He hears the bath water being turned on. The bath water makes a rush of sound.* ANDERSON *enters the bathroom and sees* HOLLAR *sitting on the edge of the bath. Interior bathroom.*)

HOLLAR: (*Quietly*) I have not yet made a copy.

ANDERSON: (*Loudly*) What?

(HOLLAR *goes up to* ANDERSON *and speaks close to* ANDERSON's *ear. The bath taps make a loud background noise.*)

HOLLAR: I have not yet made a copy. I have a bad feeling about carrying this home. (*He indicates his envelope.*) I did not expect to take it away. I ask a favour. (*Smiles.*) Ethical.

ANDERSON: (*Quietly now*) What is it?

HOLLAR: Let me leave this here and you can bring it to my apartment tomorrow – I have a safe place for it there.

(HOLLAR *takes a piece of paper and a pencil from his pocket and starts writing his address in capital letters.*)

ANDERSON: But you know my time here is very crowded – (*Then he gives in.*) Do you live nearby?

HOLLAR: It is not far. I have written my address.

(HOLLAR *gives* ANDERSON *the paper.*)

ANDERSON: (*Forgetting to be quiet*) Do you seriously – (HOLLAR *quietens* ANDERSON.)

Do you seriously expect to be searched on the way home?

HOLLAR: I don't know, but it is better to be careful. I wrote a letter to Mr Husak. Also some other things. So sometimes they follow me.

ANDERSON: But you weren't worried about bringing the thesis with you.

HOLLAR: No. If anybody watches me they want to know what books *you* give *me*.

ANDERSON: I see. Yes, all right, Hollar. I'll bring it tomorrow.

HOLLAR: Please don't leave it in your room when you go to eat. Take your briefcase.

(*They go back into the bedroom.* ANDERSON *puts Hollar's envelope into his briefcase.*)

(*Normal voice*) So perhaps you will come and meet my wife.

147

ANDERSON: Yes. Should I telephone?

HOLLAR: Unfortunately my telephone is removed. I am home all day. Saturday.

ANDERSON: Oh yes.

HOLLAR: Goodbye.

ANDERSON: Goodbye.

(HOLLAR *goes to the door, carrying his bag.*)

HOLLAR: I forgot – welcome to Prague.

(HOLLAR *leaves, closing the door.*

ANDERSON *stands still for a few moments. Then he hears footsteps approaching down the corridor. The footsteps appear to stop outside his room. But then the door to the next room is opened and the unseen man enters the room next door and loudly closes the door behind him.*)

4. INT. ANDERSON'S ROOM. MORNING

Close-up of the colloquium brochure. It is lying on Anderson's table. Then ANDERSON *picks it up. His dress and appearance, and the light outside the window, tell us that it is morning. Dressed to go out,* ANDERSON *picks up his briefcase and leaves the room.*

In the corridor he walks towards the lifts.

At the lifts he finds CRISP *waiting.* ANDERSON *stands next to* CRISP *silently for a few moments.*

ANDERSON: Good morning. (*Pause.*) Mr Crisp . . . my name is Anderson. I'm a very great admirer of yours.

CRISP: (*Chewing gum*) Oh . . . ta.

ANDERSON: Good luck this afternoon.

CRISP: Thanks. Bloody useless, the lifts in this place.

ANDERSON: Are you all staying in this hotel?

(CRISP *doesn't seem to hear this.* CRISP *sees* BROADBENT *emerging from a room.* BROADBENT *carries a zipped bag.* CRISP *has a similar bag.*)

CRISP: (*Shouts*) Here you are, Roy – it's waiting for you.

(BROADBENT *arrives.*)

ANDERSON: Good morning. Good luck this afternoon.

BROADBENT: Right. Thanks. Are you over for the match?

ANDERSON: Yes. Well, partly. I've got my ticket.

(ANDERSON *takes out of his pocket the envelope he received from the hotel* CLERK *and shows it.*)

CRISP: (*Quietly*) You didn't pull her, then?

BROADBENT: No chance.

CRISP: They don't trust you, do they?

BROADBENT: Well, they're right, aren't they? Remember Milan.

CRISP: (*Laughing*) Yeah –

(*The bell sounds to indicate that the lift is arriving.*)

About bloody time.

ANDERSON: I see from yesterday's paper that they've brought in Jirasek for Vladislav.

BROADBENT: Yes, that's right. Six foot eight, they say.

ANDERSON: He's not very good in the air unless he's got lots of space.

(BROADBENT *looks at him curiously. The lift doors open and the three of them get in. There is no one else in the lift except the female* OPERATOR.

Interior lift.)

BROADBENT: You've seen him, have you?

ANDERSON: I've seen him twice. In the UEFA Cup a few seasons ago. . . . I happened to be in Berlin for the Hegel Colloquium, er, bunfight. And then last season I was in Bratislava to receive an honorary degree.

CRISP: Tap his ankles for him. Teach him to be six foot eight.

BROADBENT: Leave off – (*He nods at the* LIFT OPERATOR.) You never know, do you?

CRISP: Yeah, maybe the lift's bugged.

ANDERSON: He scored both times from the same move, and came close twice more –

BROADBENT: Oh yes?

(*Pause.*)

ANDERSON: (*In a rush*) I realize it's none of my business – I mean you may think I'm an absolute ass, but – (*Pause.*) Look, if Halas takes a corner he's going to make it short – almost certainly – push it back to Deml or Kautsky, who pulls the defence out. Jirasek hangs about for the chip to the far post. They'll do the same thing from a set piece. Three or four times in the same match. *Really*. Short corners and free kicks.

149

(The lift stops at the third floor. BROADBENT *and* CRISP *are staring at* ANDERSON.*)*

(Lamely) Anyway, that's why they've brought Jirasek back, in my opinion.

(The lift doors open and MCKENDRICK *gets in. McKendrick's manner is breezy and bright.)*

MCKENDRICK: Good morning! You've got together then?

ANDERSON: A colleague. Mr McKendrick . . .

MCKENDRICK: You're Crisp. *(He takes* CRISP'S *hand and shakes it.)* Bill McKendrick. I hear you're doing some very interesting work in Newcastle. Great stuff. I still like to think of myself as a bit of a left-winger at Stoke. Of course, my stuff is largely empirical – I leave epistemological questions to the scholastics – eh, Anderson? *(He pokes* ANDERSON *in the ribs.)*

ANDERSON: McKendrick . . .

BROADBENT: Did you say *Stoke?*

(The lift arrives at the ground floor.)

MCKENDRICK: *(To* BROADBENT*)* We've met, haven't we? Your face is familiar . . .

*(*BROADBENT, CRISP *and* MCKENDRICK *in close attendance leave the lift.* ANDERSON *is slow on the uptake but follows.)*

ANDERSON: McKendrick –?

MCKENDRICK: *(Prattling)* There's a choice of open forums tonight – neo-Hegelians or Quinian neo-Positivists. Which do you fancy? Pity Quine couldn't be here. And Hegel for that matter.

*(*MCKENDRICK *laughs brazenly in the lobby.* BROADBENT *and* CRISP *eye him warily.* ANDERSON *winces.)*

5. INT. THE COLLOQUIUM

The general idea is that a lot of philosophers sit in a sort of theatre while on stage one of their number reads a paper from behind a lectern, with a CHAIRMAN *in attendance behind him. The set-up, however, is quite complicated. To one side are three glassed-in-booths, each one containing 'simultaneous interpreters'. These interpreters have earphones and microphones. They also have a copy of the lecture being*

*given. One of these interpreters is translating into Czech, another into
French, another into German. The audience is furnished with
earphones or with those hand-held phones which are issued in theatres
sometimes. Each of these phones can tune into any of the three
interpreters, depending upon the language of the listener. For our
purposes it is better to have the hand-held phones.*

It is important to the play, specifically to a later scene when
ANDERSON *is talking, that the hall and the audience should be
substantial.*

At the moment ANDERSON *is in the audience, sitting next to*
MCKENDRICK. MCKENDRICK *is still discomfited.* CHETWYN *is
elsewhere in the audience.*

*We begin, however, with a large close-up of the speaker, who is an
American called* STONE. *After the first sentence or two of Stone's
speech, the camera will acquaint us with the situation. At different
points during Stone's speech, there is conversation between*
ANDERSON *and* MCKENDRICK. *In this script, these conversations are
placed immediately after that part of Stone's speech which they will
cover. This applies also to any other interpolations. Obviously,* STONE
does not pause to let these other things in.

STONE: The confusion which often arises from the ambiguity of
ordinary language raises special problems for a logical
language. This is especially so when the ambiguity is not
casual and inadvertent – but when it's contrived. In fact, the
limitations of a logical language are likely to appear when we
ask ourselves whether it can accommodate a literature, or
whether poetry can be reduced to a logical language. It is
here that deliberate ambiguity for effect makes problems.

ANDERSON: Perfectly understandable mistake.

STONE: Nor must we confuse ambiguity, furthermore, with mere
synonymity. When we say that a politician ran for office, that
is not an ambiguous statement, it is merely an instance of a
word having different applications, literal, idiomatic and so
on.

MCKENDRICK: I said I knew his face.

ANDERSON: 'Match of the Day'.

STONE: The intent is clear in each application. The show ran well
on Broadway. Native Dancer ran well at Kentucky, and so

151

on. (*In the audience a Frenchman expresses dismay and bewilderment as his earphones give out a literal translation of 'a native dancer' running well at Kentucky. Likewise a German listener has the same problem.*)

And what about this word 'Well'? Again, it is applied as a qualifier with various intent – the show ran for a long time, the horse ran fast, and so on.

MCKENDRICK: So this pressing engagement of yours is a football match.

ANDERSON: A World Cup qualifier is not just a football match.

STONE: Again, there is no problem here so long as these variations are what I propose to call reliable. 'You eat well,' says Mary to John. 'You cook well,' says John to Mary. We know that when Mary says, 'You *eat* well', she does not mean that John eats *skilfully*. Just as we know that when John says, 'You cook well', he does not mean that Mary cooks *abundantly*.

ANDERSON: But I'm sorry about missing your paper, I really am.

STONE: I say that we know this, but I mean only that our general experience indicates it. The qualifier takes its meaning from the contextual force of the verb it qualifies. But it is the mark of a sound theory that it should take account not merely of our general experience but also of the particular experience, and not merely of the particular experience but also of the unique experience, and not merely of the unique experience but also of the hypothetical experience. It is when we consider the world of *possibilities*, hypothetical experience, that we get closer to ambiguity. 'You cook well,' says John to Mary. 'You eat well,' says Mary to John.

MCKENDRICK: Do you ever wonder whether all this is worthwhile?

ANDERSON: No.

MCKENDRICK: I know what you mean.

(CHETWYN *is twisting the knob on his translation phone, to try all this out in different languages. He is clearly bored. He looks at his watch.*)

STONE: No problems there. But I ask you to imagine a competition when what is being judged is table manners. (*Insert French interpreter's box – interior.*)

INTERPRETER: . . . *bonne tenue à table* . . .

STONE: John enters this competition and afterwards Mary says, 'Well, you certainly ate well!' Now Mary seems to be saying that John ate skilfully – *with refinement*. And again, I ask you to imagine a competition where the amount of food eaten is taken into account along with refinement of table manners. *Now* Mary says to John, 'Well, you didn't eat very well, but at least you ate well.'

INTERPRETER: *Alors, vous n'avez pas bien mangé . . . mais . . .*
(*All* INTERPRETERS *baffled by this.*)

STONE: Now clearly there is no way to tell whether Mary means that John ate abundantly but clumsily, or that John ate frugally but elegantly. Here we have a genuine ambiguity. To restate Mary's sentence in a logical language we would have to ask her what she meant.

MCKENDRICK: By the way, I've got you a copy of my paper.

ANDERSON: Oh, many thanks.

MCKENDRICK: It's not a long paper. You could read it comfortably during half-time.
(MCKENDRICK *gives* ANDERSON *his paper.*)

STONE: But this is to assume that Mary exists. Let us say she is a fictitious character in a story I have written. Very well, you say to me, the author, 'What did Mary mean? Well, I might reply – 'I don't know what she meant. Her ambiguity makes the necessary point of my story.' And here I think the idea of a logical language which can *only* be unambiguous breaks down.
(ANDERSON *opens his briefcase and puts McKendrick's paper into it. He fingers Hollar's envelope and broods over it.*
STONE *has concluded. He sits down to applause. The* CHAIRMAN, *who has been sitting behind him, has stood up.*)

ANDERSON: I'm going to make a discreet exit – I've got a call to make before the match.
(ANDERSON *stands up.*)

CHAIRMAN: Yes – Professor Anderson I think . . .?
(ANDERSON *is caught like a rabbit in the headlights.*
MCKENDRICK *enjoys his predicament and becomes interested in how* ANDERSON *will deal with it.*)

ANDERSON: Ah . . . I would only like to offer Professor Stone the observation that language is not the only level of human communication, and perhaps not the most important level. Whereof we cannot speak, thereof we are by no means silent. (MCKENDRICK *smiles 'Bravo'*.)
Verbal language is a technical refinement of our capacity for communication, rather than the *fons et origo* of that capacity. The likelihood is that language develops in an *ad hoc* way, so there is no reason to expect its development to be logical. (*A thought strikes him.*) The importance of language is overrated. It allows me and Professor Stone to show off a bit, and it is very useful for communicating detail – but the important truths are simple and monolithic. The essentials of a given situation speak for themselves, and language is as capable of obscuring the truth as of revealing it. Thank you.
(ANDERSON *edges his way out towards the door*.)

CHAIRMAN: (*Uncertainly*) Professor Stone . . .

STONE: Well, what was the question?

6. INT. FRONT DOOR OF THE HOLLAR APARTMENT

The apartment is one of two half-way up a large old building. The stairwell is dirty and uncared for. The Hollar front door is on a landing, and the front door of another flat is across the landing. Stairs go up and down. ANDERSON *comes up the stairs and finds the right number on the door and rings the bell. He is carrying his briefcase. All the men in this scene are Czech plain-clothes* POLICEMEN. *They will be identified in this text merely by number.* MAN 3 *is the one in charge.*
MAN 1 *comes to the door.*

ANDERSON: I'm looking for Mr Hollar.
(MAN 1 *shakes his head. He looks behind him.* MAN 2 *comes to the door.*)

MAN 2: (*In Czech*) Yes? Who are you?

ANDERSON: English? Um. *Parlez-vous français?* Er. Spreckanzydoitch?

MAN 2: (*In German*) *Deutsch? Ein Bischen.*

ANDERSON: Actually I don't. Does Mr Hollar live here? Apartment Hollar?

(MAN 2 *speaks to somebody behind him.*)

MAN 2: (*In Czech*) An Englishman. Do you know him?

(MRS HOLLAR *comes to the door. She is about the same age as* HOLLAR.)

ANDERSON: Mrs Hollar?

(MRS HOLLAR *nods.*)

Is your husband here? Pavel . . .

MRS HOLLAR: (*In Czech*) Pavel is arrested.

(*Inside, behind the door,* MAN 3 *is heard shouting, in Czech.*)

MAN 3: (*Not seen*) What's going on there?

(MAN 3 *comes to the door.*)

ANDERSON: I am looking for Mr Hollar. I am a friend from England. His Professor. My name is Anderson.

MAN 3: (*In English*) Not here. (*In Czech to* MRS HOLLAR.) He says he is a friend of your husband. Anderson.

ANDERSON: He was my student.

(MRS HOLLAR *calls out.*)

MAN 3: (*In Czech*) Shut up.

ANDERSON: Student. Philosophy.

(MRS HOLLAR *calls out.*)

MAN 3: Shut up.

(MAN 3 *and* MAN 2 *come out of the flat on to the landing, closing the door behind them.*)

ANDERSON: I just came to see him. Just to say hello. For a minute. I have a taxi waiting. Taxi.

MAN 3: Taxi.

ANDERSON: Yes. I can't stay.

MAN 3: (*In English*) Moment. OK.

ANDERSON: I can't stay.

(MAN 3 *rings the bell of the adjacent flat. A rather scared woman opens the door.* MAN 3 *asks, in Czech, to use the phone.* MAN 3 *goes inside the other flat.* ANDERSON *begins to realize the situation.*)

Well, look, if you don't mind – I'm on my way to – an engagement . . .

MAN 2: (*In Czech*) Stay here.

(*Pause.* ANDERSON *looks at his watch. Then from inside the flat* MRS HOLLAR *is shouting in Czech.*)

MRS HOLLAR: (*Unseen*) I'm entitled to a witness of my choice.

(*The door is opened violently and immediately slammed.*
ANDERSON *becomes agitated.*)

ANDERSON: What's going on in there?

MAN 2: (*In Czech*) Stay here, he won't be a minute.

(ANDERSON *can hear* MRS HOLLAR *shouting.*)

ANDERSON: Now look here –

(ANDERSON *rings the doorbell. The door is opened by* MAN 4.)
I demand to speak to Mrs Hollar.

(*Upstairs and downstairs doors are opening and people are
shouting, in Czech, 'What's going on?' And so on. There is also
shouting from inside the flat.* MAN 2 *shouts up and down the
staircase, in Czech.*)

MAN 2: (*In Czech*) Go inside!

ANDERSON: Now look here, I am the J. S. Mill Professor of
Ethics at the University of Cambridge and I demand that I be
allowed to leave or to telephone the British Ambassador!

MAN 4: (*In Czech*) Bring him inside.

MAN 2: (*In Czech*) In.

(*He pushes* ANDERSON *into the flat. Interior flat. The hallway.
Inside it is apparent that the front door leads to more than one
flat. Off the very small dirty hall there is a kitchen, a lavatory
and two other doors, not counting the door to the Hollar rooms.*)

MAN 4: (*In Czech*) Stay with him.

(*The Hollar interior door is opened from inside by* MRS HOLLAR.)

MRS HOLLAR: (*In Czech*) If he's my witness he's allowed in here.

MAN 4: (*In Czech*) Go inside – he's not your witness.

(MAN 4 *pushes* MRS HOLLAR *inside and closes the door from
within. This leaves* ANDERSON *and* MAN 2 *in the little hall.
Another door now opens, and a small girl, poorly dressed, looks
round it. She is jerked back out of sight by someone and the door
is pulled closed. The Hollar door is flung open again, by* MRS
HOLLAR.)

MRS HOLLAR: (*In Czech*) I want this door open.

MAN 2: (*In Czech*) Leave it open, then. He'll be back in a minute.

(MAN 4 *disappears back inside the flat.* MRS HOLLAR *is heard.*)

MRS HOLLAR: (*Unseen. In Czech*) Bastards.

(ANDERSON *stands in the hallway. He can hear* MRS HOLLAR
starting to cry. ANDERSON *looks completely out of his depth.*)

ANDERSON: My God . . .

>(*Then the doorbell rings.* MAN 2 *opens it to let in* MAN 3.)

MAN 2: (*In Czech*) We had to come in to shut her up.

MAN 3: (*In Czech*) Well, he's coming over. (*In English to* ANDERSON.) Captain coming. Speak English.

ANDERSON: I would like to telephone the British Ambassador.

MAN 3: (*In English*) OK. Captain coming.

ANDERSON: How long will he be? I have an appointment. (*He looks at his watch.*) Yes, by God! I do have an engagement and it starts in half an hour –

MAN 3: (*In English*) Please.

>(*A lavatory flushes. From the other interior door an* OLD MAN *comes out.* MAN 3 *nods curtly at the* OLD MAN. *The* OLD MAN *shuffles by looking at* ANDERSON. MAN 3 *becomes uneasy at being in the traffic. He decides to bring* ANDERSON *inside the flat. He does so.*
>
>*Interior Hollar's room. There are two connecting rooms. Beyond this room is a door leading to a bedroom. This door is open. The rooms seem full of people. The rooms are small and shabby. They are being thoroughly searched, and obviously have been in this process for hours. The searchers do not spoil or destroy anything. There are no torn cushions or anything like that. However, the floor of the first room is almost covered in books. The bookcases which line perhaps two of the walls are empty. The rug could be rolled up, and there could be one or two floorboards up.*
>
>MAN 1 *is going through the books, leafing through each one and looking along the spine. He is starting to put books back on the shelves one by one.* MAN 5 *has emptied drawers of their contents and is going through a pile of papers.* MRS HOLLAR *stands in the doorway between the two rooms. Beyond her* MAN 2 *can be seen searching.* [MAN 4 *is out of sight in the bedroom.*] MAN 3 *indicates a chair on which* ANDERSON *should sit.* ANDERSON *sits, putting his briefcase on the floor by his feet. He looks around. He sees a clock showing 2.35.*
>
>*Mix to clock showing 2.55.*
>
>ANDERSON *is where he was.* MAN 1 *is still on the books.* MAN 5 *is still looking through papers.* MAN 3 *is examining the inside of a radio set.*

Voices are heard faintly on the stairs. There is a man remonstrating. A woman's voice, too.
The doorbell rings.
MAN 3 *leaves the room, closing the door.* ANDERSON *hears him go to the front door. There is some conversation. The front door closes again and* MAN 3 *re-enters the room.*)

MAN 3: (*In English to* ANDERSON) Taxi.

ANDERSON: Oh – I forgot him. Dear me.

MAN 3: OK.

ANDERSON: I must pay him.

(ANDERSON *takes out his wallet.* MAN 3 *takes it from him without snatching.*)

MAN 3: OK.

(MAN 3 *looks through the wallet.*)

ANDERSON: Give that back – (*Furious*) Now, you listen to me – this has gone on quite long enough – I demand – to be allowed to leave . . .

(ANDERSON *has stood up.* MAN 3 *gently pushes him back into the chair. In Anderson's wallet* MAN 3 *finds his envelope and discovers the football ticket. He puts it back. He looks sympathetically at* ANDERSON.)

MAN 3: (*In Czech*) The old boy's got a ticket for the England match. No wonder he's furious. (*He gives the wallet back to* ANDERSON. *In English*) Taxi OK. No money. He go. Football no good.

ANDERSON: Serve me right.

MAN 5: (*In Czech*) It's on the radio. Let him have it on.

(MAN 3 *returns to the radio and turns it on.*
MRS HOLLAR *enters quickly from the bedroom and turns it off.*)

MRS HOLLAR: (*In Czech*) That's my radio.

MAN 3: (*In Czech*) Your friend wants to listen to the match.

(MRS HOLLAR *looks at* ANDERSON. *She turns the radio on. The radio is talking about the match, which is just about to begin.*)

MAN 3: (*In English*) Is good. OK?

(ANDERSON, *listening, realizes that the radio is listing the names of the English team.*
Then the match begins.
Mix to:

The same situation about half an hour later. The radio is still on.
MAN 1 *is still on the books. He has put aside three or four English books.* MAN 5 *has disappeared.* MAN 2 *is sorting out the fluff from a carpet sweeper.* MAN 4 *is standing on a chair, examining the inside of a ventilation grating.*

ANDERSON *gets up off his chair and starts to walk towards the bedroom. The three* MEN *in the room look up but don't stop him.*
ANDERSON *enters the bedroom.*
Interior bedroom.

MAN 3 *is going through pockets in a wardrobe.* MAN 5 *is looking under floorboards.* MRS HOLLAR *is sitting on the bed, watching them.*)

ANDERSON: It's half-past three. I demand to be allowed to leave or to telephone the British –

MAN 3: Please – too slow.

ANDERSON: I demand to leave –

MAN 3: OK. Who wins football?

ANDERSON: (*Pause*) No score.

(*The doorbell goes.*

MAN 3 *goes into the other room and to the door.* ANDERSON *follows him as far as the other room. On the way through* MAN 3 *signals to turn off the radio.* MAN 2 *turns off the radio.* MRS HOLLAR *comes in and turns the radio on.*)

MRS HOLLAR: (*In Czech*) Show me where it says I can't listen to my own radio.

(MAN 3 *returns from the front door with* MAN 6. MAN 6 *enters the room, saying:*)

MAN 6: (*In Czech*) I said don't let him leave – I didn't say bring him inside. (*To* ANDERSON *in English.*) Professor Anderson? I'm sorry your friend Mr Hollar has got himself into trouble.

ANDERSON: Thank Christ – now listen to me – I am a professor of philosophy. I am a guest of the Czechoslovakian government. I might almost say an honoured guest. I have been invited to speak at the Colloquium in Prague. My connections in England reach up to the highest in the land –

MAN 6: Do you know the Queen?

ANDERSON: Certainly.(*But he has rushed into that.*) No, I do not know the Queen – but I speak the truth when I say that I am

159

personally acquainted with two members of the government, one of whom has been to my house, and I assure you that unless I am allowed to leave this building immediately there is going to be a major incident about the way my liberty has been impeded by your men. I do not know what they are doing here, I do not care what they are doing here –

MAN 6: Excuse me, Professor. There is some mistake. I thought you were here as a friend of the Hollar family.

ANDERSON: I know Pavel Hollar, certainly.

MAN 6: Absolutely. You are here as a friend, at Mrs Hollar's request.

ANDERSON: I just dropped in to – what do you mean?

MAN 6: Mr Hollar unfortunately has been arrested for a serious crime against the state. It is usual for the home of an accused person to be searched for evidence, and so on. I am sure the same thing happens in your country. Well, under our law Mrs Hollar is entitled to have a friendly witness present during the search. To be frank, she is entitled to two witnesses. So if, for example, an expensive vase is broken by mistake, and the police claim it was broken before, it will not just be her word against theirs. And so on. I think you will agree that's fair.

ANDERSON: Well?

MAN 6: Well, my understanding is that she asked you to be her witness. (*In Czech to* MRS HOLLAR) Did you ask him to be your witness?

MRS HOLLAR: (*In Czech*) Yes, I did.

MAN 6: (*In English to* ANDERSON) Yes. Exactly so. (*Pause.*) You are Mr Hollar's friend, aren't you?

ANDERSON: I taught him in Cambridge after he left Czechoslovakia.

MAN 6: A brave man.

ANDERSON: Yes . . . a change of language . . . and . . .culture . . .

MAN 6: He walked across a minefield. In 1962. Brave.

ANDERSON: Perhaps he was simply desperate.

MAN 6: Perhaps a little ungrateful. The state, you know, educated him, fed him, for eighteen years. 'Thank you very much – goodbye.'

ANDERSON: Well he came back, in the spring of sixty-eight.

MAN 6: Oh yes.

ANDERSON: A miscalculation.

MAN 6: How do you mean?

ANDERSON: Well, really . . . there are a lot of things wrong in
England but it is still not 'a serious crime against the state' to
put forward a philosophical view which does not find favour
with the government.

MAN 6: Professor . . . Hollar is charged with currency offences.
There is a black market in hard currency. It is illegal. We do
not have laws about philosophy. He is an ordinary criminal.
(*Pause.*
*The radio commentary has continued softly. But in this pause it
changes pitch. It is clear to* ANDERSON, *and to us, that something
particular has occurred in the match.* MAN 6 *is listening.*)
(*In English*) Penalty. (*He listens for a moment.*) For us, I'm
afraid.

ANDERSON: Yes, I can hear.
(*This is because it is clear from the crowd noise that it's a penalty
for the home side.* MAN 6 *listens again.*)

MAN 6: (*In English*) Broadbent – a bad tackle when Deml had a
certain goal . . . a what you call it? – a necessary foul.

ANDERSON: A professional foul.

MAN 6: Yes.
(*On the radio the goal is scored. This is perfectly clear from the
crowd reaction.*)
Not good for you.
(MAN 6 *turns off the radio. Pause.* MAN 6 *considers* ANDERSON.)
So you have had a philosophical discussion with Hollar.

ANDERSON: I believe you implied that I was free to go. (*He stands
up.*) I am quite sure you know that Hollar visited me at my
hotel last night. It was a social call, which I was returning
when I walked into this. And, furthermore, I understood
nothing about being a witness – I was prevented from leaving.
I only came to say hello, and meet Pavel's wife, on my way to
the football –

MAN 6: (*With surprise*) So you came to Czechoslovakia to go to the
football match, Professor?
(*This rattles* ANDERSON.)

161

ANDERSON: Certainly not. Well, the afternoon of the Colloquium was devoted to – well, it was not a condition of my invitation that I should attend all the sessions. (*Pause.*) I was invited to *speak*, not to listen. I am speaking tomorrow morning.

MAN 6: Why should I know Hollar visited you at the hotel?

ANDERSON: He told me he was often followed.

MAN 6: Well, when a man is known to be engaged in meeting foreigners to buy currency –

ANDERSON: I don't believe any of that – he was being harassed because of his letter to Husak –

MAN 6: A letter to President Husak? What sort of letter?

ANDERSON: (*Flustered*) Your people knew about it –

MAN 6: It is not a crime to write to the President –

ANDERSON: No doubt that depends on what is written.

MAN 6: You mean he wrote some kind of slander?

ANDERSON: (*Heatedly*) I insist on leaving now.

MAN 6: Of course. You know, your taxi driver has made a complaint against you.

ANDERSON: What are you talking about?

MAN 6: He never got paid.

ANDERSON: Yes, I'm sorry but –

MAN 6: You are not to blame. My officer told him to go.

ANDERSON: Yes, that's right.

MAN 6: Still, he is very unhappy. You told him you would be five minutes, you were delivering something –

ANDERSON: How could I have told him that? I don't speak Czech.

MAN 6: You showed him five on your watch, and you did all the things people do when they talk to each other without a language. He was quite certain you were delivering something in your briefcase.

(*Pause.*)

ANDERSON: Yes. All right. But it was not money.

MAN 6: Of course not. You are not a criminal.

ANDERSON: Quite so. I promised to bring Pavel one or two of the Colloquium papers. He naturally has an interest in philosophy and I assume it is not illegal.

MAN 6: Naturally not. Then you won't mind showing me.

(ANDERSON *hesitates then opens the briefcase and takes out*

McKendrick's paper and his own and passes them over.
MAN 6 *takes them and reads their English titles.*)
'Ethical Fictions as Ethical Foundations' . . . 'Philosophy and the Catastrophe Theory'.
(MAN 6 *gives the papers back to* ANDERSON.)

MAN 6: You wish to go to the football match? You will see twenty minutes, perhaps more.

ANDERSON: No. I'm going back to the university, to the Colloquium.

MRS HOLLAR: (*In Czech*) Is he leaving?

MAN 6: Mrs Hollar would like you to remain.

ANDERSON: (*To* MRS HOLLAR) No, I'm sorry. (*A thought strikes him.*) If you spoke to the taxi driver you would have known perfectly well I was going to the England match.
(MAN 6 *doesn't reply to this either in word or expression.*
ANDERSON *closes his briefcase.*
The doorbell rings and MAN 3 *goes to open the door.*
From the bedroom MAN 5 *enters with a small parcel wrapped in old newspaper.*)

MAN 5: (*In Czech*) I found this, Chief, under the floorboards.
(MAN 5 *gives the parcel to* MAN 6, *who unwraps it to reveal a bundle of American dollars.*
MRS HOLLAR *watches this with disbelief and there is an outburst.*)

MRS HOLLAR: (*In Czech*) He's lying! (*To* ANDERSON) It's a lie –
The door reopens for MAN 3. SACHA HOLLAR, *aged ten, comes in with him. He is rather a tough little boy. He runs across to his mother, who is crying and shouting, and embraces her. It is rather as though he were a small adult comforting her.*)

ANDERSON: Oh my God . . . Mrs Hollar . . .
(ANDERSON, *out of his depth and afraid, decides abruptly to leave and does so.* MAN 3 *isn't sure whether to let him go but* MAN 6 *nods at him and* ANDERSON *leaves.*)

7. INT. HOTEL CORRIDOR. EVENING

ANDERSON *approaches his room. He is worn out. When he gets to his door and fumbles with his key he realizes that he can hear a voice in the room next door to his. He puts his ear to this other door.*

GRAYSON: (*Inside*) Yes, a new top for the running piece – OK – Prague, Saturday.

(GRAYSON *speaks not particularly slowly but with great deliberation, enunciating every consonant and splitting syllables up where necessary for clarity. He is, of course, dictating to a fast typist.*)

There'll be Czechs bouncing in the streets of Prague tonight as bankruptcy stares English football in the face, stop, new par.

(ANDERSON *knocks on the door.*)

(*Inside*) It's open!

(ANDERSON *opens the door and looks into the room. Interior room. It is of course a room very like Anderson's own room, if not identical. Its occupant, the man we had seen leave the room earlier, is* GRAYSON, *a sports reporter from England. He is on the telephone as* ANDERSON *cautiously enters the room.*)

Make no mistake, comma, the four-goal credit which these slick Slovaks netted here this afternoon will keep them in the black through the second leg of the World Cup Eliminator at Wembley next month, stop. New par – (*To* ANDERSON) Yes? (*Into phone*) You can bank on it.

ANDERSON: I'm next door.

GRAYSON: (*Into phone*) – bank on it. New par – (*To* ANDERSON) Look, can you come back? (*Into phone*) But for some determined saving by third-choice Jim Bart in the injury hyphen jinxed England goal, we would have been overdrawn by four more when the books were closed, stop. Maybe Napoleon was wrong when he said we were a nation of shopkeepers, stop. Today England looked like a nation of goalkeepers, stop. Davey, Petherbridge and Shell all made saves on the line. New par.

ANDERSON: Do you mind if I listen – I missed the match.

(GRAYSON *waves him to a chair.* ANDERSON *sits on a chair next to a door which is in fact a connecting door into the next room. Not Anderson's own room but the room on the other side of Grayson's room.*)

GRAYSON: (*Into phone*) Dickenson and Pratt were mostly left

164

standing by Wolker, with a W, and Deml, D dog, E
Edward, M mother, L London – who could go round the
halls as a telepathy act, stop. Only Crisp looked as if he had a
future outside Madame Tussaud's – a.u.d.s. – stop. He laid
on the two best chances, comma, both wasted by Pratt,
comma, who ski'ed one and stubbed his toe on the other,
stop. Crisp's, apostrophe s. comment from where I was
sitting looked salt and vinegar flavoured . . .

(ANDERSON *has become aware that another voice is cutting in
from the next room. The door between the two rooms is not quite
closed. During Grayson's last speech* ANDERSON *gently pushes
open the door and looks behind him and realizes that a colleague
of Grayson's is also dictating in the next room.*

ANDERSON *stands up and looks into the next room and is drawn
into it by the rival report.*

This room belongs to CHAMBERLAIN.

Interior CHAMBERLAIN's *room.* CHAMBERLAIN *on phone.*)

CHAMBERLAIN: Wilson, who would like to be thought the big
bad man of the English defence, merely looked slow-footed
and slow-witted stop. Deml – D.E.M. mother L. – Deml got
round him five times on the trot, bracket, literally, close
bracket, using the same swerve, comma, making Wilson
look elephantine in everything but memory, stop. On the
fifth occasion there was nothing to prevent Deml scoring
except what Broadbent took it on himself to do, which was to
scythe Deml down from behind, stop. Halas scored from the
penalty, stop.

(ANDERSON *sighs and sits down on the equivalent chair in
Chamberlain's room.* CHAMBERLAIN *sees him.*)

Can I help you –?

ANDERSON: Sorry – I'm from next door.

CHAMBERLAIN: (*Into phone*) New paragraph – (*To* ANDERSON) I
won't be long – (*Into phone*) This goal emboldened the
Czechs to move Bartók, like the composer, forward and risk
the consequences, stop. Ten minutes later, just before half-
time, comma, he was the man left over to collect a short
corner from Halas and it was his chip which Jirasek rose to
meet for a simple goal at the far post –

ANDERSON: I knew it!

>(CHAMBERLAIN *turns to look at him.*)

CHAMBERLAIN: (*Into phone*) New paragraph. As with tragic
opera, things got worse after the interval . . .

>(ANDERSON *has stood up to leave. He leaves through Grayson's*
room. GRAYSON *is on the phone, saying:*)

GRAYSON: (*Into the phone*) . . . Jirasek, unmarked at the far post,
flapped into the air like a great stork and, rising a yard higher
than Bart's outstretched hands, he put Czechoslovakia on the
road to victory.

>(ANDERSON *leaves the room without looking at* GRAYSON *or*
being noticed.)

8. INT. HOTEL DINING ROOM

The cut is to gay Czech music.
The dining room has a stage. A small group of Czech musicians and
singers in the tourist version of peasant costume is performing.
It is evening. At one of the tables STONE, *the American, and a*
FRENCHMAN *are sitting next to each other, and sharing the table are*
ANDERSON, MCKENDRICK *and* CHETWYN. *The three of them are,*
for different reasons, subdued. STONE *is unsubdued. They are*
reaching the end of the meal.

STONE: Hell's bells. Don't you understand English? When I say
to you, 'Tell me what you mean', you can only reply, 'I
would wish to say so and so.' 'Never mind what you would
wish to say,' I reply. 'Tell me what you *mean*.'

FRENCHMAN: *Mais oui*, but if you ask me in French, you must
say, '*Qu'est-ce que vous voulez dire?*' – 'What is that which you
wish to say?' *Naturellement*, it is in order for me to reply, '*Je*
veux dire etcetera.'

STONE: (*Excitedly*) But you are making *my* point – don't you see?

MCKENDRICK: What do you think the chances are of meeting a
free and easy woman in a place like this?

STONE: I *can't* ask you in French.

MCKENDRICK: I don't mean free, necessarily.

FRENCHMAN: *Pourquoi non? Qu'est-ce que vous voulez dire? Voilà!*
– now I have asked you.

CHETWYN: You don't often see goose on an English menu.

(CHETWYN *is the last to finish his main course. They have all eaten the main course. There are drinks and cups of coffee on the table.*)

STONE: The French have no verb meaning 'I mean'.

CHETWYN: Why's that I wonder.

STONE: They just don't.

CHETWYN: People are always eating goose in Dickens.

MCKENDRICK: Do you think it will be safe?

FRENCHMAN: *Par exemple. Je vous dis, 'Qu'est-ce que vous voulez dire?'*

MCKENDRICK: I mean, one wouldn't want to be photographed through a two-way mirror.

STONE: I don't want to ask you what you would wish to say. I want to ask you what you *mean*. Let's assume there is a difference.

ANDERSON: We do have goose liver. What do they do with the rest of the goose?

STONE: Now assume that you say one but mean the other.

FRENCHMAN: *Je dis quelque chose, mais je veux dire –*

STONE: Right.

MCKENDRICK: (*To* STONE) Excuse me, Brad.

STONE: Yes?

MCKENDRICK: You eat well but you're a lousy eater.

(*This is a fair comment.* STONE *has spoken with his mouth full of bread, cake, coffee, etc. and he is generally messy about it.* STONE *smiles forgivingly but hardly pauses.*)

STONE: Excuse us.

FRENCHMAN: *A bientôt.*

(STONE *and the* FRENCHMAN *get up to leave.*)

STONE: (*Leaving*) You see, what you've got is an incorrect statement which when corrected looks like itself.

(*There is a pause.*)

MCKENDRICK: Did you have a chance to read my paper?

ANDERSON: I only had time to glance at it. I look forward to reading it carefully.

CHETWYN: I read it.

ANDERSON: Weren't you there for it?

MCKENDRICK: No, he sloped off for the afternoon.

ANDERSON: Well, you sly devil, Chetwyn. I bet you had a depressing afternoon. It makes the heart sick, doesn't it.

CHETWYN: Yes, it does rather. We don't know we've been born.

MCKENDRICK: He wasn't at the football match.

CHETWYN: Oh – is that where you were?

ANDERSON: No, I got distracted.

MCKENDRICK: He's being mysterious. I think it's a woman.

ANDERSON: (*To* CHETWYN) What were you doing?

CHETWYN: I was meeting some friends.

MCKENDRICK: He's being mysterious. I don't think it's a woman.

CHETWYN: I have friends here, that's all.

ANDERSON: (*To* MCKENDRICK) Was your paper well received?

MCKENDRICK: No. They didn't get it. I could tell from the questions that there'd been some kind of communications failure.

ANDERSON: The translation phones?

MCKENDRICK: No, no – they simply didn't understand the line of argument. Most of them had never heard of catastrophe theory, so they weren't ready for what is admittedly an audacious application of it.

ANDERSON: I must admit I'm not absolutely clear about it.

MCKENDRICK: It's like a reverse gear – no – it's like a breaking point. The mistake that people make is, they think a moral principle is indefinitely extendible, that it holds good for any situation, a straight line cutting across the graph of our actual situation – here you are, you see – (*He uses a knife to score a line in front of him straight across the table-cloth, left to right in front of him*) 'Morality' down there, running parallel to 'Immorality' up here (*He scores a parallel line*) – and never the twain shall meet. They think that is what a principle means.

ANDERSON: And isn't it?

MCKENDRICK: No. The two lines are on the same plane. (*He holds out his flat hand, palm down, above the scored lines.*) They're the edges of the same plane – it's in three dimensions, you see – and if you twist the plane in a certain way, into what we call the catastrophe curve, you get a model of the sort of behaviour we find in the real world. There's a point – the catastrophe point – where your progress along one line of behaviour jumps you into the opposite line; the principle reverses itself at the point where a rational man would abandon it.

CHETWYN: Then it's not a principle.

MCKENDRICK: There aren't any principles in your sense. There are only a lot of principled people trying to behave as if there were.

ANDERSON: That's the same thing, surely.

MCKENDRICK: You're a worse case than Chetwyn and his primitive Greeks. At least he has the excuse of *believing* in goodness and beauty. You know they're fictions but you're so hung up on them you want to treat them as if they were God-given absolutes.

ANDERSON: I don't see how else they would have any practical value –

MCKENDRICK: So you end up using a moral principle as your excuse for acting against a moral interest. It's a sort of funk –

(ANDERSON, *under pressure, slams his cup back on to its saucer in a very uncharacteristic and surprising way. His anger is all the more alarming for that.*)

ANDERSON: You make your points altogether too easily, McKendrick. What need have you of moral courage when your principles reverse themselves so conveniently?

MCKENDRICK: All right! I've gone too far. As usual. Sorry. Let's talk about something else. There's quite an attractive woman hanging about outside, loitering in the vestibule.

(*The dining-room door offers a view of the lobby.*)

Do you think it is a trap? My wife said to me – now, Bill, don't do anything daft, you know what you're like, if a blonde knocked on your door with the top three buttons of her police uniform undone and asked for a cup of sugar you'd convince yourself she was a bus conductress brewing up in the next room.

ANDERSON: (*Chastened*) I'm sorry . . . you're right up to a point. There would be no moral dilemmas if moral principles worked in straight lines and never crossed each other. One meets test situations which have troubled much cleverer men than us.

CHETWYN: A good rule, I find, is to try them out on men much *less* clever than us. I often ask my son what *he* thinks.

ANDERSON: Your son?

CHETWYN: Yes. He's eight.

MCKENDRICK: She's definitely glancing this way – seriously, do you think one could chat her up?

(STONE *turns round to look through the door and we see now that the woman is* MRS HOLLAR.)

ANDERSON: Excuse me.

(*He gets up and starts to leave, but then comes back immediately and takes his briefcase from under the table and then leaves. We stay with the table.* MCKENDRICK *watches* ANDERSON *meet* MRS HOLLAR *and shake her hand and they disappear.*)

MCKENDRICK: Bloody hell, it *was* a woman. Crafty old beggar.

9. EXT. STREET. NIGHT

ANDERSON *and* MRS HOLLAR *walking.*
A park. A park bench. SACHA HOLLAR *sitting on the bench.*
ANDERSON *and* MRS HOLLAR *arrive.*

MRS HOLLAR: (*In Czech*) Here he is. (*To* ANDERSON) Sacha. (*In Czech*) Thank him for coming.

SACHA: She is saying thank you that you come.

MRS HOLLAR: (*In Czech*) We're sorry to bother him.

SACHA: She is saying sorry for the trouble.

ANDERSON: No, no I am sorry about . . . everything. Do you learn English at school?

SACHA: Yes. I am learning English two years. With my father also.

ANDERSON: You are very good.

SACHA: Not good. You are a friend of my father. Thank you.

ANDERSON: I'm afraid I've done nothing.

SACHA: You have his writing?

ANDERSON: His thesis? Yes. It's in here. (*He indicates his briefcase.*)

SACHA: (*In Czech*) It's all right, he's still got it.

(MRS HOLLAR *nods.*)

MRS HOLLAR: (*In Czech*) Tell him I didn't know who he was today.

SACHA: My mother is not knowing who you are, tomorrow at the apartment.

ANDERSON: Today.

SACHA: Today. Pardon. So she is saying, 'Come here! Come here! Come inside the apartment!' Because she is not knowing. My father is not telling her. He is telling me only.

ANDERSON: I see. What did he tell you?

SACHA: He will go see his friend the English professor. He is taking the writing.

ANDERSON: I see. Did he return home last night?

SACHA: No. He is arrested outside hotel. Then in the night they come to make search.

ANDERSON: Had they been there all night?

SACHA: At eleven o'clock they are coming. They search twenty hours.

ANDERSON: My God.

SACHA: In morning I go to Bartolomesskaya to be seeing him.

MRS HOLLAR: (*Explains*) Police.

SACHA: But I am not seeing him. They say go home. I am waiting. Then I am going home. Then I am seeing you.

ANDERSON: What were they looking for?

SACHA: (*Shrugs*) Western books. Also my father is writing things. Letters, politics, philosophy. They find nothing. Some English books they don't like but really nothing. But the dollars, of course, they pretend to find.

(MRS HOLLAR *hears the word dollars*.)

MRS HOLLAR: (*In Czech*) Tell him the dollars were put there by the police.

SACHA: Not my father's dollars. He is having no moneys.

ANDERSON: Yes. I know.

SACHA: They must arrest him for dollars because he does nothing. No bad things. He is signing something. So they are making trouble.

ANDERSON: Yes.

MRS HOLLAR: (*In Czech*) Tell him about Jan.

SACHA: You must give back my father's thesis. Not now. The next days. My mother cannot take it.

ANDERSON: He asked me to take it to England.

SACHA: Not possible now. But thank you.

ANDERSON: He asked me to take it.

SACHA: Not possible. Now they search you, I think. At the aeroport. Because they are seeing you coming to the apartment and you have too much contact. Maybe they are seeing us now.

(ANDERSON *looks around him.*)

Is possible.

ANDERSON: (*Uncomfortably*) I ought to tell you . . . (*Quickly*) I came to the apartment to give the thesis back. I refused him. But he was afraid he might be stopped – I thought he just meant searched, not arrested –

SACHA: Too quick – too quick –

(*Pause.*)

ANDERSON: What do you want me to do?

SACHA: My father's friend – he is coming to Philosophy Congress today.

ANDERSON: Tomorrow.

SACHA: Yes tomorrow. You give him the writing. Is called Jan. Is OK. Good friend.

(ANDERSON *nods.*)

ANDERSON: Jan.

SACHA: (*In Czech*) He'll bring it to the university hall for Jan tomorrow. (SACHA *stands up.*) We go home now.

(MRS HOLLAR *gets up and shakes hands with* ANDERSON.)

ANDERSON: I'm sorry . . . What will happen to him?

MRS HOLLAR: (*In Czech*) What was that?

SACHA: (*In Czech*) He wants to know what will happen to Daddy.

MRS HOLLAR: Ruzyne.

SACHA: That is the prison. Ruzyne.

(*Pause.*)

ANDERSON: I will, of course, try to help in England. I'll write letters. The Czech Ambassador . . . I have friends, too, in our government –

(ANDERSON *realizes that the boy has started to cry. He is specially taken aback because he has been talking to him like an adult.*)

Now listen – I am personally friendly with important people

– the Minister of Education – people like that.

MRS HOLLAR: (*In Czech but to* ANDERSON) Please help Pavel –

ANDERSON: Mrs Hollar – I will do everything I can for him.

>   (*He watches* MRS HOLLAR *and* SACHA *walk away into the dark.*)

10. INT. ANDERSON'S ROOM. NIGHT

ANDERSON *is lying fully dressed on the bed. His eyes open. Only light from the window. There are faint voices from Grayson's room. After a while* ANDERSON *gets up and leaves his room and knocks on Grayson's door.*

Exterior Grayson's room.

GRAYSON *opens his door.*

GRAYSON: Oh hello. Sorry, are we making too much noise?

ANDERSON: No, it's all right, but I heard you were still up and I wondered if I could ask a favour of you. I wonder if I could borrow your typewriter.

GRAYSON: My typewriter?

ANDERSON: Yes.

GRAYSON: Well, I'm leaving in the morning.

ANDERSON: I'll let you have it back first thing. I'm leaving on the afternoon plane myself.

GRAYSON: Oh – all right then.

ANDERSON: That's most kind.

>   (*During the above the voices from the room have been semi-audible.*
>   *McKendrick's voice, rather drunk, but articulate, is heard.*)

MCKENDRICK: (*His voice only, heard underneath the above dialogue*) Now, listen to me, I'm a professional philosopher. You'll do well to listen to what I have to say.

ANDERSON: That sounds as if you've got McKendrick in there.

GRAYSON: Oh – is he one of yours?

ANDERSON: I wouldn't put it like that .

GRAYSON: He's getting as tight as a tick.

ANDERSON: Yes.

GRAYSON: You couldn't collect him, could you? He's going to get clouted in a minute.

ANDERSON: Go ahead and clout him, if you like.

GRAYSON: It's not me. It's Broadbent and a couple of the lads. Your pal sort of latched on to us in the bar. He really ought to be getting home.

ANDERSON: I'll see what I can do.

(ANDERSON *follows* GRAYSON *into the room.*)

MCKENDRICK: How can you expect the kids to be little gentlemen when their heroes behave like yobs – answer me that – no – you haven't answered my question – if you've got yobs on the fields you're going to have yobs on the terraces.

(*Interior Grayson's room.*

MCKENDRICK *is the only person standing up. He is holding court, with a bottle of whisky in one hand and his glass in the other. Around this small room are* BROADBENT, CRISP, CHAMBERLAIN *and perhaps one or two members of the England squad. Signs of a bottle party.*)

GRAYSON: (*Closing his door*) I thought philosophers were quiet, studious sort of people.

ANDERSON: Well, some of us are.

MCKENDRICK: (*Shouts*) Anderson! You're the very man I want to see! We're having a philosophical discussion about the yob ethics of professional footballers –

BROADBENT: You want to watch it, mate.

MCKENDRICK: Roy here is sensitive because he gave away a penalty today, by a deliberate foul. To stop a certain goal he hacked a chap down. After all, a penalty might be saved and broken legs are quite rare –

(BROADBENT *stands up but* MCKENDRICK *pacifies him with a gesture.*)

It's perfectly all right – you were adopting the utilitarian values of the game, for the good of the team, for England! But I'm not talking about particular acts of expediency. No, I'm talking about the whole *ethos*.

ANDERSON: McKendrick, don't you think it's about time we retired?

MCKENDRICK: (*Ignoring him*) Now, I've played soccer for years. Years and *years*. I played soccer from the age of *eight* until I was *thirteen*. At which point I went to a rugger school. Even so, Tommy here will tell you that I still consider myself something of a left-winger. (*This is to* CRISP.) Sorry about that business in the lift, by the way, Tommy. Well, one thing I remember clearly from my years and *years* of soccer is that if two players go for a ball which then goes into touch, there's never any doubt *among those players* which of them touched the ball last. I can't remember one occasion in all those years and *years* when the player who touched the ball last didn't realize it. So, what I want to know *is* – why is it that on 'Match of the Day', every time the bloody ball goes into touch, *both* players claim the throw-in for their own side? I merely ask for information. Is it because they are very, very stupid or is it because a dishonest advantage is as welcome as an honest one?

CHAMBERLAIN: Well, look, it's been a long evening, old chap –

ANDERSON: Tomorrow is another day, McKendrick.

MCKENDRICK: Tomorrow, in my experience, is usually the same day. Have a drink –

ANDERSON: No thank you.

MCKENDRICK: Here's a question for anthropologists. Name me a tribe which organizes itself into teams for sporting encounters and greets every score against their opponents with paroxysms of childish glee, whooping, dancing and embracing in an ecstasy of crowing self-congratulation in the very midst of their disconsolate fellows? – Who are these primitives who pile all their responses into the immediate sensation, unaware or uncaring of the long undulations of life's fortunes? Yes, you've got it! (*He chants the 'Match of the Day' signature tune.*) It's the yob-of-the-month competition, entries on a postcard please. But the question is – is it because they're working class, or is it because financial greed has corrupted them? Or is it both?

ANDERSON: McKendrick, you are being offensive.

MCKENDRICK: Anderson is one of life's cricketers. Clap, clap. (*He claps in a well-bred sort of way and puts on a well-bred voice.*) Well played, sir. Bad luck, old chap. The comparison with cricket may suggest to you that yob ethics are working class.

(BROADBENT *comes up to* MCKENDRICK *and pushes him*

175

against the wall. MCKENDRICK *is completely unconcerned, escapes and continues without pause.*)
But you would be quite wrong. Let me refer you to a typical rugby team of Welsh miners. A score is acknowledged with pride but with restraint, the scorer himself composing his features into an expressionless mask lest he might be suspected of exulting in his opponents' misfortune – my God, it does the heart good, doesn't it? I conclude that yob ethics are caused by financial greed.

ANDERSON: Don't be such an ass.

(MCKENDRICK *takes this as an intellectual objection.*)

MCKENDRICK: You think it's the adulation, perhaps? (*To* CRISP) Is it the adulation, Tommy, which has corrupted you?

CRISP: What's he flaming on about?

CHAMBERLAIN: Well, I think it's time for my shut-eye.

CRISP: No, I want to know what he's saying about me. He's giving me the needle.

ANDERSON: (*To* MCKENDRICK) May I remind you that you profess to be something of a pragmatist yourself in matters of ethics –

MCKENDRICK: Ah yes – I –see – you think that because I don't believe in reliable signposts on the yellow brick road to rainbowland, you think I'm a bit of a yob myself – the swift kick in the kneecap on the way up the academic ladder – the Roy Broadbent of Stoke – (*To* BROADBENT) Stoke's my team, you know.

BROADBENT: Will you tell this stupid bugger his philosophy is getting up my nostrils.

GRAYSON: You're not making much sense, old boy.

MCKENDRICK: Ah! Grayson here has a fine logical mind. He has put his finger on the flaw in my argument, namely that the reason footballers are yobs may be nothing to do with being working class, or with financial greed, or with adulation, or even with being footballers. It may be simply that football attracts a certain kind of person, namely yobs –

(*This is as far as he gets when* BROADBENT *smashes him in the face.* MCKENDRICK *drops.*)

CRISP: Good on you, Roy.

(ANDERSON *goes to* MCKENDRICK, *who is flat on the floor*.)
ANDERSON: McKendrick . . .
CHAMBERLAIN: Well, I'm going to bed.
(CHAMBERLAIN *goes through the connecting door into his own room and closes the door*.)
BROADBENT: He can't say that sort of thing and get away with it.
GRAYSON: Where's his room?
ANDERSON: On the third floor.
GRAYSON: Bloody hell.
CRISP: He's waking up.
BROADBENT: He's all right.
ANDERSON: Come on, McKendrick.
(*They all lift* MCKENDRICK *to his feet*. MCKENDRICK *makes no protest. He's just about able to walk*.)
I'll take him down in the lift. (*He sees the typewriter in its case and says to* GRAYSON) I'll come back for the typewriter. (*He leads* MCKENDRICK *towards the door*.)
MCKENDRICK: (*Mutters*) All right. I went too far. Let's talk about something else.
(*But* MCKENDRICK *keeps walking or staggering*. ANDERSON *opens* GRAYSON'*s door*.)
BROADBENT: Here. That bloody Jirasek. Just like you said.
ANDERSON: Yes.
BROADBENT: They don't teach you nothing at that place, then?
ANDERSON: No.
(ANDERSON *helps* MCKENDRICK *out and closes the door*.)

11. INT. THE COLLOQUIUM

ANDERSON *comes to the lectern. There is a Czech* CHAIRMAN *behind him*.
CHETWYN *is in the audience but* MCKENDRICK *is not. We arrive as* ANDERSON *approaches the microphone*. ANDERSON *lays a sheaf of typewritten paper on the lectern*.
ANDERSON: I propose in this paper to take up a problem which many have taken up before me, namely the conflict between the rights of individuals and the rights of the community. I will be making a distinction between rights and rules.

177

(We note that the CHAIRMAN, *listening politely and intently, is suddenly puzzled. He himself has some papers and from these he extracts one, which is in fact the official copy of Anderson's official paper. He starts looking at it. It doesn't take him long to satisfy himself that* ANDERSON *is giving a different paper. These things happen while* ANDERSON *speaks. At the same time the three* INTERPRETERS *in their booths, while speaking into their microphones as* ANDERSON *speaks, are also in some difficulty because they have copies of Anderson's official paper.)* I will seek to show that rules, in so far as they are related to rights, are a secondary and consequential elaboration of primary rights, and I will be associating rules generally with communities and rights generally with individuals. I will seek to show that a conflict between the two is generally a pseudo-conflict arising out of one side or the other pressing a pseudo-right. Although claiming priority for rights over rules – where they are in conflict – I will be defining rights as fictions acting as incentives to the adoption of practical values; and I will further propose that although these rights are fictions, there is an obligation to treat them as if they were truths; and further, that although this obligation can be shown to be based on values which are based on fictions, there is an obligation to treat *that* obligation as though it were based on truth; and so on *ad infinitum.*

(At this point the CHAIRMAN *interrupts him.)*

CHAIRMAN: Pardon me – Professor – this is not your paper –

ANDERSON: In what sense? I am indisputably giving it.

CHAIRMAN: But it is not the paper you were invited to give.

ANDERSON: I wasn't invited to give a particular paper.

CHAIRMAN: You offered one.

ANDERSON: That's true.

CHAIRMAN: But this is not it.

ANDERSON: No. I changed my mind.

CHAIRMAN: But it is irregular.

ANDERSON: I didn't realize it mattered.

CHAIRMAN: It is a discourtesy.

ANDERSON: *(Taken aback)* Bad manners? I am sorry.

CHAIRMAN: You cannot give this paper. We do not have copies.

178

ANDERSON: Do you mean that philosophical papers require some sort of clearance?

CHAIRMAN: The interpreters cannot work without copies.

ANDERSON: Don't worry. It is not a technical paper. I will speak a little slower if you like. (ANDERSON *turns back to the microphone*.) If we decline to define rights as fictions, albeit with the force of truths, there are only two senses in which humans could be said to have rights. Firstly, humans might be said to have certain rights if they had collectively and mutually agreed to give each other these rights. This would merely mean that humanity is a rather large club with club rules, but it is not what is generally meant by human rights. It is not what Locke meant, and it is not what the American Founding Fathers meant when, taking the hint from Locke, they held certain rights to be inalienable – among them, life, liberty and the pursuit of happiness. The early Americans claimed these as the endowment of God – which is the *second* sense in which humans might be said to have rights. This is a view more encouraged in some communities than in others. I do not wish to dwell on it here except to say that it *is* a view and not a deduction, and that I do not hold it myself. What strikes us is the consensus about an individual's right put forward both by those who invoke God's authority and by those who invoke no authority at all other than their own idea of what is fair and sensible. The first Article of the American Constitution, guaranteeing freedom of religious observance, of expression, of the press, and of assembly, is closely echoed by Articles 28 and 32 of the no less admirable Constitution of Czechoslovakia, our generous hosts on this occasion. Likewise, protection from invasion of privacy, from unreasonable search and from interference with letters and correspondence guaranteed to the American people by Article 4 is likewise guaranteed to the Czech people by Article 31.

(*The* CHAIRMAN, *who has been more and more uncomfortable, leaves the stage at this point. He goes into the 'wings'. At some distance from* ANDERSON, *but still just in earshot of* ANDERSON, *i.e. one can hear Anderson's words clearly if faintly, is a*

telephone. Perhaps in a stage manager's office. We go with the
CHAIRMAN *but we can still hear* ANDERSON.)
Is such a consensus remarkable? Not at all. If there is a God,
we his creations would doubtless subscribe to his values.
And if there is not a God, he, our creation, would
undoubtedly be credited with values which we think to be
fair and sensible. But what is fairness? What is sense? What
are these values which we take to be self-evident? And why
are they values?

12. INT. MCKENDRICK'S ROOM

MCKENDRICK *is fully dressed and coming round from a severe
hangover. His room is untidier than Anderson's. Clothes are strewn
about. His suitcase, half full, is open. His briefcase is also in
evidence.* MCKENDRICK *looks at his watch, but it has stopped. He
goes to the telephone and dials.*

13. INT. ANDERSON'S ROOM

*The phone starts to ring. The camera pulls back from the phone and we
see that there are two men in the room, plain-clothes* POLICEMEN,
*searching the room. They look at the phone but only for a moment, and
while it rings they continue quietly. They search the room very
discreetly. We see one carefully slide open a drawer and we cut away.*

14. THE COLLOQUIUM

We have returned to Anderson's paper. There is no CHAIRMAN *on
stage.*
ANDERSON: Ethics were once regarded as a sort of monument, a
   ghostly Eiffel Tower constructed of Platonic entities like
   honesty, loyalty, fairness, and so on, all bolted together and
   consistent with each other, harmoniously stressed so as to
   keep the edifice standing up: an ideal against which we
   measured our behaviour. The tower has long been
   demolished. In our own time linguistic philosophy proposes
   that the notion of, say, justice has no existence outside the

ways in which we choose to employ the word, and indeed *consists* only of the way in which we employ it. In other words, that ethics are not the inspiration of our behaviour but merely the creation of our utterances.

(*Over the latter part of this we have gone back to the* CHAIRMAN *who is on the telephone. The* CHAIRMAN *is doing little talking and some listening.*)

And yet common observation shows us that this view demands qualification. A small child who cries 'that's not fair' when punished for something done by his brother or sister is apparently appealing to an idea of justice which is, for want of a better word, natural. And we must see that natural justice, however illusory, does inspire many people's behaviour much of the time. As an ethical utterance it seems to be an attempt to define a sense of rightness which is not simply derived from some other utterance elsewhere.

(*We cut now to a backstage area, but* ANDERSON's *voice is continuous, heard through the sort of PA system which one finds backstage at theatres.*

The CHAIRMAN *hurries along the corridor, seeking and now finding a uniformed* 'FIREMAN', *a backstage official. During this* ANDERSON *speaks.*)

Now a philosopher exploring the difficult terrain of right and wrong should not be over-impressed by the argument 'a child would know the difference'. But when, let us say, we are being persuaded that it is ethical to put someone in prison for reading or writing the wrong books, it is well to be reminded that you can persuade a man to believe almost anything provided he is clever enough, but it is much more difficult to persuade someone less clever. There is a sense of right and wrong which precedes utterance. It is individually experienced and it concerns one person's dealings with another person. From this experience we have built a system of ethics which is the sum of individual acts of recognition of individual right.

(*During this we have returned to* ANDERSON *in person. And at this point the* CHAIRMAN *re-enters the stage and goes and sits in his chair.* ANDERSON *continues, ignoring him.*)

If this is so, the implications are serious for a collective or state ethic which finds itself in conflict with individual rights, and seeks, in the name of the people, to impose its values on the very individuals who comprise the state. The illogic of this manoeuvre is an embarrassment to totalitarian systems. An attempt is sometimes made to answer it by consigning the whole argument to 'bourgeois logic', which is a concept no easier to grasp than bourgeois physics or bourgeois astronomy. No, the fallacy must lie elsewhere –

(*At this point loud bells, electric bells, ring. The fire alarm. The* CHAIRMAN *leaps up and shouts.*)

CHAIRMAN: (*In Czech*) Don't panic! There appears to be a fire. Please leave the hall in an orderly manner. (*In English*) Fire! Please leave quietly!

(*The philosophers get to their feet and start heading for the exit.* ANDERSON *calmly gathers his papers up and leaves the stage.*)

15. INT. AIRPORT

People leaving the country have to go through a baggage check. There are at least three separate but adjacent benches at which CUSTOMS MEN *and* WOMEN *search the baggage of travellers. The situation here is as follows:*

At the first bench CHETWYN *is in mid-search.*

At the second bench ANDERSON *is in mid-search.*

At the third bench a traveller is in mid-search.

There is a short queue of people waiting for each bench. The leading man in the queue waiting for the third bench is MCKENDRICK. *The search at this third bench is cursory.*

However, ANDERSON *is being searched very thoroughly. We begin on* ANDERSON. *We have not yet noted* CHETWYN.

At Anderson's bench a uniformed CUSTOMS WOMAN *is examining the contents of his suitcase, helped by a uniformed* CUSTOMS MAN. *At the same time a plain-clothes* POLICEMAN *is very carefully searching everything in Anderson's briefcase.*

We see the CUSTOMS MAN *take a cellophane-wrapped box of chocolates from Anderson's case. He strips off the cellophane and looks at the chocolates and then he digs down to look at the second layer of chocolates.* ANDERSON *watches this with amazement. The chocolate box is closed and put back in the case. Meanwhile, a nest of wooden dolls, the kind in which one doll fits inside another, is reduced to its components.*

The camera moves to find MCKENDRICK *arriving at the third desk. There is no plain-clothes* POLICEMAN *there. The* CUSTOMS OFFICER *there opens his briefcase and flips, in a rather cursory way, through McKendrick's papers. He asks* MCKENDRICK *to open his case. He digs about for a moment in McKendrick's case.*

Back at Anderson's bench the plain-clothes POLICEMAN *is taking Anderson's wallet from* ANDERSON's *hand. He goes through every piece of paper in the wallet.*

We go back to McKendrick's bench to find MCKENDRICK *closing his case and being moved on.* MCKENDRICK *turns round to* ANDERSON *to speak.*

MCKENDRICK: You picked the wrong queue, old man. Russian roulette. And Chetwyn.

(*We now discover* CHETWYN, *who is going through a similar search to Anderson's. He has a plain-clothes* POLICEMAN *too. This* POLICEMAN *is looking down the spine of a book from Chetwyn's suitcase. We now return to Anderson's bench. We find that the* CUSTOMS MAN *has discovered a suspicious bulge in the zipped compartment on the underside of the lid of Anderson's suitcase.* ANDERSON's *face tells us that he has a spasm of anxiety. The bulge suggests something about the size of Hollar's envelope. The* CUSTOMS MAN *zips open the compartment and extracts the copy of McKendrick's girlie magazine.* ANDERSON *is embarrassed.*

We return to CHETWYN, *whose briefcase is being searched paper by paper. The* CUSTOMS OFFICIAL *searching his suitcase finds a laundered shirt, nicely ironed and folded. He opens the shirt up and discovers about half a dozen sheets of writing-paper. Thin paper with typewriting on it. Also a photograph of a man. The plain-clothes* POLICEMAN *joins the* CUSTOMS OFFICIAL *and he starts looking at these pieces of paper. He looks up at* CHETWYN, *whose face has gone white.*)

16. INT. AEROPLANE

The plane is taxiing.

MCKENDRICK *and* ANDERSON *are sitting together.*

MCKENDRICK *looks shocked.*

ANDERSON: Silly bugger. Honestly.

ANDERSON: It's all right – they'll put him on the next plane.

MCKENDRICK: To Siberia.

ANDERSON: No, no, don't be ridiculous. It wouldn't look well for them, would it? All the publicity. I don't think there's anything in Czech law about being in possession of letters to Amnesty International and the UN and that sort of thing. They couldn't treat Chetwyn as though he were a Czech national anyway.

MCKENDRICK: Very unpleasant for him though.

ANDERSON: Yes.

MCKENDRICK: He took a big risk.

ANDERSON: Yes.

MCKENDRICK: I wouldn't do it. Would you?

ANDERSON: No. He should have known he'd be searched.

MCKENDRICK: Why did they search you?

ANDERSON: They thought I might have something.

MCKENDRICK: Did you have anything?

ANDERSON: I did in a way.

MCKENDRICK: What was it?

ANDERSON: A thesis. Apparently rather slanderous from the state's point of view.

MCKENDRICK: Where did you hide it?

ANDERSON: In your briefcase.

    (*Pause.*)

MCKENDRICK: You what?

ANDERSON: Last night. I'm afraid I reversed a principle.

    (MCKENDRICK *opens his briefcase and finds Hollar's envelope.*
    ANDERSON *takes it from him.* MCKENDRICK *is furious.*)

MCKENDRICK: You utter bastard.

ANDERSON: I thought you would approve.

MCKENDRICK:Don't get clever with me. (*He relapses, shaking.*) Jesus. It's not quite playing the game is it?

184

ANDERSON: No, I suppose not. But they were very unlikely to search *you*.

MCKENDRICK: That's not the bloody point.

ANDERSON: I thought it was. But you could be right. Ethics is a very complicated business. That's why they have these congresses.

(*The plane picks up speed on the runway towards take-off.*)

SQUARING THE CIRCLE
Poland 1980–81

CHARACTERS

NARRATOR	WALESA CHILDREN
LEONID BREZHNEV	DANUTA WALESA
EDWARD GIEREK	MAZOWIECKI
BREZHNEV'S AIDE	MODZELEWSKI
BABIUCH	MARIAN JURCZYK
KANIA	ANDRZEJ GWIAZDA
SZYDLAK	JAN RULEWSKI
WOJCIECH JARUZELSKI	BUJAK
BARCIKOWSKI	BOGDAN LIS
JAGIELSKI	JUDGE
FINANSKY	GANG MEMBER
FIRST ELECTRICIAN	PRIEST
SECOND ELECTRICIAN	PUBLIC PROSECUTOR
MACIEJ SZCZEPANSKI	SOVIET AMBASSADOR
JACEK KURON	GERMAN SPOKESMAN
GEREMEK	MARSHAL KULIKOV
GIEREK'S SECRETARY	WORKER
GERMAN BANKER	PARTY OFFICIAL
AMERICAN BANKER	MIECZYSLAW RAKOWSKI
SWISS BANKER	DOCTOR
GIRL	PARTY MAN
CARDINAL WYSZYNSKI	MINER
STEFAN OLSZOWSKI	KATOWICE MAN
LECH WALESA	JARUZELSKI'S SECRETARY
PRISONER	ARCHBISHOP JOSEPH GLEMP

WITNESSES, AIDES, SECRETARIES, POLICEMEN, GUARDS,
MILITARY OFFICERS, JOURNALISTS, PHOTOGRAPHERS,
WORKERS, PRIESTS, etc.

Squaring the Circle was first transmitted in May 1984 by TVS.
The cast included:

NARRATOR	Richard Crenna
LEONID BREZHNEV	Frank Middlemass
EDWARD GIEREK	John Woodvine
BABIUCH	John Bluthal
KANIA	Roy Kinnear
WOJCIECH JARUZELSKI	Richard Kane
JACEK KURON	Don Henderson
LECH WALESA	Bernard Hill
MARIAN JURCZYK	John Rogan
ANDRZEJ GWIAZDA	Jonathan Adams
JAN RULEWSKI	Tom Wilkinson
MIECZYSLAW RAKOWSKI	Alec McCowen
DIRECTOR	Mike Hodges
PRODUCTION DESIGNER	Voytek
DIRECTOR OF PHOTOGRAPHY	Michael Garfath

I

The First Secretary

Empty beach. Sea. Sky.
With the mention of his name we find EDWARD GIEREK, *a middle-aged man in a suit, overcoat, hat and lace-up shoes, walking along by the sea.*

NARRATOR: (*Voice over*) Towards the end of July 1980 Edward Gierek, First Secretary of the Polish United Workers' Party, which is to say the boss of Communist Poland, left Warsaw for his annual holiday in the Soviet Union by the Black Sea. There he met . . .
(BREZHNEV, *similarly dressed, is walking towards* GIEREK.)
. . . Leonid Brezhnev, First Secretary of the Communist Party of the USSR.
(*The two men meet and grasp each other's shoulders and kiss each other on both cheeks.*)
In an atmosphere of cordiality and complete mutual understanding the two leaders had a frank exchange of views.

BREZHNEV: Comrade! As your friends and allies in the progress towards the inevitable triumph of Marxist-Leninism, we are concerned, deeply concerned, by recent departures from Leninist norms by Polish workers manipulated by a revisionist element of the Polish intelligentsia!

GIEREK: Comrade First Secretary! As your friends and allies in the proletariat's struggle against international capitalism . . .
(GIEREK *evidently continues in the same vein.*)

NARRATOR: (*Voice over*) That isn't them, of course –
(*Close up on the* NARRATOR, *in the same location.*)
(*To camera*) – and this isn't the Black Sea. Everything is true

191

except the words and the pictures. If there was a beach, Brezhnev and Gierek probably didn't talk on it, and if they did, they probably wouldn't have been wearing, on a beach in July, those hats and coats and lace-up shoes which you get for being a Communist leader. They were after all . . .

2. EXT. SEASIDE. SUMMER DAY

NARRATOR: (*Voice over*) . . . supposed to be on holiday.
(*There are gay umbrellas and cool, brightly coloured drinks to hand. Everything in fact is highly coloured.* BREZHNEV *and* GIEREK *are now wearing brightly coloured Hawaiian shirts and slacks. They wear sunglasses. They drink from pink drinks with little purple paper umbrellas sticking out of them.* BREZHNEV, *however, is attended by two or three* AIDES, *who are dressed in dark suits. The one who is going to speak wears a suit and is carrying a file of papers ostentatiously marked 'Poland'.*)
And even if you got the look of it right, they probably didn't talk like a *Pravda* editorial, because if you're the boss of the Communist Party of the Soviet Union and if you've got twenty armoured divisions in East Germany and your supply lines have to go across Poland and the Polish railway workers are on strike, you don't say that you are deeply concerned about departures from Leninist norms, you probably say –
BREZHNEV: (*Shouting like a gangster*) What the hell is going on with you guys? Who's running the country? You or the engine drivers? Your workforce has got you by the short hairs because you're up to your neck in hock to German bankers, American bankers, Swiss bankers – you're in hock to *us* to the tune of . . . (*Glances at the* AIDE *for aid*) . . . is it millions or billions . . . ?
(*The* AIDE *panics for a second, shuffling and dropping his papers, but rises to the occasion.*)
AIDE: Zillions.
BREZHNEV: (*Triumphantly shouts*) Zillions of roubles!
AIDE: Zlotys.
BREZHNEV: (*Rounding on him*) You shut up!

192

3. EXT. SEASIDE. SUMMER DAY

NARRATOR: (*To camera*) Who knows?

All the same, there was something going on which remains true even when the words and the pictures are mostly made up. Between August 1980 and December 1981 an attempt was made in Poland to put together two ideas which wouldn't fit, the idea of freedom as it is understood in the West, and the idea of socialism as it is understood in the Soviet empire. The attempt failed because it was impossible, in the same sense as it is impossible in geometry to turn a circle into a square with the same area – not because no one has found out how to do it, but because there is no way in which it can be done. What happened in Poland was that a number of people tried for sixteen months to change the shape of the system without changing the area covered by the original shape. They failed.

4. EXT. AIRFIELD. NIGHT

So EDWARD GIEREK *is met by Prime Minister* BABIUCH. *They grasp each other's shoulders and kiss each other on the cheek.*

NARRATOR: (*Voice over*) Edward Gierek came home from the Black Sea on August 15th.

BABIUCH: Welcome home, Comrade. I'm sorry you had to cut short your holiday.

(*But* GIEREK *is immediately concerned with part of his holiday luggage, which is being taken off the plane by a uniformed* MINION. *The item is a large beach bag, out of which protrudes a snorkel and a ridiculous straw hat. The* MINION *jostles the bag, which clinks dangerously.*)

GIEREK: Careful with that . . .

(GIEREK *takes the bag from the* MINION. GIEREK *and* BABIUCH *wait for the car which is to take them away.*)

BABIUCH: Comrade Kania has been to Gdansk.

GIEREK: Why?

BABIUCH: Why? Because the Lenin shipyard in Gdansk is at a complete standstill. The Party Secretary up there telephoned yesterday in a panic.

GIEREK: I know all that. Do we have to have a member of the
    Politburo rushing to the scene whenever there's a disruption
    of working norms?
BABIUCH: You sent Jagielski to settle the railway strike.
GIEREK: The railway disruption of working norms was different.
BABIUCH: Kania says this one is different.
GIEREK: How much are they asking for?
BABIUCH: Two thousand a month, but it's not the money that
    worries us.
GIEREK: It should. It's the money we haven't got.
    (*Car pulls in front. The car door is being held open for them.*)
BABIUCH: After you, Comrade First Secretary.
GIEREK: Thank you, Comrade Prime Minister.
    (BABIUCH *takes Gierek's bag for him.*)
BABIUCH: Allow me . . .
    (GIEREK *gets into the car followed by* BABIUCH *and the beach
    bag.*)

5. INT. THE CAR. NIGHT

GIEREK *and* BABIUCH *in the back seat.* GIEREK *takes the bag from*
BABIUCH *and searches about in it during the narration.*
NARRATOR: (*Voice over*) The Prime Minister is, of course, the
    head of the government. Today, and for several days to
    come, his name is Mr Babiuch. Apart from having a prime
    minister, Poland has elections, a parliament and a head of
    state, much like Britain or France or America.
    (GIEREK *finds what he has been looking for in the bag – which he
    hands to* BABIUCH, *who is suitably grateful.*)
GIEREK: I've brought you some caviar.

6. EXT. PARTY HEADQUARTERS. NIGHT

The car draws up. GIEREK *and* BABIUCH *get out of the car and enter
the building. The door is opened by a doorman. This person is going to
pop up again in various guises throughout the film, so for simplicity's
sake he will henceforth be referred to as the* WITNESS.
The NARRATOR *enters the frame.*

NARRATOR: (*To camera*) This is where it all gets different from bourgeois Western democracy. In the East, they have the window-dressing but the shop is run by the Party. Through nominees and controlled elections the Party dominates parliament and manages the machinery of the state, and thus is in a position to fulfil its sacred trust of defending the interests of the working people . . .

7. INT. PARTY HEADQUARTERS. NIGHT

BABIUCH *is carrying Gierek's bag.* GIEREK *sees* KANIA *coming up behind and pauses to fish about in the bag, so that he is able to greet* KANIA *with another jar of caviar.*
NARRATOR: (*Voice over*) . . . with caviar and limousines.

8. EXT. PARTY HEADQUARTERS. NIGHT

The NARRATOR *has just finished addressing the camera and is interrupted by the* WITNESS.
WITNESS: A cheap shot, in my opinion. These people are not doormen. These are people with big responsibilities.
NARRATOR: Just making an observation.
WITNESS: It's not a factor. I never saw the President of France arrive anywhere on a bicycle eating a salami sandwich.
NARRATOR: Excuse me.
(*To camera*) It works like this. The Party Congress, about 2,000 delegates who meet every five years, not counting emergencies, elects a Central Committee of about 200 members who meet as and when to supervise Party policy. To implement that policy the Central Committee elects . . .

9. INT. POLITBURO MEETING. NIGHT

NARRATOR: (*Voice over*) . . . the Political Bureau.
(*There are about a dozen members of the Politburo, now seen placing themselves at a large table. They include* GIEREK, BABIUCH, KANIA, SZYDLAK, JARUZELSKI, BARCIKOWSKI, JAGIELSKI *and* FINANSKY. ['FINANSKY' *is an invented name*

195

to allow two different finance ministers to be represented in one character.]

This is not a meeting of the Government. This is the Politburo.

(GIEREK *is the chairman. He invites* KANIA *to begin.*)

GIEREK: Comrade Kania . . . ?

KANIA: At Gdansk in the Lenin shipyard they demand . . . number one, a wage increase of 2,000 zlotys a month. Number two, reinstatement of sacked troublemakers. Number three, family allowances increased to the same level enjoyed by police and security forces. Number four, earlier retirement. Number five, a monument outside the main gate . . .

GIEREK: A monument?

KANIA: Yes. To the dead of 1970. The strike spokesman is obsessed with putting up a monument. He was in the shipyard in Gdansk in 1970. He's been arrested more than once for holding demonstrations outside the gate on the anniversary . . . Actually, he's been arrested about a hundred times for one thing or another. The shipyard director tried to settle for a plaque in the dining hall but he insists on a monument, forty metres high.

GIEREK: Is he mad?

SZYDLAK: That's an idea . . .

KANIA: (*To* SZYDLAK) No.

GIEREK: Who is he?

KANIA: Walesa. You've met him.

GIEREK: When?

KANIA: Ten years ago. After the 1970 riots. You went to talk to the workers in the Baltic ports –

GIEREK: Yes.

KANIA: In Gdansk there was a three-man delegation. Walesa was one of them. Moustache. He didn't speak. You remember him?

GIEREK: No.

KANIA: Well, I think they'd settle for the money and the reinstatements. Enough of them would, anyway.

(GIEREK *looks towards* FINANSKY.)

FINANSKY: There is already more money than there are goods to

196

spend it on. The situation is inflationary, and would be more so if we did not keep food cheap artificially. The farmer buys bread to feed the pigs because it is cheaper than the wheat he sells to us. Then we buy the pigs for 130 zlotys per kilo and we sell the butcher's pork for 70 zlotys. Such subsidies are costing us 3 billion zlotys a year. As a matter of fact the same money would pay our interest to Western bankers this year.

GIEREK: (*To* KANIA) We cannot give way on the money. It buys nothing.

KANIA: It buys time.

GIEREK: Are you an economist?

KANIA: I have been to Gdansk.

GIEREK: If we give way on the money in Gdansk, Gdynia will demand the same. Then Szczecin. It'll spread everywhere.

KANIA: So will the strike if we don't stop it.

SZYDLAK: Send in the police, the state security . . .

KANIA: There's no public disorder.

SZYDLAK: A strike is a public disorder. In fact it's illegal. If the police can't handle it send in the army.

(*The members turn generally towards* JARUZELSKI, *who is in general's uniform.*)

JARUZELSKI: To do what? I said in 1970 that I wouldn't order Polish soldiers to shoot Polish workers.

SZYDLAK: But they did shoot. The army and the police. And the strikers went back to work.

JARUZELSKI: Not all of them.

SZYDLAK: All of them.

JARUZELSKI: Not the ones who were dead.

GIEREK: The Minister of Defence is quite right. We must not repeat December 1970. And if you remember, the men in the shipyards did not go back to work until I went to talk to them. January '71. The bloodstains were still on the street. I had been First Secretary for one month. The pickets at the gate didn't recognize me. I had to tell them who I was. It's not so surprising. When did the Party leader ever come to debate with the workers face to face on their own ground? And we talked. I told them how I had worked in the mines in Belgium and France. With these hands. I said to them, help us, help *me*, I'm a worker too. We can start again. I told them there was going to be a new spirit. A new Poland. A rich Poland. But the poison got back into the system. (*Helplessly*) What does one do . . . ?

KANIA: We've cut the phone lines from Gdansk.

GIEREK: No – it's time to be frank. We have to tell the country what's going on.

JARUZELSKI: Everybody listens to the foreign radio stations – they know what's going on.

GIEREK: If they know, we can afford to be frank. We must explain the shortages . . . the danger of inflation . . . we must appeal to patriotism and common sense.

BABIUCH: (*Dubiously*) Do you really think . . . ?

GIEREK: We must, of course, accept some of the blame. On the radio and television, tonight.

BABIUCH: Will you do it?

GIEREK: Me? No, you're the Prime Minister.

10. THE SAME. NIGHT

In other words, the Politburo meeting continues into the night, now without BABIUCH . . . *who is, however, present and talking, on a television set which the rest of the Politburo are watching. The formality of the meeting has disintegrated. Ties are loosened, cups and glasses are littered about. The cut is to* BABIUCH *on the television but his speech is mostly audible wallpaper for the camera's travel.*

BABIUCH: It has to be admitted that in the past we have not always managed to deal efficiently with economic difficulties. The public has not been given sufficient information about our troubles, about the state of the economy and the growing problems as and when they occurred. We have not prepared ourselves sufficiently for the difficult times which we should have seen as inevitable. Even today, not everyone realizes what our country's economic situation is like. To put it bluntly, our country's indebtedness has reached a point which must not on any account be overstepped. We have been living and developing on credit. Stopping work not only harms the national economy, it also turns against the working class and working people in general, damaging their vital interests. The opponents of People's Poland are trying to use the atmosphere of tension and emotion for their own political ends, putting forward slogans and suggestions which have nothing in common with the aspirations of the working class. (*During this*:)

KANIA: (*To* GIEREK) What do we do if it doesn't work?

GIEREK: We could try another prime minister.

KANIA: Seriously, we'll have to make them an offer.

GIEREK: How much?

KANIA: Fifteen hundred, and the reinstatement of troublemakers, and the monument.

GIEREK: Will they settle?

KANIA: Yes.

GIEREK: All right. I'm going home. I don't want to be called except in an emergency. (*Points at* BABIUCH *on the television*.) This is for Comrade Brezhnev.

BABIUCH: (*On television*) The world is watching us, wondering how we can manage in these difficult moments . . .

11. INT. CAFE. NIGHT

A café in Poland. There is a television set. BABIUCH *is continuing to speak.*

BABIUCH: (*On television*) We have reliable allies who also worry about our troubles and believe that we will be able to overcome them ourselves. They wish us success from the bottom of their hearts.

(*Among the people in the café are the* NARRATOR *and the* WITNESS.)

NARRATOR: (*To camera*) Poland's reliable ally, her neighbour to the east, had been a watchful and threatening presence since 1945.

WITNESS: 1700.

(*The* NARRATOR *is about to protest.*)

All right, 1720 but no later. You won't understand Poland's attitude to Russia until you understand some Polish history. This won't take long.

199

NARRATOR: I hope not.

(*The* WITNESS *reaches over to an adjacent table for a basket of bread rolls, which he tips over on to his own table. He pushes the bread rolls together in the middle of the table.*)

WITNESS: Nobody except the Poles remembers that for 300 years this was the biggest and freest country in Middle Europe, spanning the continent from the Baltic almost to the Black Sea and reaching hundreds of miles east into modern Russia. Russia's greatness came *after* Poland's and was achieved at Poland's expense. During the eighteenth century, Poland came under Russian domination. This alarmed the other great powers, Austria and Prussia, so in 1772 Catherine the Great gave a bit of Poland to each of them to keep them quiet.

(*He detaches a couple of bread rolls, pushing them 'west', and a couple more 'south'.*)

This was the first of three partitions which were to dismember the country by the end of the century. By the standards of the time Poland had a liberal tradition, squeezed now between three emperors. In 1793 Russia and Prussia decided to cut Poland down to size.

(*He separates two bread rolls to the 'east' and two more to the 'west'. This leaves half a dozen bread rolls in the middle of the table.*)

Poland, what was left of it, rebelled and in 1795 the three power blocks finished the job.

(*He pushes two rolls to the 'west', two to the 'east' and two to the 'south'. There is none left in the middle.*)

Poland disappeared. Of course there were still an awful lot of Poles around, and when Napoleon turned up to challenge the great powers large numbers of them joined his armies. The reward was the Duchy of Warsaw, 1807.

(*He places a single bread roll in the middle of the table.*)

It lasted as long as Napoleon lasted. And when the victors met in Vienna to carve up the map, Russia got the prize.

(*He pushes the bread roll to the 'east'.*)

For a hundred years after that Poland was mainly an idea kept alive by an underground at home and *émigrés* abroad. The period of romantic exile.

NARRATOR: Oh yes, handsome young men in lace cuffs playing the piano in Paris . . . I wondered.

WITNESS: They were waiting for a miracle. The miracle happened in 1918, with the simultaneous collapse of the Russian, Austrian and German empires. The victors met at Versailles and put Poland back on the map.

(*He pushes two bread rolls from 'east', 'west' and 'south' into the middle of the table.*)

In 1920 the old enemy, now known as Soviet Russia, invaded and was repulsed. Poland survived until the Nazi–Soviet pact in 1939.

(*He divides the six bread rolls and pushes them 'east' and 'west'.*)

The thieves fell out. Hitler lost. The allies met at Yalta to carve up the map and Churchill and Roosevelt let Stalin keep his prize.

(*He moves three bread rolls from 'west' to 'east'.*)

This is a true picture, except for the bread rolls. You don't get a basket of bread rolls put out on a café table in Poland. However, it is now possible to speak of 1945.

NARRATOR: (*To camera*) The first post-war Communist leader, Gomulka, was toppled in the Stalinist paranoia in 1948. Eight years of bad times growing steadily worse finally in 1956 touched off a huge working-class revolt which left eighty dead and brought Gomulka back as a reformer. Things got worse. This time it took fourteen years. Gomulka announced food price increases and touched off a workers' revolt in the Baltic ports in 1970. No one knows how many died, some say as many as 200. The massacre brought down Gomulka and elevated Edward Gierek.

12. INT. GIEREK'S ROOM

Telephone ringing. As GIEREK *moves through the frame:*

NARRATOR: (*Voice over*) Things got better and then the same. In 1976 Gierek announced food price increases. There were strikes. Gierek backed down. Things got better, then the same, then worse. Poland was going broke. In July 1980 Gierek announced food price increases. There were strikes.

201

Railwaymen closed one of the main lines into Russia, or, to put it another way, one of the main lines into Poland. Gierek went to the Black Sea to meet Brezhnev. On August 14th the Lenin shipyard in Gdansk closed down. Gierek flew home the next day. The Politburo met. Prime Minister Babiuch went on television. Gierek went to the country, hoping that the crisis was over.

(GIEREK *answers the telephone. He listens for a few moments, annoyed*.)

GIEREK: (*Into phone*) You told me they would settle.

13. INT. PARTY HEADQUARTERS (POLITBURO). DAY

The Politburo is meeting again.

KANIA: It was in the balance. A majority at the shipyard voted to end the strike. They were swung back by a radical element.

SZYDLAK: Reactionary. You mean a reactionary element.

KANIA: The shipyard swung back to keep solidarity with the places still on strike.

GIEREK: (*Shakes his head impatiently*) Solidarity.

KANIA: I said this one was not like the others. Now we're no longer dealing with a shipyard but a committee representing 150 plants and factories.

SZYDLAK: (*Furiously*) The scum want to set up an independent trade union! – They demand abolition of censorship – access to the media – This is not a strike. It's a bloody mutiny!

GIEREK: (*Sharply*) It's clear that the official trade unions have lost touch with the aspirations of their membership. You have forfeited their trust.

SZYDLAK: (*Surprised*) What kind of language is that?

GIEREK: You have let us down, Comrade! (*More calmly*) Independent unions are, of course, out of the question. But reform . . . yes. (*Looks directly at* SZYDLAK) A reform of the official unions. (*To* KANIA) Now I will have to talk to them.

KANIA: Do you want me to come with you?

GIEREK: No – on TV. (*To* BABIUCH) My turn.

14. INT. TELEVISION STUDIO

GIEREK *speaks to a single television camera. He is apparently in his office, sitting at a desk, the office bookcase behind him.*

GIEREK: I would like to say as frankly as I can that we are aware that quite apart from many objective factors, mistakes in economic policy have played an important part . . . We understand the working people's tiredness and impatience with the troubles of everyday life, the shortages, the queues, the rise in the cost of living . . .

(*Our camera has tilted slowly up, to find two* ELECTRICIANS *standing on a gantry, looking down on* GIEREK.)

FIRST ELECTRICIAN: I think I've seen this before . . .

SECOND ELECTRICIAN: Typical bloody August . . . nothing but repeats.

(*We cut to a different angle of* GIEREK *talking to the television camera. We see his image on a monitor, being watched by* MACIEJ SZCZEPANSKI.)

GIEREK: (*On monitor*) But strikes do not change anything for the better. Together we must find another way. We must do it for Poland's sake.

(*This is the end of Gierek's speech. He pauses a moment and then relaxes as* SZCZEPANSKI *approaches him.*)

SZCZEPANSKI: Good . . . very good. Congratulations, Comrade First Secretary.

GIEREK: Thank you.

(GIEREK *is gathering up his papers. He stands up.*)

SZCZEPANSKI: By the way, what did you think of the bookcase?

(GIEREK *looks behind him as the bookcase, which is now seen to be a fake flat, is moved aside by two* PROP MEN.)

GIEREK: Nice. Very nice.

15. INT. SZCZEPANSKI'S OFFICE

SZCZEPANSKI *is mixing cocktails.*

SZCZEPANSKI: Edward, do things look bad?

GIEREK: For you, you mean?

SZCZEPANSKI: For me? Why for me? Try and come out this

weekend, relax a little.

GIEREK: How many cars do you have, Maciej?

SZCZEPANSKI: Cars? I don't know. Who's counting?

GIEREK: Kania.

SZCZEPANSKI: Kania? And what does he make it?

GIEREK: Eighteen.

SZCZEPANSKI: Eighteen? Well, Comrade, you know . . . as Chairman of the State Committee for Radio and TV one has to get about.

GIEREK: How many houses? An aeroplane. A yacht. A health club staffed by young women with unusual qualifications. Yes, Comrade Kania has a file on you.

SZCZEPANSKI: That's his job.

GIEREK: Yes. He undoubtedly has a file on me too. How much was that little object you presented me with on my sixty-fifth birthday?

SZCZEPANSKI: Well, it was gold. All right – who built your country house? Twenty-three million zlotys. We serve the Party. The Party rewards us. What do you say, Edward?

GIEREK: I think I'll be busy this weekend.

16. INT. KURON'S FLAT. NIGHT

JACEK KURON *and* GEREMEK *are watching* GIEREK *on a television set.*

GIEREK: (*On television*) Attempts by irresponsible individuals and anarchic, anti-socialist groups to use stoppages for political ends and to incite tension are a dangerous aspect of recent events at plants on the Gdansk coast . . .

(GIEREK *continues but the* NARRATOR'*s voice takes over.*)

NARRATOR: (*Voice over*) Jacek Kuron, who now joins the story, had a strategy for freedom in a Communist state – pay lip service to Party rule while organizing into self-governing groups, like unions.

GEREMEK: I think he's talking about you, Jacek.

17. INT. GIEREK'S OFFICE. NIGHT

We see what is apparently the studio bookcase, but the middle of it is a concealed door which now opens. GIEREK *comes through the bookcase to his desk and we see that behind him there is another office with a* SECRETARY *at a desk. The phone on Gierek's desk is ringing.* GIEREK *picks it up. He listens for a moment.*

GIEREK: Lock him up.

18. EXT. STREET. NIGHT

KURON *and* GEREMEK *are walking down the street.*

NARRATOR: (*Voice Over*) Back in the sixties Kuron was a radical Marxist calling for a revolutionary workers' state. The Polish United Workers' Party did not appreciate him and put him in gaol.

(KURON, *in conversation, bursts out laughing.*)

KURON: (*Cheerfully*) Now I'm rehabilitated. But I'm still followed by the police.

(*The camera tracks with them and finds the* NARRATOR *in the foreground.*)

NARRATOR: (*To camera*) The Polish intellectuals played no part in the rebellion in 1970 which brought Edward Gierek to power. But in '76, when Gierek had to survive the first rebellion of his own, Kuron and others, shocked by the brutal police repression, formed the Workers' Defence Committee.

(*Tracking again with* KURON.)

KURON: (*To* GEREMEK) The Workers' Defence Committee was formed out of shame. When you get to Gdansk, tell them that this time we won't just leave them to it. This thing could be amazing. Workers' power, economic power, not a rebellion but a social force. No blood in the streets. That belongs to history.

GEREMEK: You think so?

KURON: Don't you?

GEREMEK: History is my subject.

(*They come to a corner and shake hands to separate.* GEREMEK *moves off. Two* POLICEMEN *approach* KURON *and arrest him, without drama, and walk him towards a nearby police car. The* NARRATOR *is in the street, watching this.*)

NARRATOR: Kuron and fourteen others were arrested on August 20th. For Gierek the subversive influence of the intellectual mavericks was the single most important factor underlying the Polish crisis . . .

(*He is interrupted by the* WITNESS, *who is now drunk.*)

WITNESS: Horse manure.

(*The* NARRATOR *turns.*)

NARRATOR: What is?

WITNESS: Kuron and his friends have been overtaken by events and they're still trying to catch up.

NARRATOR: Then why arrest them?

WITNESS: Gierek has got to arrest *someone*. Every day Brezhnev wants to know what's being done. Every day the answer is – nothing! Worse than nothing – negotiations instead of breaking heads. So Gierek arrests a few intellectuals. The Russians understand that. They've read Marx, Gierek knows it's irrelevant.

NARRATOR: Why doesn't he arrest the strikers instead?

WITNESS: He can't afford to.

NARRATOR: You mean he's scared? Or broke?

WITNESS: Try the money.

(*Another camera angle. The* WITNESS *weaves his way down the street. The* NARRATOR *faces the camera.*)

NARRATOR: Meanwhile, the economic situation was the single most important factor underlying –

(*The* WITNESS *turns round and shouts to the* NARRATOR.)

WITNESS: That's the one!

(*The camera tracks along the street, following a long fence on which graffiti have been scrawled, crude pictures illustrating the Narrator's next speech.*)

NARRATOR: (*Voice over*) Edward Gierek came to power promising political and economic reforms. He intended to go down in history as the man who turned Poland into a modern industrial nation. And for a while it worked. Life became freer and richer. The relaxation lasted a couple of years. The money lasted longer, but it was all borrowed – two billion by the middle of the decade, from the West alone. The idea was that the money would be turned into tractors, colour TVs, Polish Fiats . . . and then back into money. But almost everything Polish, except what came out of the ground, had a Western component which had to be paid for in hard currency to keep the expensive new factories in production, and with the oil crisis in 1973 those prices went up so more had to be borrowed, until Poland's industry was working just to pay the interest on a debt which, by 1980, topped 20 billion dollars.

19. INT. BOARDROOM (BANK). DAY

Formal meeting room. There is a 'round table' of BANKERS, FINANSKY *among them. The Narrator's speech overlaps into this scene.*

FINANSKY: When we met in April I proposed a loan of 500 million dollars which would enable us to refinance our accumulated debt. This agreement proposes only 325 millions. In addition you propose a rate of interest above the Eurodollar rate. This is disappointing, gentlemen. You are endangering our ability to repay. This is the truth.

GERMAN BANKER: Minister, we represent more than 400 banks from sixteen countries. To service your debt requires 95 per cent of your export revenue.

AMERICAN BANKER: American banks are badly exposed. 1.7 billion dollars. Just the commercial banks, quite apart from a billion dollars in credits from my government.

FINANSKY: American banks are lending the same to Peru.

AMERICAN BANKER: Yes, and ten times as much to Brazil. But these countries are members of the International Monetary Fund, so the money does not come without strings. We are in a position to insist on certain controls. In your case we have no control.

SWISS BANKER: Your exports are being hit now with these strikes . . .

FINANSKY: (*Sharply*) The strikes are in response to the price increases which we were left in no doubt would be welcome to *you* gentlemen when we began these present negotiations.

AMERICAN BANKER: (*To his neighbour*) Well, isn't that something? If Poland goes down the drain it'll be the fault of Chase Manhattan.

20. INT. EXECUTIVE WASHROOM. DAY

GIEREK *is using a wash-basin. When he looks into the mirror in front of him he sees two well-dressed, well-shaved, well-groomed members of the Politburo,* JAGIELSKI *and* BARCIKOWSKI. *They are standing respectfully behind him, for instruction.* GIEREK *busies himself with soap and water while he talks.*

GIEREK: (*To* JAGIELSKI) In the Lenin shipyard there is a strike committee representing 380 places of work.

(JAGIELSKI *raises his eyebrows in surprise.*)

Yes, we tried to split them with separate deals but they weren't having that. (To BARCIKOWSKI) There are 25,000 on strike in Szczecin now. You will find a strike committee waiting to negotiate.

JAGIELSKI: Kania says in Gdansk they have a list of sixteen demands.

GIEREK: Twenty-one. Well, when they add the moon it will be twenty-two.

BARCIKOWSKI: Is that what we promise them?

GIEREK: Just end the strike. (*To* JAGIELSKI) You did it with the railway workers in July. You can do it with the shipyard.

(GIEREK *ducks downs to wash his face.*)

21. INT. THE SAME

As GIEREK *straightens we see he is now dry, and tying up his tie. In the mirror he sees* JAGIELSKI *and* BARCIKOWSKI *returning now in very different shape, unshaven, looking as though they had slept in their clothes, exhausted.*

BARCIKOWSKI: In Szczecin they make thirty-six demands, beginning with free independent parties.

GIEREK: You mean unions.

BARCIKOWSKI: No. Parties. Political parties.

GIEREK: This is becoming grotesque.

BARCIKOWSKI: I told them I had come to discuss workers' grievances, not an overthrow of the political system. They accepted my point.

GIEREK: Good.

BARCIKOWSKI: And they told me that the first grievance is that the official union does not represent the workers' interest. The demand for free unions is central, absolutely central. The workers' spokesman in Szczecin is a veteran of 1970 – Marian Jurczyk – a strong Catholic. He demands also that Sunday Mass be broadcast on state radio. He is tough, very quiet, hard. When I arrived he did not even return my greeting. He said – these are our demands. The atmosphere is sober, unrelenting. No journalists, no cameras.

JAGIELSKI: Gdansk is a circus. The negotiations are in a room with a glass wall. On the other side of the glass there are hundreds of people. No, not a circus, a zoo. Scores of photographers. And every word we speak is broadcast all over the shipyard. Walesa does most of their talking. He is friendly, no intellectual but sharp, and he has the workers behind him like a football hero.

BARCIKOWSKI: The situation is very strange – some of these are our own people, *Party members*! You understand me, Comrade First Secretary? The party itself is unstable.

(GIEREK, BARCIKOWSKI, JAGIELSKI *leave the washroom. The* WITNESS, *in the role of washroom attendant, approaches the mirror to tidy up after* GIEREK.)

NARRATOR: (*Voice over*) Gierek's chief concern now was to maintain the Party line –

(The WITNESS, *busy cleaning the wash-basin, looks up into the mirror, interrupting the* NARRATOR's *speech with a shake of his head.*)

(*Correcting himself*) – was to survive.

(*The* WITNESS *nods approvingly.*)

22. INT. SZCZEPANSKI'S OFFICE. NIGHT

There are sounds of a party going on next door. SZCZEPANSKI, *drinking, is brooding alone, watching* GIEREK *mouthing silently on television. Using a remote control he switches on a video recorder and Gierek's image is replaced by a mildly pornographic film. Meanwhile, the* NARRATOR *is heard.*

NARRATOR: (*Voice over*) A crisis meeting of the Central
Committee made a dramatic show of cleaning out the stables.
Four Politburo members were sacked, including the Prime
Minister and the official trades union chief. There was a
simultaneous purge of Party men in high government posts,
including the Chairman of the State Committee for Radio
and Television. Gierek was spared, confessing to . . .
(SZCZEPANSKI *switches the television set back to* GIEREK.)

GIEREK: (*On television*) . . . errors, inconsistencies, delays and
hesitations. We owe an apology to those comrades who
pointed out irregularities, who tried to do something about
them . . .
(*The office door opens, increasing the sound of the party music. A
party guest, a* GIRL, *enters.*)

GIRL: Come on, Maciej – the party's started without you.

SZCZEPANSKI: No. It's over.

23. INT. TELEVISION STUDIO

For the moment we don't know if we are in the television studio or Gierek's actual office. GIEREK *sits at his desk, the bookcase behind him. He has evidently just finished addressing the camera. He looks shattered. Abruptly he moves his chair back. It hits the bookcase, which topples over.*

24. INT. GIEREK'S OFFICE. NIGHT

Now GIEREK *is at his 'real' desk with the 'real' bookcase behind him.* GIEREK, *evidently at the end of his tether, mutters* . . .

GIEREK: What will the Russians do?

NARRATOR: (*Voice over*) The single most important factor

underlying Poland's independence was, needless to say –
WITNESS: (*Voice over*) The Church.
(*Behind* GIEREK *the bookcase door opens. The* SECRETARY *is showing in* CARDINAL WYSZYNSKI.)

25. INT. CAFE. NIGHT

The NARRATOR *and the* WITNESS *are sitting at a café table.*
NARRATOR: (*To* WITNESS) The Church?
WITNESS: The Church. Lech Walesa wears the Black Madonna of Częstochowa on his coat. The King of Poland consecrated the nation to her as recently as 1656 and just the day before yesterday, when for the whole of the nineteenth century there was no such place, the Poles called their country the Christ among nations, and in the Church they kept alive the promise of resurrection. As with the Tsars so with Stalin. The years of terror discredited the political guardians of the nation state, and so the moral leadership fell to the Church. For the last thirty-two years that has meant to Cardinal Wyszynski.

26. INT. GIEREK'S OFFICE. NIGHT

We pick up the shot as WYSZYNSKI *is being shown into the room.*
NARRATOR: (*Voice over*) Imprisoned and conciliated, from the first years of Stalinist terror to the last years of Gierek's ramshackle version of the consumer society, Cardinal Wyszynski had been the spiritual leader of a people who, by the irony of history, constituted the most vital Catholic nation in Europe.
(*Door shuts.*)
GIEREK: Father, there will be blood. They won't listen. They will lose everything. You must talk to them before it's too late.
WYSZYNSKI: The Politburo?
GIEREK: The workers! The strikers! They demand things which cannot be given.
WYSZYNSKI: They demand nothing which is not their right. It is

you who must listen. Or there will be blood. You will lose everything.

GIEREK: No – no. The Russians will intervene if we don't go back. You must save us. Save the Church.

WYSZYNSKI: The Church needs to be defended sometimes but it does not need to be saved.

GIEREK: (*Weeping*) Then save Poland . . .

(WYSZYNSKI *gets up and leaves the room.*)

27. INT. ANTE-ROOM. CONTINUATION

KANIA *is waiting outside.*

KANIA: (*To* WYSZYNSKI) How is he?

WYSZYNSKI: Better than I have seen him for a long time.

KANIA: His nerve has gone.

WYSZYNSKI: If you like.

KANIA: Can you help?

WYSZYNSKI: The Church does not resist an appeal. I will preach on Tuesday. It is the Feast of the Black Madonna of Częstochowa. I will speak as I must for the rights of workers.

KANIA: These strikes harm the nation. We can't fulfil every demand at once.

WYSZYNSKI: I will speak the whole truth.

KANIA: How many will hear you?

WYSZYNSKI: My voice carries.

KANIA: With your permission I will assist it with television cameras.

WYSZYNSKI: Not with my permission.

28. INT. PARTY HEADQUARTERS (POLITBURO). DAY

The Politburo is meeting. GIEREK *sits in his usual place.* BABIUCH *and* SZYDLAK *have gone.* (*Two other Politburo members, anonymous ones as far as we are concerned, have also been sacked, and there are three new faces round the table.*)

KANIA: We are no longer talking about the Baltic ports. There are strikes in Wroclaw, in Warsaw, in the steel works, in the mines of Silesia.

(*The door opens as* KANIA *is speaking to admit a latecomer,* STEFAN OLSZOWSKI. OLSZOWSKI *without ceremony responds to* KANIA.)

OLSZOWSKI: What about the army?

KANIA: Welcome, Comrade Olszowski.

JARUZELSKI: Welcome back, Comrade Olszowski.

(*The* MEMBERS *get up generally and shake* OLSZOWSKI's *hand and welcome him back.* OLSZOWSKI *sits down.*)

KANIA: Congratulations on your re-election. How was Berlin?

OLSZOWSKI: (*Sitting down*) The Germans think we're soft. If we don't act now, with troops if necessary, we deserve what we get.

(*He looks directly at* JARUZELSKI.)

JARUZELSKI: Yes. But not yet.

OLSZOWSKI: When?

JARUZELSKI: When there is no alternative.

OLSZOWSKI: When is that?

JARUZELSKI: I don't know. I'll tell you.

OLSZOWSKI: Next week? Next year?

JARUZELSKI: It depends on them.

OLSZOWSKI: *On them?*

JARUZELSKI: Oh yes. We must give them what they demand and then it depends on them. They will bring us to it, slowly or quickly, but we'll get there, you have my guarantee.

OLSZOWSKI: (*To* GIEREK) Comrade First Secretary . . .

GIEREK: (*To* JAGIELSKI) Comrade Jagielski . . . go back to Gdansk and sign.

29. EXT. GDANSK SHIPYARD. DAY

There is a large crowd of noisy, celebrating DOCK WORKERS *and one man elevated above them on the shoulders of his fellow workers –* WALESA.

WITNESS: (*Voice over*) Jagielski and Lech Walesa signed the Gdansk Agreement on August 31st. The impossible had taken sixteen days. The inevitable was going to take sixteen months.

2

Solidarity

JACEK KURON *is released from a prison cell by two* GUARDS.

NARRATOR: (*Voice over*) The piece of paper signed in Gdansk guaranteed much more than an independent trade union. It spelled out the right to strike, freedom of expression, the broadcasting of Mass, economic reforms, medical, housing and welfare benefits, pensions and . . .

(*The* POLICEMAN *leads* KURON *along the catwalk.*)

. . . the freeing of political prisoners.

(KURON *and his* ESCORT *walk along a corridor lined with cells. From one of these a* PRISONER *shouts at him.*)

PRISONER: Hey, Kuron! – is it just the bloody intelligentsia who are being let out? I've redistributed more property than you'll ever see!

NARRATOR: (*Voice over*) Kuron went straight to Gdansk. For two decades the drama of his intellectual life had been the attempt to square the Communist circle inside the cornerstones of democratic socialism, and now the show had started without him.

31. EXT. STREET (GDANSK). DAY

WALESA *is coming down the street in a scrum of people, mostly* JOURNALISTS, *some with notebooks and some with tape recorders and microphones. Passers-by and general public are also drawn to the scrum, which is quite a large crowd of people altogether, thirty or forty. It is a travelling press conference, with the questions distributed among the* JOURNALISTS, *sometimes shouted from the fringe of the scrum.*

QUESTION: Lech, what are you going to do next?

WALESA: Eat dinner.

QUESTION: What is your dream?

WALESA: For Poland to be Poland.

QUESTION: What does that take?

WALESA: To eat dinner. To speak what we think. To come and go as we please.

QUESTION: Are you a Marxist?

WALESA: How do I know? I never read a book.

QUESTION: What is your badge?

WALESA: (*Touching the badge on his lapel*) The Black Madonna of Częstochowa, the holiest shrine in Poland. Here I have a picture of her –

(*He has small photographs of the Madonna, which he hands out as he walks.*)

QUESTION: What is your main task?

WALESA: To keep the movement together.

QUESTION: Why are you the leader?

WALESA: I'm the chairman. I'm not a dictator. Maybe a democratic dictator.

QUESTION: What do you want to be?

WALESA: When I was an electrician I wanted to be the best.

QUESTION: What is the first thing the union has to do?

WALESA: Survive.

QUESTION: Who is the greater danger, Russia or the Party?

WALESA: Neither. Our greatest danger is ourselves. We must learn restraint and patience or we'll tear ourselves apart.

QUESTION: Do you want to overthrow the Party?

WALESA: No – I want the Party to be strong and to be just. A weak party would be disastrous. I would have to join it.

QUESTION: Isn't the union a challenge to the Party?

WALESA: The workers challenge themselves. They let themselves down.

QUESTION: Do you want to go to America?

WALESA: I want to go everywhere and with Mother Mary on my coat I will. But now I want to go home. As a husband and father I also want to be the best. Also as a lover. I have six children and my wife won't forgive me for getting mixed up in this. I will have to give her a seventh.

(*He is extricating himself from the crowd.*)
QUESTION: Lech – are you scared?
WALESA: I am scared of nothing and nobody, only of God.
(*He has arrived at the doorway to the block of flats where he lives. He disappears inside.*)

32. INT. FLATS. DAY

WALESA *comes up the staircase. On a landing there is a small* CHILD (*one of Walesa's children*).
WALESA: What have you been doing?
CHILD: Having my picture taken.
(WALESA *takes the* CHILD *by the hand and continues up the stairs and then enters his own flat.*)

33. INT. WALESA FLAT. DAY

There are several PHOTOGRAPHERS *in the flat taking photographs of the other* CHILDREN *and of* DANUTA (*Mrs Walesa*). *She gives him a rueful look. He smiles and shrugs.*
The PHOTOGRAPHERS *turn their attention to* WALESA. *He sees that the phone is off the hook. He replaces it.*
JOURNALIST: Here, Lech . . .
(*A journalist gives* WALESA *a carton of American [Marlboro] cigarettes.* WALESA *nods and smiles. The phone rings.*)

34. INT. BATHROOM (THE FLAT). DAY

WALESA *is in the bath, pouring water over his head.*
PHOTOGRAPHER: (*Off-screen*) This way, Lech.
(*We see that there is a* PHOTOGRAPHER *in the bathroom with him. The* PHOTOGRAPHER *takes several photographs using a motordrive camera.*)
NARRATOR: (*Voice over*) Everyone knew that Lech was special. Pretty soon the outside world learned not to call him Walesser or Valesser but Vawensa.

35. INT. SOLIDARITY MEETING ROOM. DAY

The meeting room is crowded. SOLIDARITY MEMBERS *are meeting each other, shaking hands. The crowd includes Solidarity's* 'ADVISERS'. *There is a good deal of self-introduction going on as the Narrator's speech identifies several of the individuals we are going to be concerned with.*

NARRATOR: (*Voice over*) The names and faces multiply, and there were many more than these. But it sorts itself out like this . . .

The intellectuals who formed themselves around the union as unofficial advisers included . . . Kuron . . . Geremek, the historian . . . Mazowiecki, a radical Catholic journalist . . . and Modzelewski, who had gone to gaol with Kuron in 1967 when the two of them, both radical Communists and lecturers at Warsaw University, had written an open letter attacking Party rule. Maszowiecki became Solidarity's press spokesman. Jurczyk, a storeman, led the strikers at Szczecin . . . Gwiazda was the man perhaps closest to Walesa. Allowing for simple demarcations, Gwiazda . . . and Rulewski, who led one of the regional branches of the union, were radicals who were to come into conflict with Walesa's more moderate line . . . Lis personified one of the paradoxes of the situation, for he was a member of the Communist Party . . . Bujak was the union's leader in Warsaw . . . and there were others like these whose names the outside world never did get right, because –

36. EXT. SHIPYARD. DAY

NARRATOR: (*Voice over*) – the personality cult grew – sensationally – around a thirty-seven-year-old electrician whose combative, streetwise style had marked him out long before he climbed over the steel fence of the Lenin shipyard and found himself famous.

(WALESA *has been walking through the shipyard, carrying a yard-high model of the Gdansk Memorial. He is greeted on all sides by* WORKERS, *and greetings are shouted at him from distant*

217

perches on cranes and gantries. WALESA *acknowledges the
treatment like a star.*)

He liked the attention. In months to come he would be on
scores of magazine covers and travel as far as Japan, meeting
the great. It caused resentment inside Solidarity, but that
was later.

37. INT. SOLIDARITY MEETING ROOM. CONTINUATION

WALESA, *carrying the model of the memorial, enters the room. He sees*
KURON *there and shouts towards him.*

WALESA: Jacek . . . they let you out . . . do you want to make a
speech?

KURON: It's your revolution. You tell us what you want us to do.
(*The meeting settles down around* WALESA. WALESA *puts the
model of the memorial on the table.*)

WALESA: We have to make an organization. Suddenly everyone
has a free union. All over the country they're saying, we'll
have the same as Gdansk, thank you very much. I don't
know. Maybe there should be no centralization; just separate
unions.

MAZOWIECKI: No. You have to be national, otherwise the Party
will pick you off piece by piece –

GEREMEK: – or break down into chaos trying to deal with you
separately. You have to have dialogue, not a general racket
going on. Stability. Discipline.

WALESA: So a national commission representing all the regions?

MAZOWIECKI: Right.

WALESA: Yes – yes – you're right – we have to act as one.

BUJAK: You mean if we want to strike in Warsaw we have to come
to Gdansk for permission?

WALESA: Yes – definitely –

GWIAZDA: What are we going to be? An alternative bureaucracy?
A Politburo?

WALESA: How we use our authority is up to us. If we are fair we
will use it fairly. For the good of all.

GWIAZDA: That's Party language, Lech.

WALESA: No, it's the language of democracy, stolen by the Party.

We're a workers' movement, not a mob. Local strikes must have a majority at factory level first, and then they must be ratified by a majority at the National Commission in Gdansk.

JURCZYK: What is this Gdansk – Gdansk – Gdansk? We had a strike at Szczecin. *We* also had a member of the Politburo on his knees. *We* also signed an agreement. We had everything you had except foreign journalists, and you should have told them to mind their own business like we did.

WALESA: I don't care if the National Commission meets in Szczecin or Katowice. It can meet in different places. It can meet in a hot air balloon for all I care.

MAZOWIECKI: Don't say that – the damn thing would never come down.

WALESA: All right. We don't even exist yet, legally. All we have is a name. (*To* KURON) We're taking the name of the strike bulletin we published in the yard.

(*He gives* KURON *a copy of the bulletin.* KURON *looks at it.*)

KURON: Solidarity.

WALESA: We'll have legal registration in a few weeks. The statutes are being drafted now by our legal experts. You see, intellectuals have their uses – though we had trouble with them at first. They kept putting the word socialist into the manifestos, and the workers kept taking it out.

KURON: Well, we didn't know you were thinking of changing the political system.

WALESA: We aren't. We don't want to govern. We don't want to be a threat.

GWIAZDA: What are you talking about? We *are* a threat. And we are dealing with gangsters.

WALESA: We're a union, that's all.

GWIAZDA: Do you believe that?

WALESA: If we don't believe it, how can *they*? Look, it's like this. The workers want bread. A decent wage. And a proper machinery to represent them, to take their side, and also a proper influence on the way things are managed at work. We're not political.

GWIAZDA: Most of our demands are political. What's the most important thing we've gained?

219

JURCZYK: The broadcasting of Mass.

GWIAZDA: Jesus God.

JURCZYK: Please don't blaspheme.

GWIAZDA: Abolition of censorship – the right to strike – free elections for the union – no more Party hacks holding down jobs they don't know how to do – *free trade unions are political*.

MAZOWIECKI: He's right.

GWIAZDA: We're going to have to fight just to keep what we've won – even to *get* what we've won. You'll see when they start breaking their promises.

WALESA: (*To* KURON) Is he right?

KURON: I said it was a revolution. The trick is to make it a self-limiting revolution. The Party must keep the leading role.

LIS: I'm still a Party member. Lenin said the unions were the connection between the Party and the workers.

KURON: And with a union controlled by the Party there's no problem. But an uncontrolled union reverses the current of power. The Party won't forgive. It will give up ground and take its time, but in the end they still have the police and the security forces. So go slowly. You can win little by little, but remember, if you lose you will lose overnight. (*Snaps his fingers*.) Like that.

(*Everyone is sobered by this. The camera looks from face to face.* WALESA *is looking at the model of the memorial.* KURON *approaches him*.)

WALESA: Look at this, Jacek. It's going to be forty metres high, outside the gate. We used to show up there every December. With stones in our suitcases. We'd make a little monument and the police would kick it over and take us away. They won't kick this over in a hurry.

KURON: I've always said that workers shouldn't elect leaders . . . it makes it too easy for the Party to identify the enemy.

WALESA: We'll have safety in numbers. Thousands and thousands are joining. Party members, too. They understand. We're an opposition. We're reformers. The Party needs reforming more than anybody else. Don't worry. We'll have 10 million members.

(KURON *smiles at his*.)

220

I said we'd have a monument. Now I say we'll have ten million members.

38. INT. PARLIAMENT. DAY

The cut is to the members of the Politburo, who appear to be sitting in the dock of a courtroom. There are twelve of them, including JARUZELSKI, KANIA, FINANSKY, PINKOWSKI (*the Prime Minister*) *and* OLSZOWSKI. GIEREK *is absent. The 'dock' is actually the Politburo bench in parliament.*

SPEAKER ONE: What we have witnessed in Gdansk, Comrades, is an attack on the state organized by anarchists and anti-socialist groups –
(*This is greeted off-screen by loud protests.*)

SPEAKER TWO: No, that's not true – these are genuine grievances – there is a failure in the Party, and it is at the top of the Party!
(*The applause for this covers the narration.*)

NARRATOR: (*Voice over*) This was parliament five days after the Gdansk signing. The usual ventriloquist act had fallen apart. The dummy had come to life.

SPEAKER THREE: We have become a rubber stamp for a Party leadership which has lost its way. We are a sham society built on propaganda which has become a joke. We have sham planning, sham achievements in industry and science, sham debates, sham elections, sham socialism, sham justice, sham morality, and finally sham contentment because no one can any longer tell the sham from the real.
(*More applause over which –*)

NARRATOR: (*Voice over*) The other odd thing was that the First Secretary, Edward Gierek, was missing, and there was no news of him.

39. INT. HOSPITAL VESTIBULE. EVENING

KANIA, *carrying a large bunch of flowers, crosses.*

40. INT. PRIVATE WARD. EVENING

The room is so full of people that at first one doesn't realize that GIEREK *is in the hospital bed, apparently unconscious. The people in the room are the Politburo, who are animatedly discussing the situation in small groups . . . eating the grapes, drinking the barley water, examining the patient's chart.* OLSZOWSKI *is wearing headphones, the hospital radio, and manipulating the wall-switch which changes the channel. The switch is heavily labelled: 'Light music', 'Warsaw', 'Moscow', 'East Berlin', 'Prague'.*

KANIA *enters.*

JARUZELSKI: (*To* KANIA) Gierek's had a heart attack. The Central Committee is meeting tonight. We'll have a new first secretary by the morning.

KANIA: Does Stefan have hopes?

OLSZOWSKI: Quiet. I can't hear a thing.

NARRATOR: (*Voice over*) Stefan Olszowski had been in the Politburo before until a disagreement over Gierek's economic policy shunted him into the Ambassador's job in East Berlin. Now the Central Committee had brought him back. There was a hard line in the Party and Olszowski spoke for it.

OLSZOWSKI: Moscow says there are no inherent defects in the socialist system, it's in the weakness of the leadership. (*Turns the dial from 'Moscow' to 'East Berlin'.*) And as for the Germans . . . (*He reels back as the Germans nearly blow his ear out.*)

41. INT. CAFE. NIGHT

The NARRATOR *and the* WITNESS *are at a table playing chess. It seems to be the Witness's move. He is frowning at the board.*

NARRATOR: (*To camera*) But the Central Committee did not advance Stefan Olszowski. It was not the moment to attack on the left.

WITNESS: Why is it always *chess*?

NARRATOR: Ugh, well, you know, it symbolizes . . .

WITNESS: These ones with horse's heads, are they the ones which can jump over things?

NARRATOR: You're ruining it.

WITNESS: Sorry.

NARRATOR: (*To camera*) The mood was for reform, renewal, nothing too liberal, but no conservative blacklash. A middle-of-the-road *apparatchik* with a tough background in security but with nothing of the zealot about him would do. Kania had the job by 2 a.m.

42. INT. KREMLIN. DAY

BREZHNEV *and a* SECRETARY, *in an office.* BREZHNEV *is standing on a chair, being measured by a* TAILOR.

BREZHNEV: (*Dictating*) Dear Kania – get things back to normal or we'll be down on you like a ton of bricks. Read that back.

SECRETARY: Dear Comrade Kania, the working people of the Soviet Union know you as a staunch champion of the people's true interests, the ideals of Communism, the strengthening of the leading role of the Party, and the consolidation of socialism in the Polish People's Republic. (*It goes on like that but we fade him out . . .*)

NARRATOR: (*Voice over*) But Kania, in his first public statement, pledged himself to the spirit of Gdansk.

43. INT. KANIA'S OFFICE. DAY

KANIA *is behind his desk.*

KANIA: (*To camera*) The Party will reform itself, workers will work, the citizens will have more freedom, the newspapers will report the facts, radio will broadcast Mass, the hacks will be sacked, corruption will be stamped out, and Poland will be in charge of her own destiny throughout. It's all going to be all right.

44. INT. CAFE. DAY

The NARRATOR *and the* WITNESS *are now playing cards.*

WITNESS: Twist.

(*The* NARRATOR *deals him a card.*)

NARRATOR: (*To camera*) But it was a bluff and Kania knew it.
WITNESS: Bust.

45. INT. KANIA'S OFFICE. DAY

KANIA *is behind his desk as before.*
KANIA: The Soviet Union supplies us with all our crude oil,
    potash and iron ore, and 80 per cent of our natural gas and
    our timber. The August strikes have cost us zillions of zlotys
    and they aren't finished. All over the place workers have
    caught Gdansk disease. And all over the place the fat cats of
    the Party apparatus and the old union are digging in against
    what they call an anti-socialist sell-out. It's not going to be a
    picnic.

46. EXT. STEELWORKS. GDANSK. DAY

Gate with flowers in foreground.
Camera drops to take in steelworks as gates are shut.
NARRATOR: (*Voice over*)The wheel of reform was moving so
    slowly that to give it a shove the union announced a token
    one-hour strike for October 3rd. With a week to go, the
    Solidarity leadership came to Warsaw to apply for legal
    registration.
    (*Hooters go off.*)

47. INT. COURTROOM. DAY

WALESA *is alone in the room. A door opens and* KANIA *enters.*
KANIA: Comrade Walesa.
    (*They shake hands.*)
WALESA: Congratulations, Comrade First Secretary, on your
    elevation.
KANIA: Likewise. Please sit down, Comrade. Comrade Walesa,
    when I was elected First Secretary I told the Central
    Committee that I intended to use the collective wisdom of
    the people. A strike is not the act of wisdom.
WALESA: A stoppage, for one hour.

224

KANIA: But a million people, even for one hour, is a provocative symbol to our allies.

WALESA: It's going to be 3 million, Comrade First Secretary.

KANIA: I'm trying to help you but I have suspicious and angry people behind me.

WALESA: That's my position also.

(KANIA *thumps the table angrily.*)

KANIA: The proletariat cannot dictate to the Party what –

(*He collects himself. People are filing into the room. The two men begin whispering.*)

In the dictatorship of the proletariat, the Party must have the leading role.

WALESA: We accept that.

KANIA: But you haven't said so in the legal statutes which have been deposited with the Warsaw Provincial Court.

WALESA: We haven't said so because we are not a political organization. The leading role of the Party is nothing to do with us.

KANIA: The leading role of the Party is to do with everybody!

WALESA: To acknowledge it in the statutes *would* be a political act.

KANIA: To *refuse* to acknowledge it is a political act.

(*Now we see that the room is full of people.*)

WALESA: The independence of the free trade union Solidarity is not negotiable. We are waiting for the decision of the Court. Then we will know if this game is honest.

(*Close-up on a* JUDGE.)

JUDGE: The registration of the independent trade union Solidarity is allowed.

(*On the reverse shot* WALESA *smiles briefly at* GWIAZDA, *who, however, holds up his hand as if to say, 'Not so fast.'*)

But, the statutes of the union are modified to include the acknowledgement of the leading role of the –

WALESA: The Court has no power to alter the statutes!

GWIAZDA: (*Furiously to* WALESA) Now will you believe me! We're dealing with gangsters!

48. EXT. BALCONY. DAY

We see a line-up of the PARTY BOSSES, *just heads and shoulders above the parapet. They are dressed like gangsters. They look out front, possibly reviewing a parade, and talk among themselves out of the sides of their mouths.*

KANIA: The Walesa mob is calling a general strike.

OLSZOWSKI: Rub them out.

KANIA: There's three million of them!

GANG MEMBER: Four million, boss.

KANIA: Shut up!

JARUZELSKI: (*To* KANIA) It was the wrong time to pull a stunt like that.

49. EXT. STREET. DAY

NARRATOR *and* WITNESS *appear to be among the crowd looking up at the Politburo's balcony.*

WITNESS: What's all this gangster stuff?

NARRATOR: It's a metaphor.

WITNESS: Wrong. You people –

NARRATOR: All right.

50. EXT. BALCONY. DAY. CONTINUATION

Now the people on the balcony are no longer dressed as gangsters. They speak normally too.

JARUZELSKI: It was the wrong time for a confrontation.

KANIA: You haven't had Comrade Brezhnev shouting down the telephone –

JARUZELSKI: Comrade Brezhnev only demands stability. Throw the dogs a few bones. Leave the statutes of the union as they are, and put whatever you want into an appendix. Walesa will help us if we help him. And when the time comes . . .

51. INT. SOLIDARITY MEETING ROOM. DAY

WALESA, FAMILY *and* OTHERS *are kneeling. A* PRIEST *is holding Mass.*

NARRATOR: (*Voice over*) And so the deal was made. Solidarity was legal. And Mass was on the radio. The regime lost face but stood to gain a period of calm – so long as the moderate men on either side were in control.

52. INT. WARSAW SOLIDARITY OFFICE. NIGHT

A Solidarity poster is on the office window. Close-up of Solidarity poster. A group of POLICEMEN *enter the office and immediately begin ransacking it. The only occupant is* BUJAK. BUJAK *stands up.*

NARRATOR: (*Voice over*) The calm lasted nine days.

BUJAK: What the hell is going on?

(*The* OFFICER IN CHARGE *hands him the warrant. The other* OFFICERS *are emptying filing cabinet drawers on the the floor.*)

53. INT. KANIA'S BEDROOM. NIGHT

Telephone rings. Light goes on. KANIA *picks up receiver.*

KANIA: (*Angrily*) On whose orders?

54. INT. WALESA'S FLAT. NIGHT

The phone is ringing. WALESA, *in night clothes, finally answers it.*

WALESA: (*Into phone*) Yes –?

(*In the near dark he listens and feels for the light switch. He puts the light on.*)

Jesus and Mary . . .

55. INT. SOLIDARITY MEETING ROOM. GDANSK. DAY

A meeting of the Praesidium with WALESA *in the chair. There are about a dozen others, including a young woman (*ALINA PIENKOWSKA*), and* BOGDAN LIS *and* ANDRZEJ GWIAZDA. BUJAK, *talking to them, is the only one standing up.*

BUJAK: They broke into the Solidarity office in Warsaw and found what they say is a secret document. They have arrested our printer and also a clerk in the Prosecutor's office. They claim he leaked the document to us. Warsaw Solidarity has called a strike of the entire region, if both men are not released.

WALESA: Excuse me. A strike is not called by the regional office, only by the National Commission of the Union.

BUJAK: Then you'd better call it. Work has already stopped at Ursus Tractors. What's more, we are demanding as a condition of calling off the strike an investigation into the methods of the Prosecutor's office and of the security police. We're demanding cuts in the police budget and also the punishment of those who committed the police brutalities in '70 and '76.

(WALESA *looks despairing.*)

WALESA: For two arrested men? And what do we hit them with when the stakes get higher?

56. INT. KANIA'S OFFICE. DAY

KANIA *has the* PUBLIC PROSECUTOR *standing across the desk.*

KANIA: Comrade Prosecutor – are we to have a confrontation with a million workers over a miserable document?

PROSECUTOR: It is a classified document – a secret circular prepared by myself, on the organization of the anti-socialist groups. Furthermore, it is a stolen document. We have a good case for prosecution.

KANIA: (*Angrily*) The document contains nothing of importance. I have said on behalf of the Party, in public, that we offer Solidarity coexistence. These arrests merely make me look like a liar.

57. INT. SOLIDARITY MEETING ROOM. GDANSK. DAY

WALESA *and the Praesidium* (*same people as scene 55*).

WALESA: (*Strongly*) These demands against the security police – they can't be made in the name of the union. We are a

228

non-political organization. It was a pledge. Do you want to ruin everything?

It is snowing. A high shot shows us the works at a standstill. Groups of STEEL WORKERS *stand around. A small group is waiting for* WALESA, BUJAK *and* KURON, *who are walking purposefully towards the waiting delegation of* WORKERS.
When the two small groups arrive face to face we go into a closer shot.
BUJAK: Where can we talk?

BUJAK, KURON *and* WALESA *are huddled under the steps with the small group of* STEEL WORKERS, *one of whom acts as a spokesman. Snow continues to fall.*
BUJAK: It is very simple. We demanded the release of the two men. The Government has delivered them. We have to deliver the end of the strike.
STEEL WORKER: Our demands have not been satisfied.
WALESA: Your demands did not have the sanction of Gdansk.
STEEL WORKER: We are not in Gdansk. We are in Warsaw. Furthermore, our region is much bigger than the Gdansk region.
KURON: My friend, there is another reality beyond the immediate issue.
STEEL WORKER: Who is he?
KURON: I am Jacek Kuron.
STEEL WORKER: You're not a worker.
KURON: This is not an argument between you and the police. It is an argument between millions of Poles and the regime.
STEEL WORKER: No, it is between us and the police. In '76, when the Government raised prices, we went on strike and we won. They caved in. Afterwards the police made us run the gauntlet of truncheons. We were beaten unconscious, they smashed our bones. Who was ever punished for those crimes?
KURON: (*Helplessly*) Lech?

WALESA: What can I say?

BUJAK: You don't have to tell these men about the police. They have been in cells and in gaol. The Government has agreed to talk about the responsibility of the police.

STEEL WORKER: In private they will say anything.

BUJAK: The talks on police were announced on television tonight.

STEEL WORKER: Talks are not what we asked for. They guarantee nothing.

WALESA: (*Rather dramatically*) I am your guarantee! (*Self-consciously he amends this.*) We are your guarantee.

60. INT. FIRST SECRETARY'S OFFICE (KANIA). MORNING

KANIA *is being shaved, by, as it turns out, the* WITNESS.

KANIA: There are people who think that the Party boss can run the operation like a Chicago gangster. They should try sitting in this chair. I've got a Party which is losing members in droves, and half of those who remain have joined a free trade union with five million members –

WITNESS: (*Discreetly correcting*) Seven million.

KANIA: (*Taking the correction without comment*) Seven million. With the right to strike for more money which I haven't got because industrial production is down 12 per cent owing to the strikes, so I have to go cap in hand to the Soviets, who are giving us 690 million dollars in credits to keep Poland Communist. And to the United States, who are giving us 550 million dollars for the same reason. I've got a rank and file which wants to know when I'm going to reform the middle apparatus, and I've got a middle apparatus which wants to know when I'm going to stop the rot in the rank and file, and a leadership which is waiting to see which way the cat will jump. I've got a Catholic Church which doesn't want me to provoke the Russians, and a Communist Party two-thirds of whom believe in God. And to top it all off I've got a police force which can't break the habit, and a Public Prosecutor with the political nous of a bull in a china shop. As First Secretary of the Polish United Workers' Party, Al Capone wouldn't have lasted out the week.

(*The* INTERCOM *on the desk announces . . .*)

INTERCOM: His Excellency the Soviet Ambassador is here.

61. INT. KANIA'S OFFICE. ANOTHER SECTION. DAY

KANIA *leads the* AMBASSADOR *into the room, shows him to a chair.*
They sit.

KANIA: Good morning, Ambassador.

AMBASSADOR: Good morning, Comrade. You're looking tired.

KANIA: How can I help you, Ambassador?

AMBASSADOR: Comrade Brezhnev wishes to inform you that a
meeting of the leaders of the Warsaw Pact is to take place in
Moscow in eight days' time. Comrade Brezhnev asks me to
convey his fraternal greetings and looks forward to seeing
you on December 5th.

KANIA: (*Examining his diary*) I'll have to cancel a lunch. I accept
with pleasure, of course. I ask you to return my greetings
when you have an opportunity.

AMBASSADOR: I have many opportunities, Comrade First
Secretary. Comrade Brezhnev is taking a very close interest
in events here.

KANIA: Naturally. We are grateful for his interest.

AMBASSADOR: The situation is interesting. The Warsaw strike.
The general strike which is due to begin in four hours . . .

KANIA: There are no Warsaw strikes this morning. There will be
no general strike either.

AMBASSADOR: That is very good news. It is very important to us
that the Party should not show weakness.

KANIA: Quite so.

AMBASSADOR: And your two prisoners?

KANIA: Prisoners?

AMBASSADOR: The saboteurs arrested a week ago.

KANIA: You have been misinformed, Ambassador. Two men
were detained on suspicion but the suspicion proved
unfounded. The men were released very early this morning.

AMBASSADOR: I see.

KANIA: It is delightful to have seen you again.

AMBASSADOR: You won't forget? Moscow, December 5th.
(*The* AMBASSADOR *stands up and leaves the room.*)

62. INT. KREMLIN. DAY

This is the meeting of the Warsaw Pact leaders. BREZHNEV *is chairman. The Polish group consists of* KANIA, PINKOWSKI (*the last-seen prime minister*), BARCIKOWSKI *and* OLSZOWSKI *and* JARUZELSKI. *There is a little Polish flag on the table in front of them. At intervals around the large table there are the flags of Hungary, East Germany, Poland, Romania and Czechoslovakia. The only person standing is one of the Germans, who is half-way through a tirade, backed up by a pile of documents, including a sheaf of* Solidarity *magazines. He is referring to these one by one.*

GERMAN MINISTER: Item – a blatant attack on the person of the Regional Chairman of the Party. Item – a blatant attack on the office of the Public Prosecutor. Item – a blatant attack on the principle of peasant collectives. And so it goes on. These publications, openly printed and distributed by Solidarity, are an attack on socialism, an attack on everyone here, and I tell you this, Comrades, if the day comes when we in the German Democratic Republic allow the publication of filth like this, then you are free to assume that we objectively agree with it.

(*He sits down. Pause.* BREZHNEV *speaks without standing up, in a fairly friendly manner, looking straight across at the Polish leaders.*)

BREZHNEV: You know, we had our very own Soviet free trade union. I forget his name. He is in a lunatic asylum now, poor fellow . . . You see, a Communist Party which cannot defend itself is no damn use, that is the problem. If it cannot defend itself, it must be defended.

63. EXT. BUNKER. DAY

All we see is a group of perhaps half a dozen very high-ranking MILITARY OFFICERS *dressed in cold-weather greatcoats, standing at a vantage point, their attention on events in the distance, events characterized by the sounds of military vehicles and high explosives. It is a relaxed group. One or two of them may be smoking. Each of them has a pair of binoculars which he uses occasionally. The uniforms belong to*

the armies of the Warsaw Pact countries. We are concerned with
GENERAL JARUZELSKI *and* MARSHAL KULIKOV, *who are standing
next to each other. They are cold. They raise their binoculars.*

NARRATOR: (*Voice over*) During these December days reservists
were called up in the Baltic Soviet Republics. Soviet troops
camped under canvas on the Polish border, and Soviet warships
were visible from the coast. The United States Intelligence
announced that Russian invasion plans were complete.
(KULIKOV *lowers his binoculars.*)

KULIKOV: Well, I don't know what all this is doing to the Poles but
it's scaring the hell out of the Americans.

JARUZELSKI: We can deal with our own problems, Marshal.

KULIKOV: We all hope so, Wojciech.

64. EXT. THE GDANSK MEMORIAL INAUGURATION. NIGHT

*A crowd of people holding candles. It is snowing. There is the sound of
the 'Lacrimosa' from Krzysztof Penderecki's Chorale.
The floodlights illuminate the Solidarity banners.
We see WALESA dressed up for the winter cold. He wears a brown
anorak. Around him, casually but warmly dressed, are other WORKERS
and LEADERS of Solidarity. There are also the men of Warsaw in heavy
overcoats. There is a GENERAL in uniform and an ADMIRAL in
uniform. There are PRIESTS.*

NARRATOR: (*Voice over*) On December 16th, the rulers and the
ruled came together to inaugurate the Gdansk Memorial to the
dead of 1970. The Solidarity banners were consecrated by an
archbishop. There was an army general, an admiral, a deputy
member of the Politburo, a government minister and the
Head of State, the ageing Professor Jablonski. There were
diplomats of many foreign countries. There were 150,000
people gathered outside the gates of the Lenin shipyard. Lech
Walesa, unknown six months before, now leader of a union of
10 million workers, lit the flame. It was the first time in a
Communist country that a government had erected a
memorial to workers who had rebelled against the state. The
First Secretary of the Polish United Workers' Party and the
Soviet Ambassador did not attend.

3

Congress

65. INT. CONFESSIONAL. DAY

WALESA, *with his ear pressed to the grille, is listening intently and rapidly making notes in a notebook.*

NARRATOR: (*Voice over*) In the middle of January Lech Walesa went to Rome . . . and, according to Prague Radio, got his instructions straight from the Pope.

(*Caption*: Courtesy of Prague Radio)

WALESA: (*Muttering*) Yes, Father, attack the principles of socialist construction, very well, Father . . .

66. INT. SOLIDARITY MEETING ROOM. GDANSK. DAY

A large, disorganized, rowdy meeting of Solidarity people. They are members of the National Commission and we know a few of them.

NARRATOR: (*Voice over*) Solidarity was in fact in endless dispute with the Government, which seemed unable or unwilling to concede what had been agreed in Gdansk. The Government had back-tracked on the five-day week, access to the media, censorship, and the right of private farmers to set up a Rural Solidarity of their own. There were strikes and sit-ins all over the country. The National Commission tried to tidy all this up by calling for a one-hour general strike . . .

(*The meeting has suddenly pulled itself together, the background noise stilled as everybody there raises one arm in the air.*)

. . . while ordering an end to local strikes. But the second part of that had no effect . . .

(*The meeting once more disintegrates into dispute and noise.*)

The country seemed bemused and helpless in the face of all these demands. As always, there was a Polish joke for the occasion.

(*Caption*: Polish Joke)

(*The meeting is suddenly stilled as a* WORKER *shouts.*)

WORKER: I move that from now on we only work on Tuesdays!

(*The meeting agrees by acclamation. However, the* WITNESS, *who is present, raises his hand and the meeting goes quiet again to listen to him.*)

WITNESS: Do you mean every Tuesday?

67. INT. OFFICE (PRIME MINISTER). DAY

WALESA *and* PRIME MINISTER PINKOWSKI *are putting their signatures to a document.*

NARRATOR: (*Voice over*) Walesa went into a twelve-hour meeting with the Prime Minister, who at this time and for several days to come was called Mr Pinkowski. They reached an agreement which pleased neither side. On February 9th, Pinkowski was replaced. In Poland such a change was normally cosmetic, but this time it looked different.

68. EXT. STREET. DAY

An official car draws up and a fawning FUNCTIONARY *comes up to open the rear door, out of which comes* PRIME MINISTER GENERAL JARUZELSKI.

NARRATOR: (*Voice over*) The new Prime Minister liked to make unannounced visits . . .

69. INT. FOOD SHOP. DAY

NARRATOR: (*Voice over*) . . . sometimes to shops.

(*There is busy activity in the shop. Groceries of all kinds are being hastily unpacked from boxes and placed on empty shelves. When the shelves look fairly full, the* PRIME MINISTER *and his* ENTOURAGE *are seen to enter the shop. There is much handshaking and smiling as the* GENERAL *passes through.*)

JARUZELSKI: And how is the food distribution?

PARTY OFFICIAL: It is working very well, Comrade.

JARUZELSKI: Good, good.
>   (*He passes rapidly through. As soon as he has gone all the
>   groceries are quickly removed and repacked.*)
NARRATOR: (*Voice over*) Jaruzelski began by asking for a three
>   months' suspension of strike action – for, as he put it, ninety
>   peaceful days. He got thirty-eight.

70. EXT. STREET. NIGHT

The cut is to a fight. Smoke bombs. Crowds scatter. RULEWSKI *and
other men are being beaten up by a group of plain-clothes* SECURITY
POLICE.

71. INT. HOSPITAL VESTIBULE. NIGHT

A group is walking purposefully along the corridor towards us.
WALESA *is in the lead. A* PRIEST *is behind him.*
NARRATOR: (*Voice over*) The trouble happened in Bydgoszcz,
>   where the farmers, with the support of the local Solidarity
>   leader, Jan Rulewski, staged a peaceful protest against the
>   authorities' refusal to allow an independent farmers' union.
>   The uniformed militia were called but there was no violence
>   until the plain-clothes state security police moved in.
>   Rulewski was badly beaten up.
PRIEST: Wisdom. Not vengeance. Wisdom.

72. INT. HOSPITAL WARD. NIGHT

The injured RULEWSKI *is in bed.* WALESA *and the* PRIEST *enter the
ward and come to the bed.*
RULEWSKI: Yes – I heard you had a priest now.
WALESA: Jan. How are you feeling?
RULEWSKI: No – you talk.
WALESA: A warning strike within the week. A general strike after
that if we don't get satisfaction.
RULEWSKI: Somebody ordered it. This was an attack on
Solidarity by the Government.
WALESA: No. It was an attack on the Government's agreement

with Solidarity. That's the best way to play it. We'll announce a
strike in support of the Government of General Jaruzelski.

73. INT. OFFICE. NIGHT

JARUZELSKI *holding a telephone.*
JARUZELSKI: Tell him not to do us any favours.

74. INT. PARTY HEADQUARTERS (VESTIBULE). NIGHT

MIECZYSLAW RAKOWSKI *is holding a telephone to his ear, listening.*
NARRATOR: (*Voice over*) Jaruzelski's first appointment was to
    make Mieczyslaw Rakowski Deputy Prime Minister, with
    special responsibility for the unions. From now on,
    Rakowski, the editor of an influential political weekly, was
    going to do most of the talking to Solidarity.
    (RAKOWSKI *has meanwhile put the phone down and approached*
    WALESA, *who, we now see, is standing in the lobby.*)
RAKOWSKI: While we're standing here the armies of the Warsaw
    Pact are conducting exercises on Polish soil. Your warning
    strike was the greatest disruption of work in the history of
    this country.
    (WALESA *looks surprised.*)
    I mean in the history of the Polish People's Republic. If the
    general strike goes ahead we could end up with Soviet tanks
    lined up in the square outside.
WALESA: You've played the Russian card too many times. Blood
    has been spilled. Twenty-seven citizens of the Polish
    People's Republic who were not breaking any law have been
    injured in an assault by the state police in the city of
    Bydgoszcz. Three of them are in hospital. Does this have
    your approval?
RAKOWSKI: There will be an investigation, of course.
WALESA: Another card.
RAKOWSKI: We'll punish those responsible for the assault. You
    may have my guarantee. But the strike must be called off.
WALESA: It's not my decision. But your offer is not enough.
RAKOWSKI: All right, we also guarantee that the question of the

farmers' union will be examined by a parliamentary commission. And you know what that means with this parliament. It'll only be a matter of time. But we can't move faster than the Party lets us. You understand. The Party must have the leading role. That is Communism.

WALESA: And independent unions, is that Communism?

RAKOWSKI: Don't underestimate Polish Communism. We've got less than twenty-four hours before the strike goes ahead and all this is put at risk. What are you going to do?

75. INT. SOLIDARITY MEETING ROOM (GDANSK). DAY

WALESA *is there with* GWIAZDA *and* MODZELEWSKI. GWIAZDA *is angry*.

GWIAZDA: No.

WALESA: We've got most of what we wanted.

GWIAZDA: It's not up to us. The National Commission decided on the strike. If it's going to be called off, the National Commission has to meet to vote on it.

WALESA: (*Desperately*) There isn't time for that. We have to make it an executive decision.

MODZELEWSKI: You mean *your* decision. This whole business has been about as democratic as a Pharaoh's court. You're taking too much upon yourself, Lech.

WALESA: Nobody wants this strike. Do you want it?

MODZELEWSKI: I don't want the strike. I don't want any part of this decision. We went to a lot of trouble to make a democratic union. This is just getting to be Walesa's circus. I'm going back to Wroclaw to teach my students about democracy – you can get yourself another press officer.

WALESA: You're making a dogma out of procedure. Right and wrong is more important. A strike now would be wrong. And there isn't time. I'm putting this to the vote of the Praesidium. Let it be on my head. When the National Commission has time to meet, they can have it on a platter.

MODZELEWSKI: Right. I resign. (*To* GWIAZDA) How about you?

WALESA: (*To* GWIAZDA) You can only resign once, Andrzej. (MODZELEWSKI *starts to pick up his briefcase to leave*.)

GWIAZDA: They've split us.

76. INT. POLITBURO. DAY

Everybody is there and the mood is buoyant.
RAKOWSKI: (*Triumphantly*) We've split them!
(RAKOWSKI *is being slapped on the back by* JARUZELSKI . . .)
KANIA: That's it! Get them at each other's throats!
(*But this picture freezes and tears itself in half like a piece of paper with the sound of tearing paper.*)

77. INT. CAFE. DAY

The NARRATOR *is scribbling at a table. He stops and crumples up the paper and throws it away. He is being watched by the* WITNESS.
WITNESS: Try the other one.

78. INT. POLITBURO. DAY

As before.
RAKOWSKI: (*Gloomily*) We've split them!
KANIA: (*Gloomily*) How can we control them if they're at each other's throats all the time?
(*The picture freezes and tears itself in half like paper with the sound of tearing paper.*)

79. INT. CAFE. DAY

NARRATOR *and* WITNESS.
NARRATOR: I don't understand who's winning.
WITNESS: Or who's being split.
NARRATOR: (*Interested*) Is that it?
WITNESS: These people aren't smart. They're Party bosses.

80. INT. POLITBURO. DAY

As before.
KANIA: They've split us.

WITNESS: (*Voice over*) That's the one.

KANIA: In Torun there's a big Party meeting which we haven't sanctioned which wants to speed up reform. In Katowice there's another meeting which thinks Stalin is alive and well and is practically begging the Soviets to come in and save Communism. I've got hundreds of complaints from the rank and file. People want to know why we haven't punished the police who did the beating up. They want to know why we haven't expelled more Party members for bribery and theft, although we've expelled thousands. They demand an emergency Party Congress and I can't stop it. They will elect to the Congress hundreds of people we can't rely on. In the grass roots of the Party there are meetings between workers in different factories, different cities. Lenin called it the sin of horizontalism. He organized the Party on vertical lines, control from top to bottom. This is why. I'm getting demands for secret voting for the Party Congress, unlimited candidates, limited terms of office, accountability to the base instead of to the leadership. How long do you think we'd last if that happened? How long would Comrade Brezhnev and his colleagues last if it started to spread?

81. INT. KREMLIN. DAY

BREZHNEV *is dictating a letter. There is a* SECRETARY *taking it down.*

BREZHNEV: To the Central Committee of the Polish United Workers' Party from the Central Committee of the Communist Party of the Soviet Union. Dear lads. Let me spell it out for you. You were elected by the last Party Congress under Gierek, and quite obviously you're going to be out on your neck when the next Party Congress meets four weeks from now, so this is your last chance. When Kania and Jaruzelski were here in December they kept agreeing with me but ever since then they've let the Party drift into open democracy, make that bourgeois democracy, and look what happened to the Czechs just before *they* had their emergency Congress in '68 – say no more.

82. INT. POLITBURO. DAY

OLSZOWSKI *is reading Brezhnev's letter to the chastened Politburo.*

OLSZOWSKI: This letter is an invitation to the Central Committee to change the leadership. Brezhnev has lost faith in the Polish Party. And who can blame him when even Soviet war memorials in Warsaw are being defaced?

83. EXT. SOVIET WAR MEMORIAL. NIGHT

The memorial has been daubed with white paint. Sitting on top of the memorial, busy, with scrubbing brush and bucket of water, is WALESA. *Standing on the plinth, watching him, is* KURON.

WALESA: The memorials are being defaced by *provocateurs*. I've offered to scrub them with my own hands, on TV if they like. As a union we take no position on Russia.

KURON: You take every position including that one up there. You started something which you can't stop. You want a self-limiting revolution but it's like trying to limit influenza.

WALESA: Yes, it's those bloody workers. You give us freedom of choice, and we choose freedom. What I want to know is, how did *you* get to be called the intellectuals?

84. INT. BREZHNEV'S OFFICE (KREMLIN). DAY

BREZHNEV *is having a medical examination. He is stripped to the waist and is attended by a* DOCTOR.

BREZHNEV'S SECRETARY *is standing to one side holding a file.*

BREZHNEV: What's the latest?

DOCTOR: No change.

BREZHNEV: I mean him.

(*The* SECRETARY *steps forward.*)

SECRETARY: Which first sir?

BREZHNEV: Afghanistan.

(*The* SECRETARY *shuffles his files.*)

No, Poland. The Central Committee. Reaction to my letter.

SECRETARY: A strong attack on Kania's leadership in the Central Committee, and calls for his resignation.

BREZHNEV: (*Pleased*) And they think I'm losing my touch.
SECRETARY: However . . .
BREZHNEV: However what?
SECRETARY: A counter-attack arguing that if the hard-liners take over, the country will be polarized, with civil disobedience and strikes, and if we invade, Soviet Communism will be finished in Poland and *détente* with the Americans will be dead.
BREZHNEV: (*As the* DOCTOR *takes his blood pressure*) *Now* he takes my blood pressure.
SECRETARY: The entire Politburo offered themselves for a vote of confidence. The Central Committee declined the offer and proposed no changes in the leadership.
BREZHNEV: I see. And the Emergency Party Congress is still to come. I look forward to meeting the Polish leader when I go to the seaside next month. I wonder if he will be a Communist.

85. EXT. SEA SHORE. DAY

This is the same shot as scene I. The beach and the sea. Everything is the same except that KANIA *has replaced* GIEREK.
NARRATOR: (*Voice over*) In August 1981 Stanislaw Kania, First Secretary of the Polish United Workers' Party, left Warsaw for his annual holiday in the Soviet Union by the Black Sea. There he met Leonid Brezhnev, First Secretary of the Communist Party of the Soviet Union.
(*The two men, in hats, coats and lace-up shoes, come together and embrace.*)
In an atmosphere of cordiality and complete mutual understanding the two leaders had a frank exchange of views.

86. EXT. SEASIDE. DAY

KANIA *and* BREZHNEV *are now in beach clothes, wearing sunglasses, straw hats and so on. A nervous* WAITER *is hovering with a tray of brightly coloured drinks.*

NARRATOR: (*Voice over*) The July Congress of the Polish United Workers' Party was over. It had been the first ever Communist Party Congress to be composed of freely elected delegates – 2,000 of them, mostly there for the first time. They started by voting in a Central Committee which swept aside seven-eighths of the old guard, including four Politburo members. Kania, the great reformer, was re-elected First Secretary. Even so, the Congress knew that Poland was on the horns of a dilemma, and both horns made a showing in the Politburo. The hard-liner, Olszowski, made it to the top again.

BREZHNEV: Why did they keep Olszowski?

KANIA: He is respected for his economic ideas.

BREZHNEV: Why?

KANIA: Because Gierek sacked him.

BREZHNEV: And Jaruzelski?

KANIA: The Prime Minister is respected by all sides.

(*Suddenly irritated by the* WAITER, BREZHNEV *knocks the tray of drinks out of his hand.*)

BREZHNEV: (*Shouts*) Respect! (*Jabs a finger at* KANIA.) Do you know how you got into this mess?

KANIA: Comrade First Secretary, we must have strayed from the Leninist path . . .

BREZHNEV: You got into this mess by getting into debt to capitalist bankers!

87. INT. THE BANKERS' MEETING. DAY

The set-up is much the same as the first bankers' meeting (scene 19).
FINANSKY *is in the chair.*

FINANSKY: This is very harsh.

AMERICAN BANKER: I'm sorry but last March you had the unhappy distinction of being the first Communist country to request a rescheduling of its debts.

FINANSKY: We know what to do. Prices must increase two or three times over. A loaf of bread should perhaps quadruple. We know that. But you understand, we have problems.

243

88. EXT. STEELWORKS. DAY

Top shot. Meeting of fifty workers being addressed by a PARTY MAN.

NARRATOR: (*Voice over*) The Government announced food price
increases of 123 per cent. There were daily disturbances. At
workers' meetings when Party officials used the word –
(*Close up on* PARTY MAN *addressing the meeting.*)

PARTY MAN: Comrades!
(*He is greeted by sustained whistles of derision from the meeting.*)

89. INT. SOLIDARITY MEETING HALL. DAY

RAKOWSKI *is present with* WALESA *and a* SOLIDARITY TEAM,
including the KATOWICE MAN *and a* MINER.

RAKOWSKI: The attitude of Solidarity is arrogant and offensive.
You won't get eggs if you don't feed the chickens.
Production this year is down 18 per cent. Coal is down 14 per
cent. Wages are up 20 per cent.

MINER: I'm a coal miner, Comrade Rakowski. Miners are going
to work hungry – how can you expect hungry men to raise
production?

KATOWICE MAN: We're pouring steel to 40 per cent of capacity.
The whole place is run inefficiently. We could double output
if we had workers' self-management.

RAKOWSKI: For God's sake – one thing at a time.

WALESA: We don't have time. You've *had* time. It's almost
exactly a year since we signed the arrangement in Gdansk.
We are cheated, lied to, misrepresented in the press and on
TV. We've given you time. Next week we'll call a printers'
strike. We'll close down TV and radio if we don't get the
access we were promised.

RAKOWSKI: Are we here to talk about bread or TV?

MINER: Bread?

RAKOWSKI: I have to tell you from September 1st a loaf costing
seven zlotys will cost seventeen zlotys. Flour will increase
somewhat less. It will double.
(*The* SOLIDARITY MEN *look at each other silently and then get
up.*)

WALESA: We are not a poor country. We are badly managed. The question of workers' councils to take charge of production is now urgent.

MINER: (*To* WALESA) Gierek gave us those in '71. They soon got sucked under by the Party machine.

WALESA: In '71 there was no Solidarity.

(WALESA *and his* COLLEAGUES *turn and walk out of the meeting hall*.)

NARRATOR: (*Voice over*) On September 4th, the Soviet Union put 100,000 men into military manoeuvres around Poland. The following day the First National Congress of the Free Independent Union Solidarity opened in a sports stadium in Gdansk.

90. INT. SOLIDARITY CONGRESS. DAY

The cut is to a big close-up of WALESA *addressing a large gathering*.

WALESA: . . . This Congress is the heritage of the blood of 1956, of 1970, of 1976 and of all the struggles of the Polish workers. The fight has only just begun but we shall win!

(WALESA *acknowledges sustained applause*.)

NARRATOR: (*Voice over*) The Congress called for free elections to parliament, for union supervision of food production and distribution, for public control of the mass media, for workers' self-management. Jan Rulewski called for . . .

(*Mix to close-up on* RULEWSKI.)

RULEWSKI: . . . deletion of the clause recognizing the leading role of the Polish United Workers' Party . . .

(*There is a cut to* WALESA *listening. He shakes his head*.)

NARRATOR: (*Voice over*) There was worse to come.

91. INT. KANIA'S OFFICE. DAY

KANIA *and* JARUZELSKI *are present. The intercom on the desk starts to announce,* His Excellency the Soviet Ambassador, *but the furious* AMBASSADOR *is in the room waving a piece of paper before the intercom has finished*.

AMBASSADOR: I quote. 'The delegates assembled in Gdansk send

greetings and expressions of support to workers of Albania,
Bulgaria, Czechoslovakia, the German Democratic
Republic, Romania, Hungary and all nations of the Soviet
Union . . . we share the same destiny . . . despite the lies
disseminated in your countries . . . we support those of you
who embark on the struggle for a free union movement . . .' I
am ordered to make the strongest possible protest, on behalf
of the Government of the Soviet Union.

KANIA: Of course. Thank you. I agree it is most regrettable.
(*The* AMBASSADOR *waits for more but there is a pause. In the
end the* AMBASSADOR *nods a farewell and leaves the room.*
KANIA *and* JARUZELSKI *look at each other.* JARUZELSKI
begins to laugh quietly.)

JARUZELSKI: Albania . . . ! (*He finds this very funny.*) . . .
Albania . . . !

92. INT. CAFE. NIGHJT

WITNESS *and* NARRATOR.

WITNESS: It's not really funny. It's probably the end.

NARRATOR: No, they're still talking.
(*To camera*) During all this, the Government offered
Solidarity a formula for workers' self-management.
Evidently, they were still Poles talking to Poles.

WITNESS: Jaruzelski did his officer training in the Soviet Union.

NARRATOR: (*To camera*) During all this, the Government offered
Solidarity a formula for workers' management. Evidently,
the Party was playing cat and mouse with the union.

93. INT. MOVING FIAT CAR. NIGHT

WALESA *is driving.* RULEWSKI *is next to him. Two* SOLIDARITY
MEMBERS *sit in the back.*

WALESA: (*To* RULEWSKI) Jan, stick to Poland. Let the Albanians
and the Hungarians and the Bulgarians look after
themselves. I'm surprised Rakowski is still talking to us.
How are the others getting there?

RULEWSKI: It's just us four.

WALESA: That's just how I like it. A praesidium that can fit into a
Fiat.

94. INT. SOLIDARITY CONGRESS. DAY

JURCZYK *is addressing a large audience.*

JURCZYK: I move that we reprimand Lech Walesa and his
Praesidium colleagues for the undemocratic way in which
they reached this decision on workers' self-management.
Four men voted three to one, and they presumed to overturn
a resolution made by 900 of us in this hall!

WALESA: (*In close-up – shouting*) We could have come back empty-
handed! But we didn't, we made a decision. It takes no guts
at all to stand up here and complain about the world.

95. INT. OFFICE (SOLIDARITY CONGRESS). DAY

WALESA *lies exhausted across three chairs.* RULEWSKI *walks across
and looks down at him.*

RULEWSKI: I'm standing against you for the leadership.

WALESA: You're making a mistake, Jan.

RULEWSKI: Why? Do you think you're indispensable?

WALESA: No. But Marian Jurczyk is already standing against me.
You'll split the vote.

RULEWSKI: Gwiazda is standing, too.

WALESA: The three of you. All or nothing. Now or never. I've
been trying to tell you for a year. That's how to lose.
(WALESA *puts his head back and closes his eyes.* RULEWSKI
*watches him for a moment and then turns and leaves. The office
furniture, television sets etc. are being cleared away around*
WALESA. *Bulletin boards are being taken off the walls. Files are
being stacked.* WALESA *sleeps on.*)

NARRATOR: (*Voice over*) Walesa won with 55 per cent of the vote.
Marian Jurczyk polled 24 per cent, Andrzej Gwiazda 9 per
cent, and Jan Rulewski 6 per cent. The delegates left the
floor of the rented sports hall, which was then flooded and
frozen over for a hockey game.

96. INT. A DRESSING ROOM. DAY

In fact we could be anywhere because the scene is of crisp separate close-ups on a man (JARUZELSKI) *pulling on a military uniform, the belt, the hat, etc.*

NARRATOR: (*Voice over*) Talks began again between Solidarity and the Government. The union gave the Government ten days to produce results or face a national strike. Within a week there was a result of sorts.

(*The last article to be donned is the pair of tinted glasses worn by* JARUZELSKI.)

97. INT. FIRST SECRETARY'S OFFICE. DAY

A SECRETARY (*a man*) *is arranging files on the otherwise empty desk.*
JARUZELSKI *walks into the room.*
SECRETARY: Good morning, Comrade First Secretary. Everything is ready for you.
JARUZELSKI: Thank you.

(JARUZELSKI *goes to sit behind the desk.*)

NARRATOR: (*Voice over*) For the first time in a Communist country one man was head of the Party, the government and the army. It was the first Communist Party anywhere to be led by a general.

(JARUZELSKI *sits down, looks around, pleased, and gives his uniform a little flick.*)

JARUZELSKI: You don't think the effect is . . . a bit South American?

4

The General

The cut is to a close-up of GENERAL JARUZELSKI.
NARRATOR: (*Voice over*) Back in August, the General said . . .
JARUZELSKI: (*Declaiming*) How long can the patience,
    moderation and good will of the republic be put to the test?
    Polish soldiers have the right to say: enough of this
    indulgence!
    (*We cut to the* GENERAL *reviewing a line of* YOUNG
    OFFICERS.)
NARRATOR: The fact that he was speaking to a passing-out parade
    of young officers at the time made it less startling than it
    might have been . . . but nowadays there were generals in
    more and more government posts – education, money,
    transport, even a general in charge of the Polish airline. The
    only thing missing was the appointment of the Chief of the
    General Staff to the Politburo, and that came at the end of
    October.

99. INT. WALESA FLAT. EVENING

WALESA *and his wife* DANUTA *and six* CHILDREN *are eating at a
table big enough for them and two guests,* KURON *and* GWIAZDA.
DANUTA *is pregnant.*
KURON: I think political rule in Poland is already a sort of fiction.
    The army is starting to run things. *Political* power is lying in
    the gutter for somebody to pick up. Maybe the people
    nearest the gutter have the best chance – the Stalinists who
    call it socialism, the anti-Semites who call it nationalism . . .
    You have no chance at all. If you were handed power on a

plate you'd be left fighting over the plate. I thought a workers' protest movement could lead to a truly socialist Poland. It required discipline and stability. It required solidarity. The union executive is being pulled around like a tin can tied to a dog's tail.

GWIAZDA: We deserve it. The workers are activists, we're a bureaucracy.

WALESA: How else are we supposed to negotiate for them?

GWIAZDA: We negotiate, they fight.

WALESA: That's surrender. Not to the Government, to chaos. I'm going to propose a national warning strike so that at least for an hour we look like an organization again.

GWIAZDA: (*Exploding*) Jesus Christ! In Katowice there were 5,000 fighting the police with stones! Students took over the radio station! And you want to stop work for lunch!
(*It has become a loud row.*)
I don't want 5,000 people throwing stones somewhere at the other end of the country. It produces nothing except an opportunity for the generals, who can't wait to save the nation. (*To* KURON) I'm right, aren't I?
(KURON *gets up.*)

KURON: I'm going back to Warsaw. We have to start again.

WALESA: A new party?

KURON: No. A reappraisal.

GWIAZDA: A discussion group. Maybe you can write another open letter.

KURON: (*Losing his temper, too*) The Communist Manifesto was an open letter! The written word – I believe in it. When this tower of Babel collapses upon itself you'll need to be reminded what the noise was all about.
(*This takes him to the door.*)
(*More quietly*) You failed because you had no reliable framework for your actions. If you want freedom of action in a Communist state the strategy will have to be thought out better than this. Maybe it will have to be the intellectuals after all. Next time, eh?
(KURON *leaves. After a pause* WALESA *also gets up from the table and leaves, into another room, closing the door.*)

GWIAZDA: (*To* DANUTA) I'm going.
  (DANUTA *nods*.)
  Thank you. (GWIAZDA *leaves the flat*.)

100. EXT. PLAYGROUND. DAY

The NARRATOR *is there watching several of the* WALESA CHILDREN
playing with a ball.
FIRST CHILD: Poor Mr Kuron . . .
SECOND CHILD: He thinks if he leaves the Party alone . . .
THIRD CHILD: . . . the Party will leave him alone.
FIRST CHILD: Poor Mr Kuron.
WITNESS: (*Voice over*) A cheap trick, in my opinion . . . Out of
  the mouths of children . . .

101. INT. CAFE

The NARRATOR *and the* WITNESS *are drinking together. The*
WITNESS *is still speaking.*
WITNESS: . . . Why didn't you give them a puppy to make sure?
NARRATOR: Do the Walesas have a dog?
WITNESS: It's a little late to be scrupulous about detail.
NARRATOR: What's the answer to Kuron?
WITNESS: I know Kuron. In 1800 he was in nostalgic exile in
  Paris waiting for history to put the clock back. In 1900 he
  was a revolutionary Marxist in London waiting for the
  proletariat to put the clock forward. Now he's in People's
  Poland and it seems to be neither one thing nor the other, an
  independent slave-state ruled by worker-princes. No wonder
  he's disappointed.
NARRATOR: Well, then what . . .?
WITNESS: He's got it upside down, in my opinion. Theories don't
  guarantee social justice, social justice tells you if a theory is
  any good. Right and wrong are not complicated – when a
  child cries, 'That's not fair!' the child can be believed.
  Children are always right. But it was still a cheap trick.
NARRATOR: I'll take it back.

102. INT. WALESA FLAT. EVENING

As before. The scene has got to the point where KURON *is at the door, about to leave.*

KURON: Next time, eh? (*To* WALESA) I think your plan is good. Get the best deal you can for the working man. You're a union, after all.

103. INT. STEELWORKS. DAY

WALESA *is in the foreground. Low camera angle.* WORKERS *are in the gantry above. The factory is loud and busy.*

WALESA *looks at his watch. At that moment the sirens sound.*

104. INT. OPERATIONS ROOM. DAY

There is a map table and maps and city plans on the walls. Half a dozen high-ranking MILITARY OFFICERS *are crowded round the table.* JARUZELSKI *is among them, using a pointer to indicate different parts of the map. The siren sound overlaps with diminished volume, into this room. The* ARMY OFFICERS *all pause and look up, listening* . . .

105. INT. STEELWORKS. DAY

WALESA *is where he was. The siren is just finishing. The machinery is coming to a halt. So are the men who were working.*

WALESA: It's music to them . . . music . . .

106. INT. PARLIAMENT. DAY

JARUZELSKI *is at the microphone.*

JARUZELSKI: In the Central Committee, even in the Politburo, there are voices asking us to set our democratic system aside until peace is restored. What I will ask of this assembly is to prepare itself for a situation where I will have to come to you and ask for emergency laws. There are 12,000 on strike in the textile mills. If the independent union cannot control its anarchists, we will have to find some other way . . .

107. INT. GOVERNMENT MEETING ROOM. DAY

On one side of the large table is RAKOWSKI, *flanked by two*
ADVISERS. *He is faced by* WALESA, *similarly attended.*

WALESA: I was in the textile mills. I have met these anarchists . . .
12,000 women, young girls and grannies, working wives . . .
Do you think they're on strike because they want to
overthrow the Party? No, they're on strike because work
brings no reward, and it doesn't look as if the Government
knows what to do about it. They get up in the dark to stand
in line for hours to buy a pair of shoes the wrong size so that
they may have something to barter for a piece of meat –
which turns out to be rotten. They appeal to you, and you
say – oh, we can't help it, these anarchists are making life
impossible. And then it turns out *they're* the anarchists!
Listen, they can't break the circle, someone else has to. I
don't think you can do it on your own.

RAKOWSKI: I agree. You know our proposal – an action front
representing all the social forces – the Government,
Solidarity, the Church, the peasants, the official unions,
Catholic intellectuals, economists, scientists – a team of
national unity –

WALESA: You just want to water us down. But we're 10 million
and we won't sit down as equal partners with the
incompetents and hacks – the central planners, the time-
servers, the seat warmers – all the ones who had the chance
and lost it. You've failed, and the best answer now is an
economic council, independent, with real power, made up of
Solidarity and Government equally with equal voices.

RAKOWSKI: (*Angrily*) What sort of government do you expect to
hand over its authority to a committee?

WALESA: Your sort. A government with no mandate at the end of
its string.

(RAKOWSKI, *insulted, gets up from the table and walks away,
perhaps towards a window. His* ADVISERS *look stonily across the
table.* WALESA *and the* SOLIDARITY MEN *stand up and prepare
to leave.*)

RAKOWSKI: Perhaps you'd like to tell that to the General?

WALESA: (*With conscious irony*) Do you mean the Prime Minister?
RAKOWSKI: Yes, the Prime Minister. The First Secretary. The
　　General.
WALESA: How many votes does he get?

108. INT. POLITBURO VESTIBULE. DAY

The SOLIDARITY TEAM *is leaving.* RAKOWSKI *appears.*
RAKOWSKI: Comrade Walesa –
　　(WALESA *drops back.* RAKOWSKI *takes him aside. He speaks
　　quietly.*)
　　General Jaruzelski is interested in a new initiative. With
　　Archbishop Glemp. Will you meet them?
WALESA: Just the three of us?
RAKOWSKI: Just the three of you.

109. INT. SOLIDARITY MEETING ROOM (GDANSK) DAY

There are four men in the room . . . WALESA, GWIAZDA, RULEWSKI
and JURCZYK. *Because of the size of the room, some of the
conversation may be shouted across the yards of space.*
RULEWSKI: What do they want? Your autograph?
GWIAZDA: You had no authority to accept.
WALESA: Should we announce that we aren't even willing to talk
　　to the Prime Minister and the Primate of Poland?
GWIAZDA: Not we, you. Why you?
WALESA: I was asked.
GWIAZDA: You were asked because you're Jaruzelski's meat.
　　You're a babe in arms.
RULEWSKI: So is Glemp. The General wants the moral authority
　　of the Church and the social seal of approval of Solidarity.
GWIAZDA: They'll muzzle you.
WALESA: I'm going.
GWIAZDA: Lech, you're a vain fool! Your moustache is famous
　　but there is nothing above it.
WALESA: (*Over the top*) You can throw me out any time you like.
　　I'll go and I'll take the union with me. I'll dissolve it inside
　　two weeks!

(*The others look at each other in astonishment.*)

RULEWSKI: Where will you take it? To New York? In two weeks you will be the guest of the American unions. Maybe you should have taken the union with you when you went to Geneva – to Japan – to Paris – to the Vatican.

JURCZYK: We don't have to destroy ourselves, there's others willing to do it –

WALESA: Yes, that's right, Marian – and one way to destroy us is to go round making speeches calling the Government traitors, Moscow's servants, Jews – what did you mean by it?

JURCZYK: I meant they're traitors, Moscow's servants and in some cases Jews.

WALESA: As a Catholic I reject you, as a union we dissociate ourselves from such talk.

JURCZYK: Wait till you get to America. The Americans won't hear a word you say about your ideals for socialism – they'll make an anti-Russian carnival out of you.

(WALESA's *manner changes instantly as he takes this in.*)

WALESA: That's true. You're right. I won't go. The American trip is off. As of now.

(*The other three are astonished by him again.*)

(*Smiles.*) That's right. When somebody's right they don't have to argue with me. The right move and the wrong move – I don't need arguments. I can feel it – right and wrong. The meeting feels right, and I'm going to it.

IIO. INT. GOVERNMENT GUEST HOUSE. EVENING

There is a green-baize card table and three chairs. The NARRATOR *is standing by, shuffling a pack of cards.*

NARRATOR: (*To camera*) Cardinal Wyszynski had died in May. The new Primate of Poland was Archbishop Joseph Glemp. The meeting which took place between the Primate, the General and the union leader on November 4th 1981 was without precedent, not just in the Polish crisis but in the Communist world. It lasted 2 hours and 20 minutes.

(*The* NARRATOR *starts to deal the cards three ways.*)

That much is known. But as to who said what to whom . . .

(*The* WITNESS *appears with a carafe and three glasses. He puts them on the table.*)

WITNESS: Don't tell me, let me guess. Cards on the table.

NARRATOR: Playing one's hand.

WITNESS: Writers.

III. INT. THE SAME. EVENING

There is the card table and the three chairs, with a hand of cards waiting at each place. JARUZELSKI, GLEMP *and* WALESA *approach the table and sit down. Each looks at his own cards. The three men play cards as they speak. They pick up and put down cards as it becomes their turn to speak. The cards are seen to be not conventional. Their designs, in red and white, show, variously, the Polish Eagle, a Church symbol, the Solidarity symbol, the hammer and sickle . . . but there is no attempt to make the rules of the game precisely intelligible to the audience. The impression is that the game is a form of whist.*

JARUZELSKI: We are Poles. There is much we can agree on.

GLEMP: Certainly we want to settle our own problems.

WALESA: All right.

JARUZELSKI: Thank you.

> (JARUZELSKI *picks up the three cards as a 'trick'. He puts down a card.*)
> The Russians are reluctant to intervene but at a certain point they would have to overcome their reluctance. That point will be reached when socialism breaks down in this country.

GLEMP: I agree.

WALESA: We can't even agree on language. What is this socialism you're talking about? Solidarity is socialism.

JARUZELSKI: It is not Lenin's socialism.

GLEMP: Let us say that Solidarity is socialism. But is it not breaking down? Socialism is order. (*To* WALESA) Your extremists create disorder.

WALESA: (*Upset*) Father, the Government is trying to make accomplices of us by holding these Russians over our heads – 'Behave yourselves for Poland's sake!' Why should we believe it? I don't think the Russians can afford to intervene.

JARUZELSKI: They can never afford to until they can't afford not to.

(*He picks up the second 'trick'.*)

The Polish Church is unique, a stronghold of Christianity in the Communist world. Soviet intervention would change many things.

GLEMP: Not just for the Church. It would certainly be the end of the free trade unions.

WALESA: The Russian scare shouldn't change what we think or do. That's blackmail and it's not moral to give in to it. We can afford to be wrong but the Church has got to be right.

(WALESA *stands up abruptly, throwing down his cards. The picture freezes.*)

NARRATOR: (*Voice over*) But there was no fly on the wall. No one knows how little help Walesa got from Archbishop Glemp. Or how much.

(*The scene cuts back to the beginning, the game beginning again.*)

JARUZELSKI: We are Poles. There is much we can agree on.

GLEMP: Certainly we want to settle our own problems.

WALESA: All right.

JARUZELSKI: Thank you.

(JARUZELSKI *picks up the 'trick'.*)

The Russians are reluctant to intervene but they would have to overcome their reluctance if socialism breaks down in this country.

GLEMP: (*Turning on* JARUZELSKI) We can't even agree on language. What is this intervention? It is invasion and occupation to rescue a discredited dictatorship!

WALESA: (*Cautiously*) But invasion would change many things, not just for the union. The Polish Church has a unique position and it has been won at great sacrifice.

JARUZELSKI: The dictatorship of the proletariat as expressed through the Party is the only government we've got and Solidarity is not letting it govern.

GLEMP: (*Again attacking* JARUZELSKI) The Government has reneged on most of the provisions of the Gdansk Agreement. The conflict is of your creation because you deny the rights of the citizen!

(*The picture freezes again.*)

NARRATOR: (*Voice over*) Everything is true except the words and the pictures. It wasn't a card game.
(*The scene cuts back to the beginning but now it is not a card game. The table is polished wood.*)
But time was running out. There were to be elections in February and the one problem a Communist government cannot afford is to get re-elected.

JARUZELSKI: We have elections in February. (*To* WALESA) You proclaimed a trade union with no interest in politics. In the last few months, thirty-five anti-socialist groups posing as political parties have been formed. We all have reason to fear the consequences. The Russians are reluctant to intervene but at a certain point they will have to overcome their reluctance.

GLEMP: Poland's socialist dictatorship is the most democratic government we've got, and the most Polish. We are here to decide how we can best help it clothe and feed the population. Am I wrong? Without the economic problem there would be no political problem. Without the political problem there would be no Russian problem.

WALESA: No, you're not wrong.

JARUZELSKI: We have coal reserves for two more weeks. How do I get the country running again? (*To* WALESA) I've asked you to ban wildcat strikes. I've offered to sit down with you in a council for national renewal.

WALESA: With us and enough others to give you a tame majority.

GLEMP: What if Solidarity had a veto?

JARUZELSKI: No. But perhaps if every member had the right of veto . . .

WALESA: No.

JARUZELSKI: Then just Solidarity and the Government.

GLEMP: And the Church.

JARUZELSKI: That's possible. (*To* WALESA) What do you say? (*Pause.*)

WALESA: There's a meeting tonight of the Solidarity National Commission, I have to go back to Gdansk.

The meeting is noisy. The familiar faces are there. GWIAZDA *is in the chair.* WALESA (*dressed as for the Glemp/Jaruzelski meeting*) *appears.*

GWIAZDA *sees him.*

GWIAZDA: Lech!

> (*The meeting goes quiet.*)
> We didn't wait. We've made some progress.

WALESA: I've got something to put to the vote.

GWIAZDA: We already voted. A national strike in three months if the Government doesn't satisfy conditions.

WALESA: And a ban on unofficial strikes?

GWIAZDA: We voted on that too. No ban.

WALESA: Is that your idea of progress?

GWIAZDA: Yes. It is.

> (WALESA *approaches him.*)

WALESA: You're sitting in my chair.

> (GWIAZDA *vacates the chair.* WALESA *takes it. He picks up the microphone in front of him.*)
> If it's confrontation you want, that's fine because that's what you're voting for. You might as well leave now and start prising up the cobbles off the streets.
> (*The meeting goes quiet for him.*)
> I'm here with a new formula for talking with the Government – a national committee of –
> (*The meeting starts murmuring against him.*)
> Yes, I know. They lie. They cheat. They kick and bite and scratch before they give an inch – but that's how we got this union, inch by inch across the negotiating table!
> (*The meeting starts to applaud, a slow build interrupted by* GWIAZDA.)

GWIAZDA: (*Shouting*) We got it by going on strike and staying on strike.

WALESA: You're wrong. We got it because we could deliver a return to work. We've got nothing else to negotiate with, and if we can't deliver, what have they got to lose?

> (*The applause grows.*)

GWIAZDA: They've conned you, Lech! The talks are a sham.
Across the table is where they want us – all the time we're
talking they're getting ready to hit us. You keep the chair –
I'm not going to be needing it.
GWIAZDA *leaves and from different places about a dozen men,
ones who were not clapping, leave with him.*)

113. INT. PLAYGROUND (GDANSK). DAY

WALESA *and his* WIFE *and* CHILDREN *are in the playground. The*
CHILDREN *are running around at some distance and playing.*
(DANUTA *is pregnant.*)
WALESA: Andrzej's resigned. Him and others. They say my line is
too soft. Maybe it is. I read in the papers that Walesa is a
moderate and Gwiazda is a radical and I feel a sort of shame.
How brave it sounds, to be a radical.
DANUTA: You're radical enough. Solidarity is losing its halo,
Lech. The TV makes you look like saboteurs. You're getting
blamed for the shortages, for the farmers' strikes, the
student strikes, the taxi drivers' strike . . . for everything.
People are saying the government can't solve it, Solidarity
can't solve it, there's only the army left, and better ours than
theirs.
WALESA: What people?
DANUTA: Ordinary people. You know. Not the Praesidium. Not
the Government. People.
WALESA: I wish I could talk to Jacek.
DANUTA: Why can't you?

114. INT. POLICE CELL. DAY

The WITNESS, *the worse for wear, is flung into the cell.* KURON *is
lying on a bunk in the cell.*
WITNESS: Where did they get you?
KURON: At home.
WITNESS: What for?
KURON: Attempting to overthrow the state. I think. What's
happening outside?

WITNESS: The fire brigade cadets have taken over the college.
KURON: Strikers in uniform? Well, we're getting there.

115. INT. OPERATIONS ROOM. DAY

JARUZELSKI *has a visitor* – MARSHAL KULIKOV.
JARUZELSKI: We're getting there. The Western bankers have
    given us an ultimatum, the zloty is being devalued, and
    parliament won't pass a strike law. I would say . . . about a
    week. Tomorrow we move in against the fire brigade cadets.
KULIKOV: Troops?
JARUZELSKI: (*Shaking his head*) Not yet. Riot police. We'll use
    helicopters to secure the roof and go in through the main
    gate.

116. EXT. STREET

There is a lot of noise. There is a helicopter noise overhead. WALESA *is
there looking up. He is joined by a furious and triumphant* GWIAZDA.
GWIAZDA: And you're still talking to them about workers' self-
    management! It's confrontation, Lech.
WALESA: Yes. I know.

117. INT. SOLIDARITY MEETING ROOM. DAY

*This is a meeting of about twenty people, the Praesidium and
Regional Chairmen of Solidarity.* WALESA *is speaking.*
WALESA: Confrontation was always at the end of the road. I
    hoped to get there by easy stages. I think we could have got
    further, but I miscalculated. So we have to change our tactics
    and be prepared to move at lightning speed.
BUJAK: We'll liberate the radio and TV . . . we'll establish our
    own council for the national economy. It will be like a
    provisional government.

118. INT. JARUZELSKI'S OFFICE. DAY
JARUZELSKI *is listening to a tape of Bujak's speech.*

BUJAK: (*On tape*) . . . we'll establish our own council for the national economy. It will be like a provisional government.

JARUZELSKI: We're there.

(*We see that he is talking to* MARSHAL KULIKOV.)

KULIKOV: None too soon. This trap has been a long time springing.

JARUZELSKI: Forgive me, Marshal, we prefer to think of it as a regrettable outcome.

KULIKOV: We all forgive you, Wojciech.

119. INT. WALSEA BEDROOM. NIGHT

DANUTA *is in bed.* WALESA *enters without putting on the light. He sits on the bed and starts taking his shoes off.*

NARRATOR: (*Voice over*) The final meeting of the National Commission of Solidarity ended in Gdansk on Saturday night, December 12th. There was going to be a national day of protest, a general strike against strike laws, and, going all the way now, a reappraisal of the Soviet connection.

DANUTA: Remember once they arrested you when I was nearly giving birth? Which baby was that?

WALESA: Yes, I remember. Everything was simpler then. We didn't fight amongst ourselves. There was only one way to go. Then round the corner there was a fork in the road, and each fork led to a fork . . . so we got separated. Well, it's been sixteen months. We've gone further and quicker than anyone expected. Jacek said we could win little by little, or lose overnight.

DANUTA: Lech . . . ?

WALESA: They've cut the phone lines from Gdansk. I'm sorry. We may be apart for a while.

DANUTA: You don't know that. Lech . . . ?

WALESA: I think I've always known.

120. INT. POLICE CELL. DAY

The WITNESS *is asleep.* KURON *apparently doesn't know it, for he is pacing the cell, talking angrily.*

KURON: It was not a conflict between ideologists – trying to make one system fit with another. (*Scornfully*) Marxist-Leninism! – what would Lenin have thought of the Polish Church? Or Polish agriculture – 80 per cent privately owned. Ideology is as dead as Lenin. All Brezhnev demanded from us was a political guarantee of the military alliance, and reliable railways for the army. All the rest is self-delusion.

121. INT. AIRFIELD. NIGHT

There is a parked helicopter with its rotors spinning. WALESA *is escorted into the helicopter, which then takes flight.*

NARRATOR: (*Voice over*) By dawn on Sunday, December 13th almost the entire Solidarity leadership was under arrest. The military council which announced itself as Poland's saviour also arrested the former First Secretary, Edward Gierek, together with five others who had helped him to bring the Party and the country to the point in August 1980 when the shipyard workers on the Baltic Coast went on strike and demanded the right to form a free and independent trade union.

122. EXT. SEA SHORE. DAY

The beach and sea again. Everything is the same except that JARUZELSKI *has replaced* KANIA.

NARRATOR: (*Voice over*) When the summer came, Wojciech Jaruzelski, First Secretary of the Polish United Workers' Party, left Warsaw for his holiday in the Soviet Union by the Black Sea. There he met Leonid Brezhnev, First Secretary of the Communist Party of the Soviet Union.
(BREZHNEV *approaches, and the two men come together and embrace.*)
In an atmosphere of cordiality and complete mutual understanding the two leaders had a frank exchange of views.

BREZHNEV: Greetings, Comrade!

JARUZELSKI: Greetings, Comrade First Secretary!

BREZHNEV: So, how's tricks?
JARUZELSKI: Fine.
BREZHNEV: And Mrs Jaruzelski?
JARUZELSKI: Who? – Oh, fine. And you?
BREZHNEV: To tell you the truth, I haven't been feeling too well.
  (*They walk together up the beach.*)

DATE DUE

~~FEB 18 1997~~		
~~NOV 05 2003~~		
APR 10 2006		
MAY 10 2006		
AUG 14 2006		

Demco, Inc. 38-293